The GEFILTE MANIFESTO

The GEFILTE MANIFESTO

New Recipes for Old World Jewish Foods

JEFFREY YOSKOWITZ & LIZ ALPERN

Photography by Lauren Volo

FLATIRON
BOOKS
NEW YORK

www.flatironbooks.com

Illustrations by Sun Young Park

Background images: (butcher paper) BW Folsom/Shutterstock.com and (parchment paper) Evgeny Karandaev/Shuttertock.com

Designed by Toni Tajima

The Library of Congress Cataloging-in-Publication Data is available upon request.

ISBN 978-1-250-07138-5 (paper over board)
ISBN 978-1-250-07143-9 (e-book)

Our books may be purchased in bulk for promotional, educational, or business use. Please contact your local bookseller or Macmillan Corporate and Premium Sales Department at 1-800-221-7945, extension 5442, or by e-mail at MacmillanSpecialMarkets@macmillan.com.

First Edition: September 2016

10 9 8 7 6 5 4 3 2 1

To the generations of cooks who breathed life into Ashkenazi food traditions and moved this cuisine forward in such an inspiring way

CONTENTS

Rockfish Imperial
For each lb of fish use:
1 tbs. Seafood seasoning
2 tsp. salt
1/4 cup vinegar
1/4 cup water
    Place fish in pan & pour
the combined seafood seasoning,
salt, vinegar & water over fish
cover. Bring to a boil; reduce
heat & allow to steam 20 min.
(Stir once, coating fish with
spiced liquid) Remove from
heat & drain. Remove bones &
flake fish (large pieces)
For 1lb of fish (flaked)
  1 egg
  1 slice wht. bread (crumbled)
  1/2 cup mayonnaise
  1 Tsp. dry mustard
  1 Tsp. Worcestershire sauce
  1 Tbs. green pepper
  Mix above ing. together & then
mix with fish. Put in crab
shells & bake 20-30 minutes at
400°
            Evelyn Green
                  50

Pickled Herring
  10 Hard herring
    (Soak herring over night
    and change water about
    2 or 3 times)
Boil 1 qt. vinegar with 1 qt. water
and 1 box pickling spice for
about 1 hour. Let cool and pour
over the herring that is placed
in jar.
  When herring is placed in
jar put one layer herring,
(cut in pieces) one layer sliced
onions, continue on until jar
is filled, then place sliced
carrots around sides of jar -
close lid tightly and shake
jar. Let stand for about 1 week.
            Eleanor Harris

                  51

FOREWORD

THE GEFILTE MANIFESTO

In today's reality, most families don't store a live carp in the bathtub before the holidays anymore, or spend all day preparing labor-intensive foods. Under the banner of convenience, the past several decades have seen treasured food traditions stuffed into jars and neglected, gefilte included.

Gefilte fish was once an innovative way to stretch how far one fish could go to feed a family, a powerful symbol of European peasantry. The canned variety, by contrast, is a poignant reminder of how far we've strayed from the old days, so much so that gefilte has become synonymous with the outdated, the gray, the antiquated, and the Old World.

But we need not accept the extinction of this tradition, or of the robust, colorful, fresh flavors of Ashkenazi cuisine. We know that gefilte—like borscht and kvass and so many Old World foods—is excellent when done right. It comes down to the basics of quality, freshness, care, and creativity.

Gefilte is not just about your bubbe. *It is not about kitsch or a foodie revolution. Gefilte is about reclaiming our time-honored foods and caring how they taste and how they're sourced. It is about serving a dish with pride, not simply out of deference to hollow convention. It is about taking food traditions seriously and reclaiming the glory of Ashkenazi food—what it has been and what it can be.*

We of The Gefilteria plan to bring our foods out of the jar and back to the street, to the pushcarts where we began, to the flavors of the people.

—JEFFREY YOSKOWITZ, LIZ ALPERN & JACKIE LILINSHTEIN,
UPON CO-FOUNDING THE GEFILTERIA IN 2011

RECIPES

Appetizers & Beverages   Barbecues   Breads & Pastries

DISH

PREPARATION TIME
NUMBER OF SERVINGS
SOURCE OF RECIPE

Cooking Jewish

Cookbook
res in Jewish Cooking

INTRODUCTION

JEFFREY Standing in a tiny, narrow kitchen in an East Village synagogue, Liz and I are preparing hundreds of pounds of gefilte fish and horseradish relish. It's our first holiday in business, and we've recruited a small group of friends to help with the epic undertaking. After several hours of grinding fillets, dicing onions, and grating horseradish, the tinny sounds of a clarinet drift through the kitchen doors. A klezmer band is setting up in the adjacent room, and soon, dozens of fans, young and old, are dancing to traditional eastern European Jewish music. We dance, too, stirring and chopping to the beat of the upright bass and the bellowing of the trumpet, which helps relieve the stress of filling our very first orders. As the familiar smells from our kitchen waft into the auditorium, curious concertgoers peek in to see a group of millennials bopping to the beat, elbows deep in mixing bowls full of ground fish.

A year earlier, Liz and I were hardly gefilte fish mavens, though we grew up similarly, she in Long Island and I in New Jersey. Our families served standard Jewish fare: brisket, gefilte fish, kugel, and other specialties for Passover, as well as challah, chicken, and potatoes every Friday night for Shabbat dinner. The rest of the time it was the usual: spaghetti and meatballs, tuna noodle casserole, and grilled cheese sandwiches—about as American as you can get. But inspired by our families' holidays, we both developed a deep affection for the flavors of the Jewish table, as well as an appreciation of the stories behind these foods.

I moved to New York City when I was in my midtwenties. No longer around for Shabbat meals with my parents or family outings to the 2nd Ave Deli before Broadway shows, my Jewish identity and the food that reinforced it were now in my own hands. I wasn't doing a great job keeping it alive, even though I regularly felt pangs of longing for pastrami, matzo ball soup, and kreplach. Occasionally I'd visit a deli, which would relieve my yearning for a bit, but generally, I no longer felt like I was living by the rhythm of the holidays or the cuisine as I did in my family's home. When a few of my favorite delis and appetizing shops in New York closed, I started to panic. I sensed that I wasn't the only one. I confided in Liz, who clearly shared my passion for Jewish food, describing my fears of a world without the smells of chicken soup and apple strudel in a Yiddish kitchen. She had the same fears.

After much discussion, we decided that we had to do something about it. While we weren't technically chefs, we had both trained on farms and worked in professional kitchens, bakeries, pickle kitchens, test kitchens, and food trucks. Our shared passion and drive brought us together and became the basis for both a long-standing friendship and a professional partnership.

We brought our good friend Jackie Lilinshtein into the fold and made plans for a gefilte fish revival that we hoped would help spark a greater Ashkenazi culinary renaissance. We began cooking together—and have yet to stop. We penned a "gefilte manifesto" (see page ix), then spent about a year researching and developing recipes before committing to our first holiday production. Eventually, we named the small operation The Gefilteria.

We initially began manufacturing gefilte fish for local stores, then for shops around the country. Soon, we looked beyond gefilte and began producing pickles, horseradish relish, borscht, black-and-white cookies, and beet kvass for New York's outdoor food markets. Eventually, The Gefilteria was catering elaborate meals in pop-up spaces around the country.

Since that very first klezmer kitchen dance session, Liz and I have shared a commitment to digging deep into our personal food traditions, connecting with seasoned chefs, and poring over timeworn cookbooks. We've come to see that the wisdom of Jewish cooks from the Old World, and the knowledge they brought with them and applied to their kitchens in North America, offers incredible insights that should inform how we all cook today.

THE BASICS OF ASHKENAZI COOKING

JEFFREY

Let's clarify a few terms. *Ashkenazi* refers to those Jews who trace their roots to central and eastern Europe, including the regions that now comprise Germany, Russia, Poland, Belarus, Lithuania, Hungary, Ukraine, Romania, and beyond, as well as the culture and cuisine that defined their lives. Yiddish, in various dialects, was the primary language of most of these Jews. Although deeply rooted in folk traditions, Yiddish language and culture transformed and adapted to modern ideas and changing sensibilities with surprising ease—much like the cuisine. Of course, food played an important role not just in the sustenance of the Jewish community, but in the rhythm of life, from marking sacred days and preparing holiday feasts to the seasonal preservation of summer and fall harvests.

The terrain and climate is quite similar across parts of central and much of eastern Europe, and as a result Jews from various cities and shtetls—small towns—who already shared religious customs and holidays, cultivated similar crops and raised the same livestock. Sure, the Galitsianers (from Galicia in southwestern Poland) liked sugar in everything, the Litvaks (from Lithuania and northeastern Poland) preferred pepper, and the Hungarians doubled down on paprika, but a common cuisine developed despite these regional variations. Yes, it was frequently similar to the cuisine of their gentile neighbors, but it was also distinctly Jewish—and, more often than not, adhered to religious dietary proscriptions, which clearly delineated what was kosher (permitted) from what was not.

And while the laws of kashrut (Jewish dietary laws) and the climate set up the framework for Ashkenazi cuisine, it was the resourcefulness of Jewish cooks, an economic necessity, which we reference and highlight so often throughout this book, that connected the cuisine as a whole. During harvest seasons, Ashkenazi Jews utilized every part of what they had. Scraps of animal fat and vegetable tops were never discarded. Dairy was precious and preserved in any way possible. Dishes were improvised based on availability, and even the wealthiest households operated under the understanding that food sources were finite.

Millions of Jewish immigrants left Europe for North America beginning at the turn of the twentieth century. Most settled in urban areas, where geographic distinctions more or less eroded. Romanian, Polish, and Lithuanian foods found their place in German-influenced Jewish delicatessens. Galitsianers married Litvaks and culinary styles were altered. Once Ashkenazi Jews Americanized, a social and economic process that involved a significant step up from the poverty they'd faced back home, their lives were changed. Thanks to advances and differences in food production and availability, they were no longer living in sync with the seasons. The traditional wisdom of the Old Country— preserving summer and fall harvests, storing produce in root cellars, pairing sour cream and potatoes to make a complete protein, and naturally leavening breads with wild yeasts—was less relevant in the tenement blocks of major cities. Some foods and traditions remained, but a great deal was also lost.

WHAT THIS BOOK IS REALLY ALL ABOUT

LIZ

I distinctly remember the chilly fall Friday when I realized the extent to which Jeffrey and I weren't just researching and cooking these Ashkenazi foods, but actually living them. It was during a magical year when our apartments were directly across the street from each other and we regularly hosted joint Shabbat dinners for friends. We would cook in our respective kitchens and then transport loaves of bread, pots of soup, and trays of roasted vegetables from his place to mine (since my living room was larger).

One Friday, I realized I was out of barley for my cholent, so I ran across to his place and nabbed what he had, along with our shared slow cooker. A couple of hours later, Jeffrey needed extra rye flour for the challah he was baking, and I had enough for months. Just before dinner, I went to his place to help him carry loaves of marble rye challah, stacks of plates, and a big jug of rye kvass he'd been fermenting for the occasion. Back at my place, where the smell of cholent sat heavy in the air, we set the table as the sun was setting. Our friends began to arrive. It felt like we had invited them to enter our world, even if just for an evening.

With this book, we're inviting you to enter our world as well, where Ashkenazi foods and the kitchens in which they're lovingly made are surprisingly modern and relevant. That's what makes this a different kind of Jewish cookbook. Rather than attempting to preserve old recipes or soon-to-be-forgotten ingredients, we're presenting an old approach to a new way of eating. Or is it a new approach to an old way of eating? Perhaps a pickle analogy will be helpful here: Think of a cucumber, which, when preserved, doesn't remain a simple cucumber for long. As it ferments, it changes, transforms, intensifies, and deepens in flavor. So it is with this food. Its preservation is never static, but the spiritual core remains the same.

We focus on recipes that tell the story of a rich ethnic cuisine that can too often be misunderstood and undervalued. "Jewish cooking today has a reputation for blandness, not entirely unearned," writes Jane Ziegelman in *97 Orchard*. "A hundred years ago, however, the label would have never stuck." Indeed, this cuisine contains strong flavors of garlic and onion, palate-opening sweets and sours, and earthy tastes of forest mushrooms and grains.

Ashkenazi cooking fits naturally into our contemporary lives. When prepared with care and thoughtfulness, this food's components are as balanced and nutrient rich as any of the popular diets we deem healthy today. The key is avoiding the adulterations of midcentury America, which saw margarine replace butter and the humble pastrami sandwich morph into a tower of fatty meat. Yes, Jews of eastern Europe ate vegetables, nourishing broths, and herring. These fresh items, as well as pickled and preserved vegetables, fruits, dairy, meats, and fish, were critical to balancing the Ashkenazi diet once the bounty from the fall harvest season came to an end.

There's a lighter and brighter side to this cuisine, too, the kinds of foods you'd eat in the summertime, like fresh greens, radishes,

sour cream, all sorts of pickles, smoked fish with freshly baked bialys, and chilled fruit soups. And the colors! Lilya's beet borscht with swirls of sour cream may be the most stunning shade of magenta in the natural world, and carrot citrus horseradish is the brightest condiment in our Ashkenazi pantry. We like to think of these as picnic foods, or the staples you'd find at a New York bagel shop or the old dairy restaurants, most of which no longer remain.

Whether your roots are Ashkenazi or not, the recipes in these pages will make you feel warm and nurtured. These are universal comfort foods, and they are adaptable to personal preference and multicultural flair. We hope you'll love them as much as we do.

THINGS TO KEEP IN MIND WHEN USING THIS BOOK

LIZ

This cookbook is a snapshot of Ashkenazi cooking through our eyes and is hardly a compendium of every recipe in the Jewish canon. We have fun within the confines of the tradition, so there are a few recipes that our great-grandmothers could never have conceived of, like Fried Sour Pickles with Garlic Aioli (page 54) or Dark Chocolate and Roasted Beet Ice Cream (page 275). There's also a good number of vegetarian and gluten-free recipes since, let's face it, we all have friends and loved ones with specialized diets. If you don't find your favorite Ashkenazi dish in this book, it doesn't mean we don't know about it or love it. If only we had more pages! Also, we've grouped our recipes into sections inspired by institutions, ingredients, and methodologies, rather than by Jewish holidays. We do include sample menus for holiday planning (see page 313), however, and encourage you to reference them for ideas and inspiration.

You'll note that Jeffrey and I switch our voices regularly throughout these pages. We both have strong connections to many of the dishes in this book and the stories behind them, so we take turns introducing the chapters and the individual recipes. Rest assured, all the following recipes and stories are products of our mutual collaboration.

Some of the recipes in this book are quick and easy; others are lengthier and more complicated. Be sure to read each recipe through before beginning. Many recipes build on each other. The recipe for farmer's cheese can be used to make the filling for cheese blintzes, for example. When possible, we make use of leftovers and elements of other recipes, such as pickle brine, which we use in breads, salad dressings, and cocktails. After all, resourcefulness is a central tenet of Ashkenazi cuisine.

And while the recipes in this book feature precise lists, measurements, and instructions for making these Ashkenazi dishes at home, you should have fun with these foods and, once you feel comfortable, feel free to put your own spin on them. If you're an experienced home cook, you'll see lots of room to play with spices and ratios, plating, and ingredients. That's the spirit of Ashkenazi cuisine. Our great-grandmothers rarely, if ever, followed recipes. Here, we've outlined a few important notes that will be helpful to keep in mind before you begin.

FERMENTATION OF VEGETABLES, GRAINS, AND DAIRY The process of fermentation is highly variable. We generally tell first-time fermenters (whether they are working with vegetables, fruit, dairy, or grains) that there are tons of variables that can affect a batch. These include temperature, freshness of the produce, and even the soil on the farm from which the produce comes. We encourage you to be as hygienic as possible when working with fermented food products and to refer to government guidelines for additional food handling instructions. Following our fermentation guide (page 44) and our recipes should yield safe, healthy, and delicious results.

WATER BATH CANNING Water bath canning is a simple method for safely sealing high-acid foods and creating shelf-stable items that will last for months. The foods in this book that we specify as good for canning are high-acid foods and therefore take well to this method. Water bath canning is not the same as pressure canning, and you should never water bath can low-acid foods or meats. After canning, if your jam or pickles or applesauce jars do not seal properly according to the signposts outlined in Water Bath Canning 101 (page 325), which happens from time to time, do not leave them at room temperature. Treat them as you would an opened (unsealed) jar of jam, pickles, or applesauce and store them in the fridge.

When sealed safely and effectively, water bath canning is a safe method. If not, dangerous bacteria, molds, and viruses can develop. We encourage canning enthusiasts to conduct further research using the fantastic tools provided by the National Center for Home Food Preservation (nchfp.uga.edu).

STOCKING YOUR KITCHEN The ingredients in this book are, for the most part, easy to source and totally affordable. Your typical supermarket or farmers' market should have everything you need. There are a few pieces of equipment that come up repeatedly in this book: widemouthed quart-size mason jars, parchment paper, cheesecloth, a food processor, heavy-bottomed pots, nonstick pans, a kitchen thermometer, a kitchen scale, an immersion blender, roasting pans, fine-mesh strainers (small, medium, and large), and a slow cooker.

ROOM TEMPERATURE At many points in this book, we mention leaving your food at room temperature. Often, the exact range we're referring to isn't terribly important; in other cases it is. Our ideal room temperature range is between 65° and 75°F. This is important to keep in mind when working with fermented dairy and grains, like Old Country Sour Cream (page 24), Cultured Cream Cheese (page 25), Żurek (page 124), and Jewish Rye (page 100), as well as all types of fermented vegetables, such as Classic Sour Dills (page 50), Crisp Garlic Dilly Beans (page 56), Sauerruben (page 65) and Sauerkraut (page 60), and the four different types of kvass in our beverage chapter (pages 285–307).

FILTERED WATER VS. TAP WATER In many of our recipes for fermented foods and beverages, we call for filtered water. Tap water often contains chlorine, and chlorine kills bacteria. When making rye starters or kombucha or a vegetable ferment like dill pickles, bacteria are critical for a successful outcome. Filtered water provides a stronger guarantee that the good bacteria will live, and therefore, of success. Note that some home filters will not clear out all the chlorine from the water supply. If you live in an area with highly chlorinated water, bottled water is a good solution.

KOSHER SALT VS. SEA SALT VS. TABLE SALT All the recipes in this book were tested using Diamond Crystal Kosher Salt. We prefer kosher salt because it contains no iodine, and therefore works better when making fermented foods. We also prefer its coarse granulation. If you do not have kosher salt, you can substitute either sea salt or table salt. Coarse sea salt is very similar to kosher salt and swaps in easily in any of the recipes in this book. Table salt granules are generally finer than those of sea salt, so you'll always want to use less table salt than the suggested amount of kosher salt to start off. Note that many table salts do contain iodine, known to inhibit the growth of bacteria, so do not use table salt for any recipes that require fermentation.

KOSHER CHICKEN AND MEAT The recipes in this book were mainly tested using kosher meat and poultry. This means that the meat went through a koshering process using salt. As such, kosher meat and chicken are often a touch saltier than nonkosher meats and poultry. If you are cooking with nonkosher meat, we recommend taking this into account and adjusting the salt to taste.

LOCAL AND SEASONAL PRODUCE, MEAT, AND DAIRY Local and seasonal foods are part of a larger ethos of how we think about Ashkenazi cuisine, which is, at its core, sustainably oriented and seasonal. Generations of our ancestors in eastern Europe ate food grown close to home, without pesticides, additives, or industrial processing of any kind. That's part of what made it delicious, even though it was often very simple food.

~~ ONE ~~

PANTRY STAPLES

JEFFREY I once asked my grandma Ruth what food she missed most from the Old Country. I expected her to miss exotic foods like fresh gooseberries or forest mushrooms, or even timeless classics like apple strudel. Instead, Grandma Ruth surprised me: "Butter on toast," she said.

It turns out that Grandma Ruth's family owned a dairy cow, which resided right next to her childhood brick home in Szumsk, a village in what was once eastern Poland (now Ukraine). Her family also raised chickens and geese. Drinking warm milk from the pail is one of her fondest memories from her life before the Second World War. In the spring and summer, her parents would skim the cream and churn it into fresh butter. "Butter was so fresh and flavorful in Poland," she always said, and then, with disdain, "The American stuff has no taste."

My grandmother's Polish kitchen was a do-it-yourselfer's dream. There weren't any supermarkets or corner stores in Szumsk, so her mother, my great-grandmother Frieda, made everything from scratch. Truth is, everyone did. Frieda transformed apples, pears, and plums from trees outside her kitchen window into sauces and compotes. She lined cellar shelves with jars of preserves made from currants, plums, and strawberries, cooking down the fruit slowly in copper kettles over a small fire. She toasted and crushed stale bread into bread crumbs. For meat dishes, she rendered fat into schmaltz for cooking. For dairy meals, she used that famous butter.

My great-grandmother Frieda was an astounding woman—a badass *balabusta*, as I like to say. She raised four children and kept them all well fed in a harsh climate without any of the comforts— like refrigeration—that I take for granted today. Frieda created her own staples from the produce in her yard, milk from her cow, and fat from her geese and chickens. She later kept herself and her family nourished through five years of imprisonment in Siberia during the Second World War, pulling together potato peels and scraps of animal fat to concoct sustaining meals however she could.

The kitchen instincts and techniques that were deeply ingrained in Great-Grandma Frieda (and had been passed on to Grandma Ruth) were lost when my family arrived in the New World. While my grandmother spoke Yiddish and cooked blintzes and mushroom and barley soup for her family, my mother focused on learning English and eating American foods—quite a common story among Jewish immigrants, especially in the fifties. Fortunately for me, my survival doesn't exactly hang in the balance. Living in New York City, I have access to a refrigerator and a bodega two doors down. At two a.m., I can buy organic butter from upstate New York, or I can order pad thai for dinner when I'm feeling lazy. I'm not complaining. But it's been an uphill battle to develop instincts retroactively, to learn to cook with my gut and make real food. I'm still learning.

That's why Liz and I chose to begin with the basics. Making the essentials in this chapter helped us to learn how to cook with our *kishkes*—our guts. It's been important for us personally and professionally.

I can remember one specific time when I returned home for Passover and put those Ashkenazi methods to use. I rendered fat into schmaltz (which hadn't ever been seen in my parents' house) and crisped up *gribenes* (see page 35), which I handed directly to Grandma Ruth. As we munched on the fried chicken skins together, Grandma Ruth—who hadn't eaten *gribenes* in the forty years since Great-Grandma Frieda passed away—told me she was impressed. I like to think she saw something of her mother in me. Learning to create Old World pantry staples and the instinct to do so continually bring me closer to tasting a piece of my grandmother's past.

$\sim\sim$

LIZ →

A decade ago, I knew nothing of schmaltz. I had no clue about canning or cheese making or pickling. Unlike Jeffrey, I didn't think of myself as one of those DIY food nerds. Why would I spend time making jam when the small-batch preserves at the farmers' market were so delicious? And who would attempt to age their own cheese when the process takes so damn long? I loved to cook, but I hated the fuss.

My perspective changed as I dug deeper into Ashkenazi cuisine. While working as an assistant to Joan Nathan, the doyenne of Jewish food in America, I tested recipes that required a lot of advance planning and high-quality ingredients. I'll never forget making gravlax with her for the first time. It took us only a few minutes to coat the thick side of salmon with salt and dill, but we had to wait for what felt like ages to actually eat it. I huffed every time I saw that luminous orange flesh in the fridge, teasing me and testing my patience. Then there was the day I spent running around Washington, D.C., frantically searching for fresh fava beans, shell peas, and artichokes to use in Joan's Passover spring vegetable ragout. If I'd paid more attention to what was available at the farmers' market the first time around, I would have been able to track them down exactly when they were in season. Sigh.

As I continued to cook with Joan, I learned that some dishes simply couldn't be improvised. She encouraged me to start from scratch and plan ahead, and showed me how to go a level deeper than my typical hodgepodge cooking techniques. We made Tunisian *brik*, starting with the dough, then making the meat filling, then carefully folding each individual pastry and frying it. We made vegetables stuffed with rice, hollowing out the vegetables and eventually slow-cooking them in a Dutch oven. With time, I actually learned to enjoy cooking this way: slowly, with preparedness and a focus on the basics.

Schmaltz, for example, became a given in my kitchen. I developed a respect for its rich flavor and its ubiquity in Ashkenazi cooking, as well as its borderline sacred status in Europe. In Hungary at the turn of the twentieth century, containers that stored rendered fats ("schmaltz" for Jews and "lard" for gentiles) were designed with a strap that could be padlocked. "People wanted to guard the valuable rendered fat," recounted András Koerner of his great-grandmother's kitchen in western Hungary, in his book, *A Taste of the Past*. Sour cream, too, for all its simplicity, had an elevated status. It was one of the primary ways to extend the life of cream from fresh milk, and it added a velvety texture and sour flavor to otherwise bland dishes like boiled potatoes. Sour cream even served to balance out the starch-heavy eastern European diet by providing crucial vitamins A and D. Clearly, the DIY food projects I had long resisted were not just flights of fancy for people with too much spare time. They were the essence of shtetl cookery.

PANTRY STAPLES
=RECIPES=

EVERYTHING BAGEL BUTTER

LIZ

In my childhood home, butter materialized only on special occasions and came whipped and salted. Nutritionists vilified butter for decades, so health-conscious moms like mine replaced butter with margarine. Margarine also contained neither meat nor dairy, so using it made it easier to follow Jewish dietary laws. Only in adulthood did I realize how bizarre it was to have eaten chemically processed fats instead of natural butter. And now nutritionists have changed their tune, too.

Making butter is so simple; it requires only heavy cream (the fresher it is, the better the taste) and a simple hand mixer. The flavor is much lighter and much creamier than that of the butter you buy in the store, where even the highest-quality brands may have been sitting on the shelf for several months. The seeded version bursts with Ashkenazi flavor and adds flair to any breakfast or brunch spread. If you don't have time to make the butter from scratch, you can mix in the same ratio of seasonings with two sticks (1 cup) of store-bought butter.

Churning butter makes a fun and accessible project for kitchen beginners of all ages, and the finished product freezes well if you make too much. The process also leaves you with a fair amount of old-fashioned buttermilk, which will add a creamy tang to baked goods like biscuits, cakes, cookies, and pancakes. Note that this is not the same as cultured buttermilk and cannot be used in recipes that specifically call for cultured buttermilk.

MAKES 12 TO 16 OUNCES BUTTER (PLUS 2 CUPS BUTTERMILK)

FOR THE EVERYTHING BAGEL SEASONING:

3 tablespoons dried minced onion

2 tablespoons white sesame seeds

1 tablespoon black sesame seeds

1 tablespoon poppy seeds

1 tablespoon onion powder

1½ teaspoons kosher salt

FOR THE BUTTER:

1 quart heavy cream

1. TO MAKE THE EVERYTHING BAGEL SEASONING: In a small bowl, combine the minced onion, sesame seeds, poppy seeds, onion powder, and salt. Set aside.

2. TO MAKE THE BUTTER: In a large bowl using a hand mixer, or in the bowl of a stand mixer fitted with the whisk

(continued) ▶

attachment, whip the cream on high speed. Be sure to use a deep bowl or you'll make a mess. If using a stand mixer, drape a clean kitchen towel around the top of the bowl to keep splashes of milk from flying out. After 5 to 7 minutes (or a little less if using a stand mixer), the heavy cream will thicken to become whipped cream (the kind you'd eat with cake). Keep whipping. After 6 to 8 minutes more, you'll notice the cream will begin to separate into yellowish clumps and watery liquid. The clumps are butterfat, and the liquid is buttermilk.

3. When there's substantial buttermilk at the bottom of the bowl, and no more seems to be coming from the clumps, 10 to 15 minutes total, turn the mixer off. Pour the buttermilk into a jar and store in the refrigerator for baking or drinking.

4. Fill a small pitcher with ice and water. Using your hands, form the butter into one solid mass and place it in a bowl. Pour some of the ice water over the butter and use your hands to lift up the butter and squeeze out the excess liquid—this is called "washing" the butter. Washing removes any remaining buttermilk from the butterfat and helps keep it from going rancid. The purer the fat, the longer the butter will last. Let the liquid run into the bowl. Continue to pour ice water over the butter and squeeze until the liquid draining off into the bottom of the bowl becomes clear. Drain the liquid from the bowl every couple of times you "wash" the butter. Keep towels nearby to dry your hands between squeezes.

5. When you've extracted as much liquid as possible, your butter is good to go. If you're leaving it plain, shape it however you like—into a log, a stick, or a square—wrap it in wax paper or place it in an airtight container, and refrigerate. The butter will keep in the refrigerator for about 2 weeks and also freezes well. If making the seasoned butter, proceed to the next step before refrigerating.

6. In a large, clean bowl using a hand mixer, or in the bowl of a stand mixer fitted with the paddle attachment, beat together the butter and the seed mixture until thoroughly mixed. You can also use a fork to mix in the seeds. Shape the butter into a log (or whatever shape you'd like) and wrap it in wax paper or place it in an airtight container. Serve at room temperature for easy spreading. Everything Bagel Butter, if most of the water is successfully removed, will keep in the refrigerator for up to a month.

QUICK AND CREAMY FARMER'S CHEESE

 **LIZ** A few years back, Jeffrey taught me the simple cheese-making process he had learned years ago from a friend who was a goat herder. Not for the first time, Jeffrey filled the role of the Jewish grandmother I never quite had. He was more familiar with DIY kitchen tips than I was, and he loved watching over my shoulder as I tried them myself. Together, we stood over a large pot of milk, and the cheese we strained that day was fresher and creamier than I knew farmer's cheese could be.

Farmer's cheese (and its less-crumbly cousin, pot cheese) tends to be fairly bland on its own. Higher-quality milk makes for richer flavor, but we also like to add salt and fresh herbs. For something really deluxe, place your farmer's cheese in olive oil and herbs and let it sit in the refrigerator for a couple of days before serving with bread or crackers. We use homemade farmer's cheese for our Sweet Blintzes (see page 224), Pierogi (page 140), and Cheesecake with Currant Glaze and Caraway Crust (page 271). This recipe calls for a cooking thermometer, which isn't necessary, but is helpful to know exactly when to remove your milk from the heat and to ensure the maximum yield. Note that the yield may vary slightly.

MAKES 1½ POUNDS FARMER'S CHEESE (ABOUT 3 CUPS)

---

1 gallon whole milk

½ cup distilled white vinegar

2 tablespoons minced garlic (optional)

2 heaping teaspoons finely minced fresh herbs, such as chives, parsley, and sage (optional)

1 teaspoon kosher salt (optional)

---

1. In a heavy-bottomed medium pot or saucepan, heat the milk over medium-low heat, stirring frequently to avoid burning, for 15 to 20 minutes, or until the milk reaches 180° to 190°F. The time will vary depending on the size of your pot and your stovetop. Look for a bubbly white foam to form all over the surface of the milk, but do not let the milk boil. Remove from the heat.

2. Immediately pour in the vinegar and stir gently. The milk will instantly begin to curdle. Milk solids will form and separate from the yellowish whey. Let sit for 15 minutes.

3. While the cheese curdles, drape a large piece of cheesecloth over a colander or large, fine-mesh strainer set over a large bowl. Gently pour or ladle the milk

(continued) ▶

▶ (Quick and Creamy Farmer's Cheese, *continued*)

solids and the yellowish whey into the cheesecloth. Either discard the whey that collects in the bowl or set it aside for another use. Run the cheese curds under cold water for about 5 seconds. Let drain in the sink in the colander for a few minutes.

4. Tie the corners of the cheesecloth into a knot. Hang the bundle from the knot on a hook, ideally over the sink or a bowl, and let the cheese drip for about an hour to remove excess whey. You may have to improvise to find a way to hang your cheesecloth if you don't have a hook handy. Hooks on wire hangers work well.

5. After about an hour, open your cheesecloth bundle. If desired, transfer the cheese to a bowl and stir in the garlic, herbs, and salt, or just leave the cheese plain. Pack the cheese into an airtight container and refrigerate or use immediately in another recipe. Farmer's cheese will keep in the refrigerator for 5 to 7 days. It also freezes well—just defrost it in the fridge for 4 hours before using as filling for Sweet Blintzes (see page 224).

OLD COUNTRY SOUR CREAM

JEFFREY

In a world without refrigeration, soured cream was practical and delicious. The process wasn't much of a to-do, either: you just let unpasteurized cream sit and the result was an all-purpose condiment with a velvety texture and a strong sour flavor. Dolloped on soups, dumplings, potatoes, and blintzes or mixed with herring or fruit, sour cream could enhance a wide range of Ashkenazi foods—which made it a prized accompaniment. The classical Yiddish author I. L. Peretz captured sour cream's perceived value in his short story *In the Mail Coach* (1893): "And her face always looked strained and worried, as if her shipload of sour cream had just sunk."

Note that because homemade sour cream lacks chemical coagulates, it will be runnier than store-bought sour cream. Add a hearty dollop of sour cream to a bowl of fresh berries, juicy peaches, or, like my father does, sliced banana. My ideal ratio is 2 to 3 tablespoons sour cream to every cup of fruit. Be sure to appreciate how the sour tang enhances the fruit's sugars. Serve on Sweet or Savory Blintzes (page 224), Pierogi (page 140), and Root Vegetable Latkes (page 204). Add a dollop to Lilya's Summer Beet Borscht (page 117). Or serve atop a baked potato.

MAKES 1½ CUPS
SOUR CREAM

---

1 cup heavy cream

¼ cup store-bought cultured buttermilk

1. Pour the heavy cream and buttermilk into a clean pint- or quart-size glass jar with a lid.

2. Seal tightly and shake vigorously for about 1 minute. Let the jar sit on the countertop at room temperature, out of direct sunlight, for 24 to 48 hours. The longer it sits, the sourer it will become. You may notice liquid separation occurring. It's hard to judge from the looks of your sour cream when it's ready, so taste to see if it's at a sour level you're comfortable with within the 24- to 48-hour window. The warmer it is, the faster it will sour. If the mixture becomes yellow or chunky, which could occur if the temperature in the room is too hot, toss it out and try again.

3. Place the jar of sour cream in the fridge and enjoy for up to a week. Shake before each use to reincorporate any liquid that has separated.

CULTURED CREAM CHEESE (SCHMEAR)

JEFFREY

As the story goes, a Jewish dairyman from upstate New York accidentally added too much cream to a batch of soft cheese sometime in the late 1800s, and the spill changed bagel culture forever. Now it's almost unfathomable to think of bagels having ever existed without cream cheese.

Homemade cream cheese is not nearly as dense as the store-bought variety, making it better for light spreading on bagels or toast. Cream cheese requires a bit of science and planning. You'll need to purchase cheese cultures and rennet, which are inexpensive and sold on many websites. A simple kitchen thermometer is also essential since cream cheese is quite temperature sensitive.

MAKES 1½ POUNDS CREAM CHEESE

1 quart whole milk

1 quart heavy cream (or half-and-half, for a lighter cream cheese)

¼ teaspoon standard (mesophilic) cheese starter culture (see Resources, page 327)

4 drops liquid vegetable rennet (see Resources, page 327), mixed with 2 tablespoons water

½ teaspoon kosher salt

½ cup finely chopped scallions (optional)

1. In a heavy-bottomed pot, heat the milk and cream over low heat until the mixture registers 75°F on a kitchen thermometer. Remove from the heat.

2. Sprinkle the cheese starter culture on top and let the mixture sit, uncovered, for 5 minutes, then gently stir to incorporate the culture. Add the rennet-water mixture, stirring carefully with a few gentle strokes. Cover the mixture and let sit at room temperature overnight.

3. The next morning, drape cheesecloth over a colander or fine-mesh strainer set over a bowl. Pour the creamy mixture through the cheesecloth. Discard the liquid in the bowl. Tie the corners of the cheesecloth and hang the bundle from the knot on a hook above the sink or a bowl. Let the cream cheese drip for 12 hours, or until the cream cheese is soft, pliable, and no longer runny. If the mixture still seems too saturated, place the cream cheese, still in the cheesecloth, in an airtight container and let sit in the refrigerator overnight. More liquid will drain out. The next day, drain all remaining liquid and transfer the cream cheese to a bowl. Mix in the salt and scallions (if using). Cream cheese is best after it has hardened in the refrigerator, but feel free to schmear it on a bagel (page 106) with lox right away. Store in an airtight container in the refrigerator for up to 2 weeks.

APPLE-PEAR SAUCE

JEFFREY

Grandma Ruth used to make blush red applesauce from local Massachusetts apples that she sweetened with pears and plums and spiced with cinnamon. I would've gulped it straight from the jar, had my mother let me. But Grandma never visited us in New Jersey for Hanukkah, when apples were at the end of their season in the Northeast and when latkes required gobs of the stuff, so my mother and I took matters into our own hands. It soon became our ritual. My job was to run the fruit, with seeds and skin, through the food mill, extracting all the saucy pulp. I haven't stopped since.

Applesauce is a great way to utilize bruised or imperfect fruit. The variety of apple doesn't matter too much; the sweeter the apple, the sweeter the sauce. This recipe also calls for pears, which provide natural sweetness, as well as apple juice or cider, which adds a deeper and sweeter flavor. (But water is a fine substitute for juice or cider—it means one less item to purchase, and depending on how I'm consuming my applesauce, I sometimes prefer it a little less sweet.) Serve on Pierogi (page 140) and Root Vegetable Latkes (page 204). You can also swirl some into Grandma Fay's Applesauce Cake (page 277) or gulp it from a jar at the kitchen counter. This apple-pear sauce freezes and cans well, so do not hesitate to double the recipe and save some for later use.

If you have a food mill, simply quarter your unpeeled apples and pears—no need to core them. In step 2, run the fruit through the food mill into a large bowl instead of mashing or pureeing.

MAKES 5 TO 6 CUPS SAUCE

2 pounds baking apples (about 6 medium), such as McIntosh, peeled, cored, and quartered

2 pounds sweet pears (about 5 medium), such as Bartlett, peeled, cored, and quartered

½ cup apple juice, apple cider, or water

2 cinnamon sticks

1 to 4 tablespoons maple syrup or sugar (optional)

2 tablespoons fresh lemon juice (optional)

1. In a large, heavy-bottomed pot, combine the apple and pear quarters, apple juice, and cinnamon sticks and bring to a boil over high heat. Reduce the heat to low and simmer, stirring occasionally, for 30 to 40 minutes. The apples will soften and puff up a bit as the heat draws out their liquid. When you can smush the fruit by pressing on it with a spoon, it has finished cooking.

(continued) ▶

▶ (Apple-Pear Sauce, *continued*)

2. Turn off the heat and remove the cinnamon sticks. Mash the mixture with a potato masher or an improvised masher (an empty jar works well). For a smooth applesauce, puree using an immersion blender or food processor.

3. If you'd like your sauce sweeter, stir in the maple syrup or sugar (start with 1 tablespoon and add more if needed).

Stir in the lemon juice, if using, which adds a bit of tartness to balance out the sweetness. Let the sauce cool.

4. Serve at room temperature. The sauce will keep in the refrigerator for about a month. If storing for later use, transfer to an airtight container and freeze, or follow the canning instructions on page 325.

BACK CUPBOARD VINEGAR

I always have so many bottles of opened wine left over from dinner parties. I use some of it for cooking, of course, but sometimes, when I've left it for too long, it begins to taste vinegary. But what would happen if we let it sit for longer? That was the wormhole we went down that led to this recipe.

It takes a long time to turn wine into vinegar. The key is to keep it in a cool, dark corner, preferably in a cabinet you will not be going into very often. That said, making homemade vinegar is rewarding and simple. Experiment with sauvignon blanc, Chardonnay, or other wine varietals, and each time you'll have a different end result. Use your homemade vinegar to make salad dressings (page 80) or just sprinkle on vegetables with olive oil. Note that this recipe calls for a quick prep time (only about four minutes) but an extended wait time of 8 to 12 weeks.

**MAKES ABOUT
3 CUPS VINEGAR**

¼ cup high-quality unfiltered apple cider vinegar

3¾ cups wine (opened within the last week)

1. Pour the vinegar into a sterilized quart-size jar. Seal the jar and turn to coat the entire inside of the jar with the vinegar. Open the jar and pour in the wine.

2. Place a piece of cheesecloth over the mouth of the jar and secure it with a rubber band or twine. Place the jar in a dark cabinet with a steady cool temperature.

3. Vinegar develops in about 8 weeks. Depending on the temperature of your kitchen, it may need to sit a bit longer—up to 12 weeks. Vinegar has finished actively fermenting when its wine characteristics disappear and the liquid tastes acidic and, well, vinegary.

4. Remove and discard the cheesecloth. Close the jar with a lid and let the vinegar sit in the refrigerator for about 1 week before using. This mellows the flavor. It will keep in the refrigerator for up to a year.

SUMMER HARVEST JAMS

 LIZ

You don't need the fanciest berries or stone fruits to make excellent jam—just fresh fruit and sugar. This recipe is a terrific way to preserve and honor the short season for the blueberries and currants and strawberries that define our summers in New York. Come early fall, when the Concord grapes are ready to harvest in my parents' backyard on Long Island, I mark the occasion with a homemade grape jam.

If you have a heavy-bottomed pot, that's ideal. If not, just stir continuously and be sure not to burn the fruit. For a less-sweet jam, reduce the sugar to 1½ cups. You'll notice that it won't gel as thickly, but it's still fantastic. The recipe calls for placing the jam in the refrigerator, but it can be canned, too: just follow the instructions on page 325. Definitely use homemade currant jam for hamantaschen filling (see page 264) and strawberry jam for Ruth's Apple Strudel (page 278), and spread gooseberry jam on toast with fresh butter. If working with strawberries, be sure to hull and quarter them before measuring.

MAKES 2 CUPS JAM

~~~~~~

4 cups fresh raspberries, blueberries, black-berries, red or black currants, goose-berries, Concord grapes, or quartered strawberries

2 cups sugar

1. Place three metal spoons in your freezer. Place the fruit in a heavy-bottomed saucepan and crush it using the bottom of a clean jar or a heavy wooden spoon. Set the saucepan over low heat and cook, stirring continuously, for about 2 minutes. The fruit will begin to cook down and release liquid.

2. Bring the fruit and its liquid to a boil, stirring occasionally, 5 to 8 minutes, depending on the size of the fruit at the start. Pour in the sugar and cook, stirring continuously to ensure that the fruit doesn't burn, for 10 to 15 minutes more (the exact time will depend on the type of pan you are using and the variety of fruit). Skim off any foam that forms on the surface. The jam will begin to gel.

3. You can now perform a gel test to see if the jam is ready. Remove one of the spoons from the freezer and dip it into the fruit mixture. Turn the spoon sideways. If the jam gels and a thick coating remains on the back of the spoon, it's ready. If the jam mixture quickly slides off the spoon, cook for 2 minutes more and repeat the gel test with a clean spoon until the jam sticks.

4. Pour the jam into a clean glass jar and cover. It can be stored in the refrigerator for 6 months or longer. If you prefer a shelf-stable jam, see page 325 for canning information.

SPICY WHOLE-GRAIN MUSTARD

JEFFREY

Mustard is a key player in Ashkenazi cooking. The mustard plant, a member of the Brassica family, has some pretty important relatives in cabbage and horseradish. Can you imagine eastern European Jewish cooking without them? Probably not. And you also probably can't imagine a hot deli pastrami sandwich without spicy ground mustard. Personally, I can't fathom life without a hot deli pastrami sandwich.

Why make your own mustard? Some store-bought mustard contains thickeners and unnamed "spices." But more important, homemade mustard is just really good. Liz and I cooked a four-course pop-up dinner one January night at Barjot, a restaurant in Seattle. We made almost everything ourselves, from the schmaltz to the pastries. But we didn't make mustard because Barjot makes its own. After the meal, a guest pulled me aside and said, "Everything was great, but the mustard is out of this world." Oof. It was time for us to make our own. This recipe is inspired by Barjot's.

Ashkenazi mustard should have bite and texture. Smear it on Home-Cured Pastrami (page 210) and Home-Cured Corned Beef (page 207), eat it with savory Roasted Garlic Potato Knishes (see page 195), and use it for salad dressings.

MAKES 2 CUPS MUSTARD

---

1 cup whole brown
mustard seeds

1¼ cups apple
cider vinegar

¼ cup mustard
powder

2½ tablespoons
honey

½ teaspoon
kosher salt

1. Place the mustard seeds and vinegar in an airtight glass container and let sit at room temperature until the seeds absorb the vinegar and plump up, at least overnight or up to 24 hours.

2. Pour the seed mixture into a food processor and add the mustard powder, honey, and salt. Process for a minute or two until a paste forms.

3. Scoop the mustard into a clean glass jar, seal, and refrigerate for about 2 days to allow the flavor to mellow out. Don't be alarmed if the initial smell is rather pungent. The mustard will keep in the refrigerator for 4 to 6 months.

SCHMALTZ AND GRIBENES

JEFFREY

Rendered poultry fats were the linchpin of Jewish cooking in eastern Europe. "Schmaltz became to Ashkenazi cooking what olive oil was to Mediterranean food," wrote Gil Marks in the *Encyclopedia of Jewish Food*. Unfortunately, many cooks stopped using it in the twentieth century, when natural animal fats were replaced by "healthier" fats. But times have changed, and animal fat has been reanointed as the cooking fat du jour. Schmaltz ("liquid gold") is back on the map.

Whenever you're preparing chicken, duck, or goose, trim off any excess fat and skin and store both in the freezer until you accumulate about 8 ounces (1 cup). You can also purchase chicken skin or straight poultry fat from your local butcher. Chicken skin contains a lot of fat in and of itself. A tip: When you're in need of more schmaltz, purchase a small whole chicken or fatty chicken thighs, trim the skin and fat for schmaltz, and then use the meat for Classic Chicken Soup (page 130). Fried poultry skins make a delightful, though admittedly indulgent, snack or recipe topper. These *gribenes*, as they're called, are delicious on their own or as garnish for Chopped Liver Pâté (page 189).

Goose fat is especially incredible; it's mild in taste, not nearly as greasy as chicken or duck fat, and has a high smoke point, which makes it excellent for frying and roasting. This recipe calls for water and onions: the water prevents burning if you're just using skin, no fat, and the onions add flavor. But if you're working with copious amounts of straight goose or duck fat, you really don't need them. Happy rendering!

MAKES ABOUT ¼ CUP SCHMALTZ AND 1 CUP GRIBENES

---

1 cup poultry fat and/or poultry skin, cut into 1-inch strips (6 to 8 ounces)

¼ cup water (optional)

1 small onion (about 4 ounces), sliced (optional)

---

1. In a heavy-bottomed pan, combine the poultry fat and/or skin and ¼ cup water (if using) and set the pan over low heat. Once a thin layer of liquid fat has collected on the bottom of the pan, add the onion (if using). Increase the heat to medium-low and cook for 45 minutes to 1½ hours, stirring regularly to avoid burning or browning. Good schmaltz is

(continued) ▶

clear, so adjust the heat accordingly and take it slow. The more straight fat you're using, the faster the process will go; if you're using fatty skin, the process may take longer.

2. When the poultry skins and onions turn a bit brown (but not burnt), remove the pan from the heat. Carefully strain the schmaltz through a fine-mesh strainer into a glass jar. (If making *gribenes*, use tongs to remove the chicken skins from the strainer and set aside. Discard the onions.) Cover the schmaltz and refrigerate for later use. It will keep in the refrigerator for 2 to 3 months. You can also transfer it to an airtight plastic container and freeze it. It will last for 6 months or longer.

3. IF MAKING THE *GRIBENES*: Preheat the oven to 400°F. Discard any pieces of onion stuck to the reserved chicken skins. Place the skins on a rimmed baking sheet. Bake for 7 to 10 minutes, or until puffy and crispy. Remove from the oven and let cool on a paper towel–lined plate. The *gribenes* will keep in an airtight container at room temperature for up to 2 weeks.

THOUGHTS ON GOOSE FAT

JEFFREY Goose, which I thought for years was exclusively a Christmas food, actually plays a big role in Ashkenazi culinary history. My father always tells me how much Grandpa Julius loved goose—it was his meat of choice when he was growing up in Poland. Jews have been rearing geese and ducks for centuries in Europe because the birds possess valuable stores of fat between their skin and meat, which makes for excellent schmaltz. Geese were also prized for their down feathers, which were used for bedding, and for their fattened livers, which Jews sold for foie gras in Alsace-Lorraine. Because geese are foragers and cannot subsist on pure grain, as chickens do, they have fallen out of fashion in today's factory farm system.

Goose schmaltz was used throughout the year, but at no time was it more important than during Hanukkah, when fried foods are traditionally eaten and when latkes fried in goose fat are unbelievably delicious. I didn't believe it until I tried it myself. "The smell of smoking goose fat became the traditional scent of Hanukkah," writes Michael Wex in his book *Rhapsody in Schmaltz*. Sadly, the traditional Hanukkah goose (not unlike the Christmas goose) that was once commonplace has now all but disappeared. For the most part, latkes are no longer fried in goose fat in the United States, but in flavorless vegetable oils. In my mind, the holiday has never recovered.

SEASONED CROUTONS AND BREAD CRUMBS

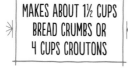

LIZ It breaks my heart to throw out a loaf of stale bread, so I've taken to turning past-its-prime bread into bread crumbs and croutons, and finding more recipes that call for them. Our spiced bread crumbs can be used in Cauliflower and Mushroom Kugel (page 198), Root Vegetable Latkes (page 204), and Kimchi-Stuffed Cabbage (page 245). The croutons can top leek soup (page 122), Autumn Kale Salad (page 154), or any soup or salad, really. Feel free to go wild and use any bread you have (stale or not). If you're gluten-free, try the same method with commercial gluten-free breads. I've tried it for gluten-free friends and was pleased with the results.

MAKES ABOUT 1½ CUPS BREAD CRUMBS OR 4 CUPS CROUTONS

6 slices stale bread (rye, pumpernickel, challah, etc.; about 6 ounces)

Pinch of salt

1 tablespoon caraway seeds or sesame seeds (optional)

3 tablespoons olive oil, for croutons

FOR BREAD CRUMBS:

1. Preheat the oven to 400°F. Toast the bread directly on the oven rack(s) for about 7 minutes, or until the bread is well toasted and completely firm when pressed in the middle of the slice.

2. Break up the slices, transfer to a food processor, and add the salt and caraway seeds (if using). Pulse until fine crumbs are formed. If the crumbs aren't breaking down, spread them on a baking sheet and return to the oven for 5 minutes, then pulse again. Let cool to room temperature. The bread crumbs will keep in an airtight container at room temperature for 6 months.

FOR CROUTONS:

1. Preheat the oven to 350°F. Cut the bread into bite-size squares (1-inch squares or the size of your preference) and place them in a bowl. Coat with the oil and sprinkle with the caraway seeds (if using). Spread them out on a heavy rimmed baking sheet. Bake for 12 to 15 minutes, or until the croutons are completely crisp. Stir halfway through to ensure even browning, and keep an eye on them to make sure they don't burn.

2. Let cool to room temperature. The croutons will keep in an airtight container at room temperature for up to 6 weeks.

~~~ TWO ~~~

PICKLES

JEFFREY → When I was twenty-two, I moved onto a pickle farm—think: hippie vegan co-op meets Israeli kibbutz in the Berkshire Mountains. I was a suburban New Jersey boy who had never planted an onion bulb or worn steel-toed work boots. I certainly hadn't ever pickled my own vegetables.

On one particularly hot day, I helped pack bushels of cucumbers, dill, and garlic straight from the field into the bed of an old Chevy truck and haul them to the "picklearium." Under the instruction of Adamah Farm's pickler, I cleaned and submerged the veggies in salted water, sealed them with a large lid, and left them to sit at room temperature in giant blue barrels. Like magic, one week later, the fifty-gallon drums were filled with perfect sour pickles. My mind was blown.

The pickles were delicious. There was a fizziness to them. They conjured up childhood memories of the New York deli, but they were bolder and crisper. I couldn't believe it. We hadn't done anything to make this happen. The pickler explained that it was all about letting the bacteria do their thing. These pickles were lacto-fermented, meaning the good bacteria naturally found on vegetable skins and leaves did all the work. As old-fashioned picklers, our role was merely to create the right environment for the natural bacteria to thrive. Unlike the sterile, mass-market vinegar-brined stuff on grocery store shelves, lacto-fermented pickles were live-cultured and probiotic. They provided just the right combination of science, flavor, and rebelliousness to hook me for good.

The director of Adamah Farm—whose parents had immigrated from Hungary—managed to connect many dots for me and thirteen other farm fellows by explaining how Jewish history, centuries of shtetl wisdom, and larger food systems all came together to create the best damn pickle I'd ever eaten. He explained how the process we employed on the farm mirrored the techniques in prewar Polish shtetls. When making sauerkraut by feeding endless heads of cabbage into the industrial shredder with a team of farm fellows, I couldn't help but imagine my ancestors in eastern Europe shredding cabbages by hand into wooden barrels, preserving their own harvests together as a community. I pictured women and children collecting the produce from the garden, then stomping on cabbage leaves with their feet to release the cabbage juices, after which bearded men would lug the barrels down to the root cellar, where the future sauerkraut would join the drums of pickles, soon to be joined by sacks of beets, turnips, and potatoes as the harvest continued.

Pickles revealed to me the Jewish folk wisdom that my family either lost or shed when becoming American and assimilating to life in the New World. It seemed so basic. How could they not have covered this in Jewish Day School? Cucumbers, dill, and garlic were all harvested at the same time in the summer. Caraway seeds—a standard Ashkenazi flavor agent for sauerkraut—are harvested in the fall, the same time as cabbage. It's best to wait for the first frost to harvest cabbage for sauerkraut, when sugars shoot from the core into the leaf.

We began to eat differently at Adamah in late fall, after the cold hit. There were fewer fresh vegetables and fruits available. We ate heartier meals, with more starches and fatty meats, which we balanced with soured vegetables from the picklearium. "In other societies people digested their heavy starch diet with the assistance of sauces, chili peppers, olive oil, or sugar-based products," culinary historian John Cooper wrote in *Eat and Be Satisfied*. For eastern European Jews, it was the pickle. Pickled foods were my ancestors' survival strategy for making summer and fall vegetables last through long, harsh winters; they were nutrient-packed foods in an otherwise meager diet that helped digest fatty meats. Eating pickles with my pastrami sandwich suddenly took on a much deeper significance.

〰

LIZ

I had always assumed pickling was complicated, requiring sterilized jars and expensive pressure-canning equipment. Not to mention that canning felt like something *foreign*, some vestige of pioneer life on the American prairie. But lacto-fermented pickling, which I came to know because of Jeffrey, defied my expectations.

In the stark industrial kitchen deep in Queens, where Jeffrey and I first started cooking together on a large scale, Jeffrey would open the pickle bucket lids and marvel at the cloudlike white formations on the surface. "They're like snowflakes," he'd exclaim, "each one unique." He talked about pickling *a lot*.

With practice, I learned to appreciate the art of saltwater pickling myself. I'd mix vegetables with salted water and spices. Then wait. The bacteria *Lactobacillus*, found naturally on vegetable skins, converted sugars into lactic acid. The acid transformed the salty water into increasingly sour brine, nature's preservative. After several days or several weeks, I'd open the bucket lid and marvel, just like Jeffrey did. The process required me to cultivate a level of patience I never thought I had.

Cucumbers, I'll admit, were a bit difficult for me to get right on a small scale at first. My first experiment in a quart-size jar on my kitchen counter didn't come out well. I fermented the cucumbers for six days and ended up with results that were way too soft and mushy. There were a few issues with my technique, which I was able to troubleshoot with Jeffrey's help.

I persisted in my pickling efforts despite those early mishaps, and a few months and many batches later, my pickle confidence was through the roof. I made a new batch of sour dill pickles in an elegant straight-sided jar, wrapped it with a bow, and gave it as a wedding gift to my brother and sister-in-law. They love pickles, which I knew. And they were especially impressed with mine. Apparently, they ate the entire jar that night. From that moment on, pickles became a solid part of my repertoire, and hopefully they'll become part of yours, too. We've included lots of lacto-fermented pickles in this chapter, like Classic Sour Dills (page 50), Crisp Garlic Dilly Beans (page 56), Ashkenazi Kimchi (page 68), and Sauerruben (page 65).

The yin to lacto-fermentation's yang is hot brine vinegar pickling, which is more common today. Making vinegar pickles is also really simple and easy. Just pour hot brine over vegetables (or fruits), which cooks them slightly. Once the jars are filled, close the lid and wait a day before you dig in, or place the jars in the refrigerator. Vinegar creates the right kind of sterile environment and pH levels for canning, which is how pickles can sit on store shelves for years without spoiling—great for supermarkets and emergency shelter stockpiles. (See page 325 for information on canning.) Vinegar brines can lead to some pretty exciting combinations, even if the predominant flavor will always be vinegar. So while I'm firmly in the saltwater camp, Jeffrey and I nevertheless included recipes in this book for several vinegar pickles we adore, including Quick Pickled Shallots (page 71), Clove and Spice Pickled Beets (page 72), Sweet Pickled Watermelon Rind (page 75), and Cardamom Pickled Grapes (page 79).

LACTO-FERMENTATION 101

1. **SALT** regulates the fermentation process, helping to create a mini ecosystem that encourages the growth of good bacteria and inhibits the growth of bad bacteria, which cause vegetables to spoil. Salt also draws out the water from vegetables, concentrating their flavors and keeping the vegetables crunchy. There's no need to purchase special "canning" or "pickling" salts. Noniodized kosher salt will do (iodine is known to inhibit the growth of bacteria, good or bad).

2. **SALT RATIOS** matter for your brine and are a major key to pickling success. Our recipes stick to a 3½ to 5 percent salt solution for fermented pickles. Old-fashioned recipes call for about 10 percent of the pickle brine to be salt (quite salty), and those pickles would last longer without refrigeration, but they have to be rinsed with water multiple times before serving. Refrigeration allows for less

salty brines ready to be eaten straight from the jar. For dry-salting recipes, like sauerkraut or sauerruben, the salt ratio is 3 tablespoons kosher salt to about 5 pounds vegetables, according to the USDA.

3. The **TEMPERATURE** of your kitchen can make or break a batch of pickles. Generally speaking, warmer temperatures speed up the fermentation process and cooler temperatures slow it down. For warmer temperatures, be sure to monitor your creations closely. In the case of cooler temperatures, cultivate patience and plan ahead for longer fermentation times. If your kitchen is sweltering or near-freezing, you may want to wait for the heat wave or cold spell to pass before throwing down a batch of sauerkraut or brewing beet kvass. A good moderate temperature is somewhere in the range of 65° to 75°F. In addition to pickling, room temperature plays an important role when working with fermented dairy and grains, like Old Country Sour Cream (page 24), Cultured Cream Cheese (page 25), and Jewish Rye (page 100), as well as different types of kvass (pages 290–296).

4. **VEGETABLES** for pickling should be the freshest available. Generally, the smaller the cucumber or green bean or radish, the better. They'll be less watery and thus have a more concentrated flavor and better crunch.

5. **SEAL AND SUBMERGE** your vegetables, forcing them to remain beneath the brine. This ensures that they're not exposed to oxygen in the air while still allowing the bubbles (carbon dioxide is a by-product of the process) to be released. Any part of the vegetable exposed to oxygen will turn slightly yeasty or moldy. Note that creating a seal for fermented pickles is not the same as sealing a jar when canning.

   a. If you're fermenting in a wide ceramic **CROCK**, use a glass or ceramic plate or wooden sauerkraut board to push the veggies beneath the brine. Top the plate with a weight (such as a glass jar filled with water) to ensure that it is pressing down on the vegetables. You may then drape a clean kitchen towel over the crock to keep out any bugs or dust (see photo, page 59).

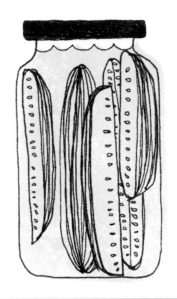

The brine line

"Sealing"—crock and plate method

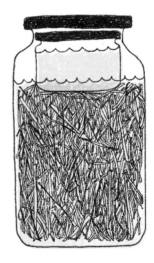

"Sealing"—jar within a jar method

b. If you're fermenting in a **JAR**, you may be able to pack the vegetables into the jar tightly enough that they will remain below the brine naturally, as is often the case with dill pickles or pickled string beans. Place an unscrewed lid loosely on the top of the jar to keep out any bugs or dust. If fermenting sauerkraut, sauerruben, or any other vegetable that won't stay below the brine easily, find an even smaller glass jar, fill it with water, and use it as a weight to press down on the vegetables. If possible, screw on the jar lid and use it to apply pressure to the smaller jar inside (see illustration page 46). When your lid is sealed tightly, you must "burp" it once a day to release the carbon dioxide that builds up in the jar during the fermentation process. Burping is easy: simply unscrew the lid for a moment and then tighten it again.

6. **PATIENCE** is the critical ingredient. The process of fermentation involves waiting as the bacteria do their work, tasting your experiments, and sometimes more waiting. After the appropriate number of days, when your pickles are at their desired flavor point, place them in the refrigerator to stop—or at least slow to a near halt—the fermentation process.

Additional Tips

- **CRUNCH:** Tannins in leaves such as bay leaves, horseradish leaves, currant leaves, grape leaves, oak leaves, tea leaves, etc., help keep fermented vegetables crunchy by inhibiting an enzyme (pectinase) that is known to soften cucumbers. Soaking cucumbers in **ICE WATER** before pickling helps firm them up, too.

- **CERAMIC, GLASS, AND WOOD:** Make sauerkraut or pickles in crocks, bowls, and jars made of ceramic, glass, or wood. Don't use metal, a reactive material. You can even reuse jars from store-bought pickles, tomato sauce, etc. For larger quantities and more street cred in the pickling community, spring for a ceramic crock. There are several plastics that are food-grade and considered safe, but it's not always simple to know what's what, so either use a number 2 HDPE food-grade plastic bucket, or just stick to glass and ceramic crocks or jars. Wash your jars before use, though at home it's not necessary to sanitize them as you would if canning.

- **FILTERED WATER VS. TAP WATER:** Tap water often contains chlorine, which kills bacteria. When making a vegetable ferment such as Classic Sour Dills (page 50), the bacteria are critical for a successful outcome, and filtered water provides a stronger guarantee of success. However, there are two easy ways to get around using filtered water:

  a. Boil water, then let it cool to room temperature.

  b. Let the water sit, uncovered, for at least 30 minutes but ideally several hours to let the chlorine evaporate.

  We've had success with both of these methods, but if we have access to filtered water, we'll take it.

- **MOLD:** White yeast or mold, which commonly forms on the surface of lacto-fermented vegetable brines, is harmless. Just scrape it off and the vegetables should be good to eat. On the off chance that you find black, pink, or green fuzz on the surface of your brine or on your vegetables, be extra vigilant to ensure that you don't ingest it. If the smell is funky or otherwise off (you'll know), you may have to toss the batch and start over. The more you ferment, the more you'll find that odors and colors tell you what's going on in your crock. If a batch doesn't work out, don't feel guilty about tossing it. It's part of the learning process. It's also a good opportunity to brainstorm what could be done differently.

- **MURKINESS:** With any brined pickles, white sediment can form at the bottom of the jar as a by-product of lacto-fermentation. It's healthy. If shaken up, it can make the brine look cloudy—that's fine.

- **BLUE GARLIC:** Don't be afraid of blue garlic in your lacto-fermented experiments. Garlic contains a special enzyme that turns itself bluish green when exposed to copper and aluminum, both of which are found in most tap water. Just warn your friends.

PICKLES
⫸ RECIPES ⫷

CLASSIC SOUR DILLS

JEFFREY

My mission to spread the sour pickle gospel brought me to Poland. I had been asked to lead a pickle demo during the Festival of Jewish Culture in Krakow. Why conference organizers wanted a New Yorker to teach Poles about pickling was beyond me. I stood at the front of a room crowded with older Polish women. "Who here has made pickles before?" I asked through my translator. Every single hand shot up. *Uh-oh. What do I say to thirty or so women who have been making pickles as long as I've been alive?* Not much—I decided I'd rather learn from them. Our discussion quickly turned contentious. "You use too much salt," one woman yelled. Another told me that I wasn't letting the pickles ferment long enough. And while we all could agree that a mushy pickle is a pox on your house, their tricks to keep cucumbers crunchy ranged from tannin-rich leaves to ice-water baths to horseradish root.

The demo concluded with a discussion of the best cucumber varieties to use for pickling. Finally, a simple topic. Always select thin, small cucumbers. The lower the water content in the cucumber, the better. In the United States, the best cucumbers for pickling are usually Kirby cucumbers. Persian cucumbers work, too, but not as consistently, we've found. Avoid long, waxy English cucumbers. On the pickle farm we called them "slicers" with as much derision as we could muster.

Note that this recipe calls for an extended wait time of up to 7 days. Also, pickling your cucumbers whole increases the likelihood of a crunchy pickle. Slice or spear your cucumbers only once they're finished for best results. The brine will likely look cloudy and a bit fizzy. That's 100 percent normal and healthy. Once you're done with the pickles, save the brine for salad dressings (page 80), Pickle Brine Bread (page 96), and Sour Dill Martinis (page 306).

 MAKES 1 GALLON PICKLES

---

5 pounds whole unpeeled Kirby cucumbers (the smaller the better)

½ gallon filtered water

½ cup kosher salt

1 cinnamon stick

3 bay leaves (dried or fresh)

1 dried whole chile pepper

1 teaspoon whole coriander seeds

1 teaspoon yellow mustard seeds

1 teaspoon whole black peppercorns

½ teaspoon whole cloves

¼ bunch fresh dill, washed (leave the stems on)

1½ heads garlic, cloves separated and crushed

1. If desired, fill a large bowl or bucket with ice and water and place the cucumbers in it. Let sit for 45 minutes or up to 5 hours. This helps firm the cucumbers so they retain crunch during the fermentation process, but it's not absolutely necessary.

2. Fill a large ceramic crock or glass jar (gallon-size is ideal) halfway with the filtered water. Add the salt and stir until it has dissolved.

3. Add the remaining ingredients to the salted water, then add the cucumbers. Make sure the spices, herbs, and garlic are not simply floating on the surface.

4. CREATE A SEAL: If fermenting in a crock, use a plate or a wooden board to force the vegetables beneath the brine. If necessary, top with a clean glass growler or jar filled with water to ensure that the weight applies pressure on the vegetables, keeping them submerged. If fermenting in a jar, use a smaller jar filled with water to do the same (see page 45 for sealing instructions). Cover with a towel to keep out dust and bugs.

5. Let the soon-to-be-pickles sit at room temperature for 3 to 7 days. The longer they sit and ferment, the sourer they will become. At a stable room temperature, half sour pickles should take 2 to 3 days to ferment and full sour pickles should take 5 to 7 days (the amount of time may vary based on air temperature and even elevation). You'll notice that the pickles will turn paler as they ferment.

6. Once the pickles reach the desired flavor, remove any white yeast or mold (or moldy pickles) from the top of the vessel and discard them. Yeasts and molds are a natural part of the process and typically occur only on the surface, where oxygen meets the vegetables. Don't worry. (For more information on mold and yeast, see page 48.) Pack your pickles into smaller glass jars, then cover completely with brine and place directly in the refrigerator. They will keep in the refrigerator for up to 6 months.

FRIED SOUR PICKLES WITH GARLIC AIOLI

JEFFREY

At the Rosendale International Pickle Festival in upstate New York, I stumbled upon a fried pickle truck. There was a long line of folks waiting to get a taste. As a recent convert to lacto-fermentation, I was skeptical of anything involving sweet vinegary pickles, and doubly unsure of putting them in the deep fryer. But the long line spoke for itself, so I tried them. And loved them. They were crisp and juicy, and tasted of Southern county fairs I'd never actually attended. They offered a brand-new way for me to enjoy the exalted pickle, though I couldn't help but wonder what it would be like to fry a Jewish pickle.

Liz and I began frying up our Classic Sour Dills (page 50) and never turned back. It's a great way to use pickle batches that don't turn out as crunchy as you would like, though don't hesitate to use your crunchiest batch. If you haven't made homemade pickles yet, the recipe also works with store-bought sours. Fried pickles make a great hors d'oeuvre, especially with the garlic aioli. Sweet pickles will definitely work in place of sour pickles, but may put your Ashkenazi street cred in jeopardy. Note that a thermometer is important for this recipe.

SERVES 8

FOR THE AIOLI:

1 large egg

1 egg yolk

2 tablespoons fresh lemon juice

1 tablespoon spicy brown mustard, homemade (page 32) or store-bought

2 garlic cloves, crushed

½ cup grapeseed oil

Kosher salt and freshly ground black pepper

FOR THE FRIED PICKLES:

Peanut or canola oil, for frying

6 large sour or half sour dill pickles, store-bought or homemade (page 50), cut into ½-inch-thick rounds

2 tablespoons all-purpose flour

4 large eggs, beaten

1 cup panko bread crumbs

1 teaspoon ground coriander

¼ teaspoon mustard powder

1 teaspoon kosher salt

1. TO MAKE THE AIOLI: In a blender or food processor, combine the egg, egg yolk, lemon juice, mustard, and garlic. With the machine running, slowly drizzle in the oil and blend until the aioli thickens. (Your blender or food processor will do this easily and quickly, but you can also make the aioli in a large bowl and whisk the oil in by hand.) Season with salt and pepper to taste. Transfer to a small bowl, cover, and refrigerate until ready to serve.

2. TO MAKE THE FRIED PICKLES: Fill a large, heavy-bottomed pot with at least 2 inches of oil for effective frying and attach a thermometer to the side. (The thermometer is critical here.) Heat the oil over medium heat to 325°F. Be patient. This may take a few minutes. Monitor the temperature and do not let it go above 325°F.

3. Meanwhile, set up four wide, shallow bowls near your stovetop. In one, place the pickle rounds; in the next, place the flour; in the next, place the eggs; and in the last, place the panko, coriander, mustard, and salt and whisk with a fork to combine. Finally, line a wide plate with paper towels and set it nearby.

4. Once your oil has reached 325°F, you're ready to fry. Coat a pickle round in flour, then dip it in the egg, then in the panko. Carefully drop it in the hot oil—avoid splashing. It's important that the temperature doesn't dip too low, so work on about 4 pickle rounds at a time and don't crowd the pot. Fry the pickle rounds until the coating turns golden brown. This should take about 1 minute per batch. We recommend timing this. You don't want them to get any darker and burn.

5. Using a small mesh strainer or spider (or even a fork, but be careful), transfer the fried pickles to the paper towel–lined plate. Repeat with the remaining pickle rounds. Fried foods are best served immediately, so if you are serving these for a party or other gathering, set up your frying station in advance and start frying when everyone has arrived. Serve with the aioli on the side for dipping.

CRISP GARLIC DILLY BEANS

LIZ

Jeffrey and I taught a month-long culinary course to high school students, and we made dilly beans with the students on the first day of class. "Are you sure we only need salt and water?" the students asked, as if we were playing some kind of joke on them. We submerged green beans, garlic, and dill in salt water, then watched our dilly beans transform each day in the brine. By day 5, they were munching on some of the crispiest pickles they'd ever eaten. And all they'd needed was salt and water.

We love the sense of wonder that arises when folks are pickling for the first time. Since dilly beans are some of the easiest lacto-fermented pickles to make, they're usually where we begin. Look for thinner, smaller beans. The fresher and crisper they are, the crunchier they'll be. As you become more proficient, you can make larger quantities in a crock or larger jar quite easily by scaling up the recipe and using the methods on page 45 to create a seal. Whether you're a novice or an experienced pickler, these beans will make for an endlessly satisfying snack. Use them as garnishes for our Pickle Brine Bloody Marys (page 305), and after you've eaten your beans, save any brine for Sour Dill Martinis (page 306). Note that this recipe calls for an extended wait time.

MAKES 1 QUART PICKLES

2 cups filtered water, plus more if needed

1 tablespoon plus 1 teaspoon kosher salt, plus more if needed

½ teaspoon yellow mustard seeds

½ teaspoon whole black peppercorns

1 bay leaf (dried or fresh)

2 sprigs fresh dill

3 garlic cloves, crushed

½ pound green or pole beans

1. Pour the filtered water into a clean widemouthed quart-size jar. Pour the salt into the water, cover with a tight-fitting lid and shake to dissolve the salt.

2. Add the mustard seeds, peppercorns, bay leaf, dill, and garlic, then add the green beans. Pack the beans in tightly, squeezing as many as possible into the jar, making sure the brine covers the vegetables. If it doesn't cover the beans, mix a heaping 1½ teaspoons of salt with 1 cup of water, then pour in enough to cover the vegetables. Seal the jar.

3. Let the beans sit at room temperature for 5 to 7 days, briefly opening the jar once every couple of days to "burp"

it (releasing carbon dioxide). You'll
notice that the beans will turn pale after
about 2 days. The time the beans take
to ferment fully will vary depending on
air temperature and elevation. Taste the
beans each day after the fifth day until
the desired level of sourness is reached.
The brine will begin to appear cloudy
and may be a bit fizzy. That's fine.

4. When you are happy with the taste of
    the beans, remove all white yeast or
    mold from the top of your jar, if any has
    appeared. Cover the jar and place the
    pickled beans directly in the refrigerator.
    They will keep for up to 6 months.

SAUERKRAUT

JEFFREY

Believe it or not, sauerkraut making wasn't always gender neutral. "Krauting" in eastern Europe was considered a manly pursuit. "It's not quite cooking," David Bezmozgis writes in *The New Yorker*. "There are few ingredients and the work required is part wrestling match, part science experiment." In the pickle kitchen at the Adamah Farm, I was always heaving, smashing, and chopping. Yet women in the shtetls of eastern Europe were no backseat krauters. They were working alongside their husbands and brothers, smashing and chopping. Families with enough money even hired women as seasonal workers just for the task. Try not to feel restricted by Old World gender norms in your sauerkraut pursuits.

Making sauerkraut is actually quite simple and meditative. The salty cabbage mixture you'll be making can handle the addition of various spices and even other vegetables or fruits, like carrots, radishes, and even apples, so feel free to get creative. And definitely scale up as you become proficient at the process. Sauerkraut is tangy and refreshing and delicious on a hot dog or sandwich, or in Kimchi-Stuffed Cabbage (page 245), Braised Sauerkraut and Potato Gratin (page 222), or Pierogi (page 140). Sauerkraut is classically paired in the German tradition with sausage and potatoes. It's nice with a Riesling, too. But the truth is, it's best on its own, straight from the jar. A bit of folk wisdom I picked up along the way recommends using part of the cabbage core in your kraut to keep it from making you gassy. Note that this recipe calls for an extended wait time.

MAKES 2 QUARTS SAUERKRAUT

---

3 pounds green and/or purple cabbage (about 1 small head)

1½ tablespoons kosher salt, plus more if needed

OPTIONAL SPICES (CHOOSE JUST ONE):

1½ teaspoons caraway seeds

2 garlic cloves, finely minced

1½ teaspoons whole black peppercorns

1½ teaspoons mustard seeds

1 tablespoon juniper berries

Filtered water, if needed

---

1. Remove any dirty or discolored outer leaves from the cabbage and rinse the head under cold water. Using a long, sharp knife, slice off the stem of the cabbage, carefully quarter the cabbage, and remove the core.

2. Using a knife or a mandoline, slice the cabbage quarters into long, thin shreds, the thinner the better, placing the cut pieces in a large bowl as you work. Sprinkle the salt into the bowl and, using clean hands, coat the shredded cabbage with the salt, pressing down occasionally to release liquid. You'll notice quickly that the cabbage begins to "sweat" and reduce in volume.

3. Lightly massage the cabbage, stirring the cabbage from the bottom to the top of the bowl over and over again, for 10 to 15 minutes total. To retain the crunchy texture, be gentle. If you prefer softer sauerkraut and want to save time, you can be rough. The cabbage will reduce in volume by about one-quarter. It should also glisten; it turns iridescent and light in color as it gains moisture. The cabbage is ready when you can firmly squeeze a handful in your fist and juices drip out.

4. Mix in the spice of your choice (if using). Pack the cabbage and any liquid from the bowl into two separate widemouthed quart-size jars or a small ceramic crock. Be careful not to lose any liquid. (A canning funnel helps avoid spills.) Pack tightly, pushing on the cabbage forcefully with your fingers or fist to release more liquid and remove any air bubbles. The cabbage juices will rise above the cabbage. If they do not rise above right away, let the cabbage sit for about 2 hours and try pressing down again. Occasionally, depending on the cabbage, the liquid will still not rise above the cabbage, even after some time. In this case, simply mix 1 cup filtered water with 1 teaspoon kosher salt and pour some of the salty water over the cabbage until it is completely submerged.

5. CREATE A SEAL: If fermenting in a crock, use a plate or a wooden board to force the cabbage beneath the brine. Top with a clean glass growler or jar filled with water to ensure that the weight applies pressure on the cabbage, keeping it submerged. If fermenting in a jar, use a smaller jar filled with water to do the same (see page 45 for sealing instructions). Cover with a towel to keep out dust and bugs. Let the cabbage ferment at room temperature, out of direct sunlight, for 7 to 10 days. The longer it sits, the sourer it becomes. When the cabbage shreds become translucent, that's a good sign that it's close to ready. You may notice foam or bubbles during fermentation. That's okay. When the sauerkraut has reached your desired level of sourness, transfer to a jar with a lid (if you've used a crock), cover, and refrigerate. Enjoy for up to 9 months.

 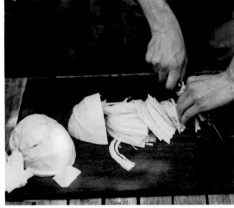 

WINE-BRAISED SAUERKRAUT AND MUSHROOMS

If you love the tangy and salty notes of sauerkraut, try this recipe. Wine-Braised Sauerkraut and Mushrooms is an incredible topping for grilled sausage paired with crusty bread, and is used to build our rich and hearty Braised Sauerkraut and Potato Gratin (page 222). It can also be served as a savory side with Alsatian Roasted Goose or Duck with Apples and Onions (page 234).

If you've made your own flavored sauerkraut according to our instructions (see page 60), any variety we suggest except for peppercorn or juniper berry will work well for this recipe, as the peppercorns and juniper berries become bitter when cooked.

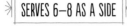

SERVES 6–8 AS A SIDE

---

2 tablespoons unsalted butter or vegetable oil

1 medium onion, thinly sliced

1 pound fresh mushrooms (porcinis are delicious but any garden variety of mushroom you find at the store will work great), dry-scrubbed and thinly sliced

1 pound fermented sauerkraut, home-made (page 60) or store-bought (about 2 cups)

2½ teaspoons sugar, plus more as needed

½ cup dry white wine (whatever leftover wine's in your fridge works well)

½ cup vegetable broth, homemade (page 123) or store-bought

---

1. In a heavy-bottomed pan, melt the butter over medium-low heat. Add the onion and cook, stirring frequently, until the onion begins to brown but remains moist, about 8 minutes. Add the mushrooms and cook, stirring frequently, until the mushrooms are fully cooked but not shriveled, about 10 minutes more. Add the sauerkraut and sugar and stir to incorporate.

2. Increase the heat to high and cook rapidly for about 2 minutes. Add the wine and stir well. Reduce the heat to low and simmer for about 2 minutes while some of the alcohol evaporates, then pour in the broth. Simmer for about 10 minutes, or until some of the liquid has begun to evaporate. Taste the mixture. If it is too sour, add another teaspoon of sugar. The final mixture will be liquidy.

3. Serve the braised sauerkraut right away or reheat the next day for an even richer flavor.

SAUERRUBEN

JEFFREY

Turnips used to be the go-to Ashkenazi root vegetable. They rivaled beets and were cheap and available before the potato even dared to cross the Atlantic. So what happened? They got labeled the poor person's root. Even the rabbis from the Talmud knew this. "Woe to the house where the turnip is common," they wrote. The potato soon took over, and it hasn't relinquished its hold on Ashkenazi cuisine in nearly two centuries.

But we love turnips. They pickle well, and their strong flavor complements most sandwiches and salads without dominating them. Sauerruben makes for a healthy midnight snack, and you will be pleasantly surprised by the horseradish notes that develop as it ferments. Can the potato say that? I think not.

MAKES 1 QUART
SAUERRUBEN

2 pounds whole turnips (rutabaga works, too)

1 tablespoon plus 1 teaspoon kosher salt

1. Using the medium holes on the box grater or the shredder plate on a food processor, shred the turnips. Sprinkle 1 tablespoon of the salt on the turnips, mixing the shreds with your hands to coat them evenly with the salt. Liquid will begin to appear at the bottom of the bowl. After a few minutes, sprinkle in the remaining 1 teaspoon salt. Continue to mix with your hands for a few minutes more, pressing down occasionally to release more liquid. Take a fistful of shredded turnips and squeeze—if liquid oozes out, then you're ready.

2. Place the turnips in a quart-size jar, being careful not to lose any of the liquid. (A canning funnel helps avoid spills.) Create a seal: Use a smaller jar that fits into the mouth of the quart-size jar, fill it with water, and place on top of the turnips to force them beneath the brine and to ensure that the weight applies pressure, keeping the turnip shreds submerged (see page 45 for sealing instructions). Cover with a towel to keep out dust and bugs. Let the turnips sit at room temperature for 3 to 6 days. Taste after 3 days to see if it's sour enough for your liking. If not, reseal and taste daily.

3. Once the desired flavor is reached, cover the jar and refrigerate. Note that the top layer may dry out. If this happens, just scrape it off. Sauerruben will remain delicious in the refrigerator for up to 3 months.

FRONT: **Ashkenazi Kimchi** (page 68);
BACK: **Sauerruben** (page 65)

TO SPICE, OR NOT TO SPICE

LIZ While Ashkenazi cuisine is hardly lacking in strong flavors, it isn't generally known for the type of heat that dominates Asian cuisines or Sephardi or Mizrachi (Middle Eastern) Jewish foods. That said, spice is part of the contemporary culinary vernacular. Open the fridge in any of my friends' houses, and I bet you'll see at least three different types of hot sauce. Even in new Jewish restaurants, you can sometimes find spicy matzo balls and jalapeño herring. And while we don't take it quite that far, we have incorporated a few spicy dishes into this book. Ashkenazi Kimchi (page 68), Spicy Hungarian Cholent (page 239), Kimchi-Stuffed Cabbage (page 245), and our Pickle Brine Bloody Mary (page 305) are among my favorites.

Jeffrey claims he is concerned about our mothers, who are sensitive to spice and always order dishes "mild" when eating out at Thai or Indian restaurants. He thinks, in deference to the women who birthed us, we should start our recipes off mild and suggest that spice lovers increase the levels to whatever they might prefer. I, on the other hand, think we should start big and tell those who can't handle the heat (including our moms) to deal with it.

Naturally, there are echoes of a famous first century BCE Talmudic argument between Rabbi Hillel and Rabbi Shamai in our debate. Hillel argued that when lighting Hanukkah candles, you should light just one on the first night and increase the number of candles that you light each subsequent night so by the eighth you'd have a fully lit candelabra. Shamai, on the other hand, argued that one should start with eight candles and decrease until there was just one. If we were to apply these arguments to our spice debate, Hillel would side with Jeffrey and Shamai with me. Annoyingly, Hillel won the argument and Jewish practice follows the Hillel lighting scheme. But I didn't go down so easily. I forced a compromise, and we made most of the spicy elements in the book optional. Jeffrey thinks he won, and maybe he did just a little bit, but I'm okay with that since I have a spice-averse Jewish mother, too.

〉〈

ASHKENAZI KIMCHI

JEFFREY

How can there be kimchi, a Korean fermented staple, in an Ashkenazi cookbook? Fair question. In 2009, I was writing an article about the Lower East Side's annual Pickle Day. I met a number of young Korean Americans who had started kimchi companies, building something new from an age-old tradition. I liked that sentiment so much that a few years later, I looked to those entrepreneurs for inspiration when conceiving of The Gefilteria. Plus, kimchi is to Korean cuisine what sauerkraut is to eastern European cuisine, though fermented cabbage may be even more revered on the Korean Peninsula. In fact, when there was a shortage of napa cabbage a few years ago, the South Korean government instituted an emergency kimchi bailout program.

We've given this kimchi a Yiddish accent by including green cabbage, turnips, and hot Hungarian paprika. If you want a spicy kimchi, include spicy chile peppers like serrano or cayenne. If you'd like a more mild kimchi, leave out the hot paprika and opt for milder peppers like ancho chiles or banana peppers. I opt for no ginger, but Liz feels pretty strongly that the ginger belongs. Use this kimchi in your Kimchi-Stuffed Cabbage (page 245) for a spicy and distinctive take on a classic. It also makes a great palate opener or side. Just know that each time you open a jar, the smell will linger for a few moments. You'll learn to love it. Note that this recipe calls for an extended wait time.

MAKES 2 QUARTS KIMCHI

1 pound green cabbage, outer leaves removed, cored and thinly shredded

1 pound napa cabbage, outer leaves removed, cored and coarsely chopped

1 pound turnips or daikon radishes, halved and cut into ¼-inch-thick half-moons

1 pound carrots, cut into ¼-inch-thick rounds

2 scallions, sliced

8 cups filtered water

½ cup kosher salt

FOR THE PASTE:

1 medium red onion, quartered

4 garlic cloves

2 chile peppers, fresh or dried, mild to hot based on your preference

1 tablespoon hot Hungarian paprika (optional)

3 tablespoons grated peeled fresh ginger (optional)

1. Place the prepared vegetables in a large bowl. In a separate container, combine the filtered water and salt and stir until the salt has dissolved. Pour the saltwater brine over the vegetables, weigh down the vegetables with a plate to ensure that they stay below the brine, and let sit at room temperature for 1½ hours.

2. Drain the vegetables, reserving 1 cup of the brine, and return them to the bowl.

3. TO MAKE THE PASTE: In a food processor, combine all the paste ingredients and process for about 15 seconds, or until the ingredients break down and combine to form a rough paste. (If you don't have a food processor, you can do this using a mortar and pestle.)

4. Using a wooden spoon or your hands (we prefer our hands—but keep in mind that the mixture is spicy), coat the vegetables with the paste. Once well coated, pack the vegetables *very* lightly into two quart-size jars or a small ceramic crock so that the brine rises to cover them. If there is not enough liquid in the jar to keep the vegetables submerged, pour in enough of the reserved brine to cover them.

5. CREATE A SEAL: If fermenting in a crock, use a plate or a wooden board to force the vegetables beneath the brine. Top with a clean glass growler or jar filled with water to ensure that the weight applies pressure on the vegetables, keeping them submerged. If fermenting in a jar, use a smaller jar filled with water to do the same (see page 45 for sealing instructions). Cover with a towel to keep out dust and bugs. Let the kimchi ferment on your kitchen counter, out of direct sunlight, for 3 to 7 days, or longer to taste. Fermentation times vary significantly with temperature, so it is critical to taste the kimchi each day after 2 days. When the kimchi reaches the desired taste, cover the jar and refrigerate. Kimchi will remain delicious in your refrigerator for up to 6 months.

QUICK PICKLED SHALLOTS

LIZ

I think shallots are the ideal vegetable for hot vinegar brining. After they're pickled, they lose any harshness, but they retain their gorgeous color. They're also so easy to make and so delicious on everything that I feel like a fool when I don't have them on hand.

Pickled shallots belong in egg scrambles, tacos, ramen, grilled cheese, and, of course, on a bagel with lox and schmear. Mix them into Autumn Kale Salad (page 154) or use the brine for a salad dressing (page 80). You can swap the shallots for red onions to great effect. And while fennel seeds and thyme or marjoram add great flavor, you don't need them.

MAKES 1 QUART PICKLES

1 pound shallots (or red onions)

2 teaspoons whole black peppercorns

2 teaspoons fennel seeds

6 dried bay leaves

2 or 3 sprigs fresh herbs, such as thyme or marjoram (optional)

2 cups distilled white vinegar

1 cup sugar

3 tablespoons kosher salt

1. Slice the shallots as thinly as possible with a sharp knife. Hand slicing is fine, but using a mandoline on the ⅛-inch setting is ideal. The key is to slice them as evenly as possible. You should have about 2 cups sliced shallots. Place them in a clean quart-size glass jar.

2. Make a spice bundle by tying the peppercorns, fennel seeds, bay leaves, and herb sprigs (if using) in a square of cheesecloth. Place the spice bundle in a small saucepan and add the vinegar, sugar, and salt. Bring the mixture to a boil over high heat, stirring to dissolve the sugar and salt. Reduce the heat to low and simmer for 3 minutes.

3. Open the spice bundle and place its contents in the jar with the shallots, then pour the brine over the shallots, making sure they're completely covered. Close the lid immediately and let cool to room temperature before refrigerating. Let the shallots sit for at least 24 hours before eating. They will keep in the refrigerator for up to 6 months. If you prefer shelf-stable pickled shallots, leave the spice bundle intact and see page 325 for canning information.

CLOVE AND SPICE PICKLED BEETS

LIZ

On a freezing-cold Valentine's Day in 2012, we were huddled in our kitchen straining Beet and Ginger Kvass (page 290). The heat was barely running and the work was difficult. On top of my cynicism about Valentine's Day in general, it was deflating to be in a cold, dark kitchen on a day when everyone is celebrating with flowers and chocolates. I needed a cheering up, so I found a cookie cutter and began shaping excess beet slices into hearts. I pickled them using warming spices. There and then, the heartbeet was born.

That day, everyone received a jar—from store managers who bought our products to friends we ran into on the street to our mashgiach (kosher supervisor), who definitely did not celebrate Valentine's Day. As an Ashkenazi cook, I felt giving out beets was the ultimate expression of love.

These clove and spice pickles don't need to be cut into heart shapes. If you have extra fresh beets on hand from the farmers' market, this is a great way to keep crunchy snacks in your fridge for months. They go well when paired with goat cheese on a salad, and if you've made Beet and Ginger Kvass (page 290), you can use the leftover beets for this recipe, though you may want to add a bit of the kvass to the jar once the brine is added since *rossel* beets, as they're called, are quite pallid.

MAKES 1 QUART PICKLES

1½ pounds fresh or *rossel* beets (from about 2 pounds whole beets with tops)

½ gallon water

½ cup plus 1 tablespoon white vinegar

1 cup apple cider vinegar

½ cup plus 2 tablespoons sugar

1½ teaspoons kosher salt

½ teaspoon whole cloves

½ teaspoon celery seeds

½ teaspoon whole allspice berries

2 dried bay leaves

1 small cinnamon stick

¼ cup Beet and Ginger Kvass (page 290; optional, if using *rossel* beets)

1. Slice the beets into ¼- to ⅛-inch half-moons, then into quarters if the beets are larger, so that they look like mini pizza slices. While slicing, bring the water to a boil in a large pot.

2. When the water is boiling, add the beet slices and 1 tablespoon of the white vinegar to the water (the vinegar helps the beets retain their vibrant color).

(continued) ▶

Return the water to a boil and cook for about 7 minutes. The beets should be tender, but not fully cooked (a tad bit softer than al dente pasta). Remove from the heat, drain, and place the beets in a clean widemouthed quart-size jar.

3. In a small saucepan, combine the remaining ingredients (except for the kvass, if using) to make a brine. Bring to a boil over high heat, then reduce the heat to low and simmer for 3 minutes.

4. Remove the brine from the heat. Using a fine-mesh sieve, strain the hot brine into a glass vessel and immediately pour it into the jar over the beets. You may have some extra brine. That's okay. (If you're using leftover beets from your kvass production, leave a bit of room and add the kvass at this point to add color.) Cover the jar and let cool to room temperature before refrigerating. Let the beets sit in the refrigerator for 24 hours before eating. Pickled beets will keep in the refrigerator for up to 6 months. For longer storage, see the canning information on page 325.

SWEET PICKLED WATERMELON RIND

JEFFREY

The first time I tried pickled watermelon rind, I was sitting in the parking lot of a Russian supermarket in the city of Ashdod, Israel. I spit it out. It was gross, and way too salty. I tried it again a few months later in Brighton Beach in Brooklyn. Again, I wasn't feeling it. I usually can't say no to a lacto-fermented pickle, but this was a definite *nyet*.

When I first moved to Brooklyn, I sold fruit at the farmers' market. In the summer, I occasionally wound up biking home with a watermelon in my bag. After eating the fruit, there was always so much rind left over. It felt like a shame to discard it all, so, somewhat reluctantly, I gave pickled watermelon one more try. I used the hot vinegar brine method instead of lacto-fermentation, making a more Southern-style pickled rind. Bingo. Even the aesthetics improved. I started leaving a ⅛-inch-thick piece of pink flesh on the rind, and now this pickle gets *oohs* and *ahhs* whenever it's served.

MAKES 1 QUART PICKLES

This recipe starts with 5 pounds of whole watermelon, including rinds and flesh, so enjoy the fruit and save the rinds for pickling.

---

1 (5-pound) watermelon	6 tablespoons kosher salt	1½ cups sugar	½ teaspoon whole black peppercorns
8 cups water	1½ cups distilled white vinegar	½ teaspoon yellow mustard seeds	6 dried chile peppers

1. Using a long, sharp knife, cut the watermelon in half lengthwise so it lies flat and is easier to work with. Cut each half in half. Using a smaller knife, carve out the flesh of the watermelon, leaving ⅛ inch of the pink flesh connected to the rind all around. (Cut the remaining watermelon flesh into large chunks for noshing.) Don't worry about getting every bit of the flesh. You can clean up your pieces later on. A 5-pound watermelon should yield about 2½ pounds rind.

2. Using a vegetable peeler, peel the tough green outer skin from the watermelon. Don't push too hard. You will still want to see the veins and the light green hue of the fruit after peeling.

3. Slice the rind into ½-inch-wide by 2-inch-long strips. Clean off any excess chunks of pink flesh. You do not want more than a hint of the pink flesh to remain on the inside of each piece, or it will turn soggy when pickled.

(continued) ▶

4. In a medium saucepan, combine the water and the salt and bring to a boil. Add the rinds to the boiling water and cook for about 5 minutes, or until the rinds soften slightly and begin to pale in color. Drain and set aside. They'll have shrunk considerably.

5. In the same saucepan, combine the remaining ingredients to make a brine. Bring to a boil, stirring to dissolve the sugar. Return the rind to the saucepan and cook over medium heat until almost translucent, 5 to 8 minutes.

6. Using a slotted spoon, carefully transfer the rind to a clean quart-size jar. Pour the hot brine over the rind and close the lid. Let cool to room temperature before refrigerating. Let the rind sit in the refrigerator overnight before eating. Pickled rind will stay delicious in the refrigerator for up to 6 weeks. It will get sweeter and more intense in flavor over time. For longer storage, see the canning information on page 325.

CLOCKWISE FROM TOP LEFT: **Quick Pickled Shallots** (page 71), **Clove and Spice Pickled Beets** (page 72), **Cardamom Pickled Grapes** (page 79), **Sweet Pickled Watermelon Rind** (page 75)

CARDAMOM PICKLED GRAPES

LIZ

As active picklers, Jeffrey and I are always looking for something new to keep our creative juices flowing. Grapes, we realized, have just the right makeup for vinegar pickling: they're firm yet full of water, and they're sweet with a touch of tart. When we settled on the recipe below, we were pleasantly surprised to discover that kids, who are sometimes critical of pickles, really loved these.

Add these pickled grapes to a cheese plate or bring them to a picnic in the park. You can even pulse them lightly in the food processor to make a relish to pair with soft cheeses and crackers.

MAKES 1 QUART PICKLES

1½ pounds seedless red or black grapes

1½ cups white wine vinegar

1½ cups sugar

¼ teaspoon kosher salt, plus a pinch

1½ teaspoons whole black peppercorns

1 cinnamon stick

1½ heaping teaspoons green cardamom pods, lightly crushed

1 dried chile pepper

¾ teaspoon ground allspice

1. Wash the grapes well and remove them from the stems. Place in a clean quart-size jar.

2. In a small saucepan, combine the remaining ingredients to make a brine. Bring to a boil, stirring to dissolve the sugar. Reduce the heat to low and simmer for 3 minutes, stirring well.

3. Remove the brine from the heat and let cool until warm but not hot.

4. Pour the brine over the grapes and close the jar. Let cool to room temperature before refrigerating. Let sit for 24 hours in the refrigerator before serving. The grapes will stay delicious in the refrigerator for about 3 weeks.

PICKLE BRINE SALAD DRESSINGS

 LIZ I'm always stuck with jars of leftover brine. Jeffrey, ever the pickle eccentric, happily drinks these liquids straight, sometimes encouraging friends to shoot lacto-fermented brine as a chaser. "It replenishes your body with electrolytes," he says. I roll my eyes. Luckily, I discovered a much more practical use for these brines: salad dressings.

We've created these salad dressings based on the amount of brine you'll have left over after making many of the recipes in this chapter. If you have pickle brines on hand, these dressings are an extremely quick recipe. Dill pickle brine makes for a simple dilly vinaigrette, sauerruben brine dressing pairs well with salads that include fruit and blue cheese or Gorgonzola, and shallot brine dressing is for tahini lovers (and is my personal favorite).

FOR DILL PICKLE BRINE DRESSING:

½ cup leftover brine, from Classic Sour Dills (page 50) or Crisp Garlic Dilly Beans (page 56)

2 teaspoons olive oil

¼ cup distilled white vinegar

1 garlic clove, minced or pressed

2 teaspoons Dijon mustard, store-bought or homemade (page 32)

½ teaspoon dried dill

½ shallot, minced (about 1 tablespoon)

FOR SHALLOT BRINE DRESSING:

⅓ cup leftover pickled shallot brine (from Quick Pickled Shallots, page 71)

2 tablespoons olive oil

1½ tablespoons tahini

1 tablespoon pure maple syrup

¼ teaspoon kosher salt

⅛ teaspoon freshly ground black pepper

FOR SAUERRUBEN BRINE DRESSING:

3 tablespoons leftover sauerruben brine (from Sauerruben, page 65)

2 tablespoons olive oil

1½ tablespoons horseradish relish, store-bought or homemade (page 174 or 176)

1½ tablespoons mustard, store-bought Dijon or homemade (page 32)

1½ teaspoons honey

1 garlic clove, minced

¼ teaspoon kosher salt

1. The process is the same for each salad dressing: Combine the ingredients in a small jar, seal with a lid, and shake. Adjust the seasoning to taste, adding more brine if you'd like.

~~~ THREE ~~~

BREADS

LIZ Call me unoriginal, but my primary association with Jewish bread is challah. During college, my social life revolved around a synagogue in the upstairs of a narrow row house. My tiny apartment down the block was known for its particularly epic Friday night feasts. As part of my weekly ritual, I began baking challah.

One night, a friend tore into one of my loaves and said, "This is so good, I'd pay for it!" The challah was eggy and rich, but what was really special about it was that it was homemade and fresh. There was no Jewish bakery nearby, so, recognizing an oppportunity, I launched my first entrepreneurial venture, Challah Back Bakers. I took orders throughout the week, shopped for giant bags of flour, and mixed and kneaded dough in a plastic bowl nearly the size of a kiddie pool. On Thursday night, friends came over to help, which was really just an excuse to drink strong beer and chat about life and love. On Friday morning, customers dropped by to pick up their loaves. I "bribed" my landlord with challah each week so she wouldn't be upset by the chaos. Luckily, she was incredibly generous and even let me use her oven in the apartment downstairs to fill especially large orders.

Looking back now, it took serious chutzpah to launch a business with no training and no real plan. But I was passionate about challah and dedicated to my community of friends who gathered together each week. Baking challah came to define my college experience more than any course I took. I baked until I graduated, and promised myself that if I didn't like having a "real" job after graduation, I'd return to challah. And I suppose that's just what I did.

To this day, home-baked breads are central to most events Jeffrey and I host together. "It is impossible to think of any good meal, no matter how plain or elegant, without soup or bread in it," wrote M. F. K. Fisher. I couldn't agree more. Seeded Honey Rye Pull-Apart rolls (page 98) are perfect for brunch. Rachel's Buckwheat Bread (page 103) is an earthy, nutty loaf to pair with dinner whether you're gluten-free or not. Our homemade matzo (page 94) will add an artisanal spark to your Passover seder.

And the recipes in this book are only a small smattering of what is possible with bread. Some call for old-fashioned techniques, and some are a bit more modern. Baking bread may not be quick, or even easy all the time, but it's certainly worth the effort. Bread brings people together like no other food I know.

〜〜〜

JEFFREY

I didn't realize just how deep my affections for Jewish breads were until I cut them out of my diet when experimenting with gluten-free living for a couple of years. Walking the streets of New York City, the aroma of bagels, seeded ryes, and challahs taunted me. I couldn't find a decent gluten-free bread back then, let alone one with Jewish character. I wound up hungry all the time. At a Jewish deli, I ordered pastrami and mustard, "hold the rye." The waiter looked confused, like I'd just asked for a pizza. It was humiliating. Come Passover, I found myself lusting for matzo. Matzo! Worst of all, however, was turning down challah at Shabbat dinner. Occasionally, at friends' homes, I'd pinch crumbs of the egg-washed crust to taste what I was missing. And on certain rare occasions, I completely broke down, ripping into the loaves with an intensity that frightened me and likely some of my dining companions.

I started thinking more intensely about the sustaining role of bread in Jewish life, coming back regularly to images of the Second World War and stories of family members surviving on bread rations alone. In my younger years, I had imagined these rations as dainty slices of whole wheat sandwich bread and been skeptical of how they could have possibly provided enough sustenance. But this bread of survival did not come presliced. It was the dense rye bread of eastern Europe, so nutrient rich that it relieved the feeling of hunger for hours longer than sandwich bread from an American supermarket.

In many Jewish communities throughout eastern Europe before the Second World War, families followed what is effectively a "bread calendar," eating loaves of dense, dark rye made from whole kernels six days of the week. "Then on the seventh, the Sabbath," writes food historian Andrew Coe, "they enjoyed light and golden challah," which they blessed at the start of the Sabbath meal. Rye was cheap and widely available in eastern Europe and an all-around tough bread that, when naturally leavened, could stay fresh for up to a week or longer (far longer than wheat breads).

Rye bread was a nutritional foundation of the Ashkenazi diet, often eaten with fermented sauerkraut or sour milk, which complemented it to create a package of essential nutrients. "It is no wonder that the aroma of fresh baked rye bread smelled like perfume," wrote Lithuanian educator and memoirist Hirsz Abramowicz of prewar Lithuania. "People could do even the most strenuous work having eaten only plain rye bread with sour soup or with barley soup laced with a little milk." Wheat, whose perfect amount of gluten makes bread that holds its shape and rises significantly, was more expensive and more precious. Challah was made from wheat and eggs, making it an even more luxurious proposition. In her memoir at the turn of the twentieth century, author Mary Antin wrote of the lean years in her Belarussian shtetl as "eating black bread on holidays" instead of challah.

Fortunate to not have any real sensitivities or celiac disease, I got back on the bread wagon. At the same time, I decided to take agency over my own sustenance and learn to bake bread myself. Something about the process, however, felt like it required a certain forethought and precision that I just didn't have. Stand mixers, compressed dry yeasts, and sourdough starters intimidated me. Liz was always the baker, and I was the pickler. But it turns out I have what it takes. The fermentation geek in me fell in love with keeping a rye starter—a natural leavening agent—in my kitchen like a pet, with regular feedings of flour and water. I began to relish the unexpected fruity flavor of the starter as it bubbled. And I find that I'm endlessly satisfied and delighted when pulling from the oven a perfectly formed Jewish Rye (page 100), a tray of Bialys (page 109), or a loaf of Rachel's Buckwheat Bread (page 103). As I learned from my two-year gluten-free experiment, life is simply more satisfying with freshly baked bread.

BREADS
RECIPES

CLASSIC CHALLAH WITH A MARBLE RYE TWIST

LIZ →

A while back, I joined baker and food writer Shannon Sarna for a challah-baking session in her home. Shannon does things to challah I've never even dreamed of, like king cake challah for Mardi Gras, candy-stuffed challah for Halloween, challah filled with PB&J. We decided to play with the idea of a (more) Ashkenazi challah, as if that were necessary. Shannon suggested a two-tone challah, and I loved it. The results were promising, so I went home, tested a number of different variations, and worked on developing the formula for the marble rye challah you'll find here.

This recipe calls for making separate traditional challah dough and a darker, richer rye dough, then intertwining them into a single marbled loaf. If you're a challah novice, or just looking to bake something simple, start with the classic challah recipe below. Once you've mastered the basics, feel free to take on the second part of the recipe (page 92) and make the extraordinary marble loaf. The rye dough is tougher and a bit harder to roll out and braid, so you'll want to have some experience before you begin. It also tastes great when baked on its own. Wherever you are in your challah journey, it'll be delicious. Note that making challah, or any bread, requires patience and waiting at various stages, and the addition of the marble rye twist requires some additional time and effort. Slightly stale challah also makes incredible French toast.

※ MAKES 2 MEDIUM CLASSIC LOAVES ※

~~~~~~

CLASSIC CHALLAH:

2 (¼-ounce) packets active dry yeast (4½ teaspoons)

⅔ cup plus 2 tablespoons sugar

⅓ cup lukewarm water

1 cup boiling water

¼ cup vegetable oil or grapeseed oil

1½ teaspoons kosher salt

4 large eggs, lightly beaten

5 to 6 cups all-purpose or bread flour, plus more as needed

Sesame seeds or poppy seeds, for sprinkling (optional)

1. If making the marble loaf, start by making the Marble Rye Twist (page 92). Then in a small bowl, combine the yeast, 2 tablespoons of the sugar, and the lukewarm water. Stir and set aside.

(continued) ▶

In a large bowl or in the bowl of a stand mixer, combine the remaining ⅔ cup sugar, the boiling water, oil, and salt. Stir until the sugar has dissolved. Add the beaten eggs (reserve about 1 tablespoon of the eggs for coating the loaves at the end), pour in the yeast mixture, and stir to combine.

2. Add the flour 1 cup at a time. Start by stirring in the flour with a fork, then switch to kneading by hand or using the stand mixer fitted with the dough hook. Don't be afraid to add more flour. You do not want sticky dough. Knead the dough until it is soft and pliable and bounces back when you poke it with your finger, about 12 minutes if kneading by hand. If you're using a stand mixer, you'll want to let it run on speed one or two until it forms a ball of dough and pulls off the sides of the bowl, about 7 minutes.

3. Transfer the dough to a clean bowl and cover with a kitchen towel or plastic wrap. Let rise in a warm place for at least 2 hours, or until the dough has doubled in size. Do not rush this first rising. Leave the dough for as long as it takes to double in size (up to 4 hours, if necessary).

4. When the dough has risen, punch it down and lightly knead it on a floured surface. Separate the dough into

12 pieces about the size of golf balls. Roll each piece into a ball and then roll each ball into a long rope. Each rope should be about 8 inches long.

5. Braid the ropes into two large challahs using the six-braid method (see page 91). Place the braided loaves on a baking sheet lined with parchment paper. Using a pastry brush or your fingers, coat each loaf with the reserved egg and sprinkle with sesame or poppy seeds if you like. Set aside to rise for 45 minutes, until they are puffy.

6. Preheat the oven to 350°F. Bake the challah for 30 minutes, moving the loaves from the top rack to the bottom rack halfway through the baking time. At 30 minutes, check the challah by (carefully) lifting each one up and tapping the bottom with a knuckle. If it sounds hollow and the outside of the challah is a brownish color, it's ready. If it sounds completely solid or is still pale in color or doughy in the places where the braids meet, bake for 5 to 10 minutes more and test again.

7. Remove the loaves from the oven and let cool on a wire rack. Serve warm or at room temperature. Challah freezes well and can be thawed and reheated before serving.

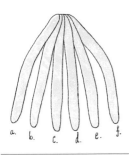

1. Join six strands of dough at the top.

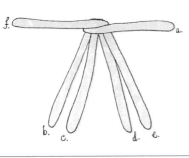

2. Move both strands on the far sides (strands A and F) across the center, creating three zones: top left, top right, and four center strands.

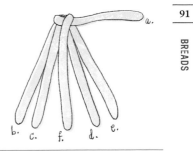

3. Bring strand F from the top left and place it in the middle of the four center strands.

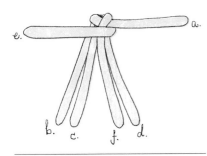

4. Move strand E from the outer right side of the four center strands and bring to the top left. Strand E has now re-created the top left zone.

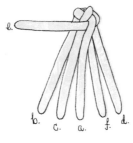

5. Bring strand A from the top right zone and move it to the middle of the four center strands.

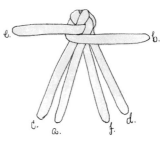

6. Bring strand B from the outer left side of the four center strands and bring to the top right, re-creating the top right zone.

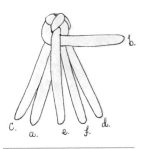

7. Take strand E from the top left and bring to the middle of the new four center strands.

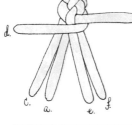

8. Move strand D from the outer right side of the four center strands to the top left.

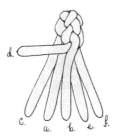

9. Continue as above. Move the top right strand, B, to the middle of the four center strands.

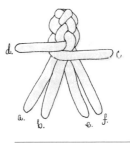

10. Take the outer opposite side of the four center strands, C, at this point, and bring it to the top right. Repeat.

11. When you can no longer braid (it will become more difficult as the strands get braided), pinch the challah strands together at the bottom of the loaf.

(continued) ▶

Marble Rye Twist

MAKES 4 MEDIUM
MARBLE RYE LOAVES

If making the marble challah combination, *make the rye dough first,* as it will take longer to rise than the classic white flour dough. If a yield of four loaves seems like a lot, freeze one or two loaves in an airtight plastic bag once they cool. To defrost, simply take out of the freezer a couple of hours before serving and warm in the oven just before serving.

2 (¼-ounce) packets active dry yeast (4½ teaspoons)

⅔ cup plus 2 tablespoons sugar

⅓ cup lukewarm water

⅔ cup hot coffee

½ cup vegetable oil or grapeseed oil

1½ tablespoons caraway seeds, plus more for sprinkling

1½ tablespoons unsweetened cocoa powder

¾ tablespoon kosher salt

3 large eggs, lightly beaten

4 to 5 cups all-purpose or bread flour, plus more as needed

2 cups rye flour

Classic Challah dough (page 88), prepared without seeds

1. In a small bowl, combine the yeast, 2 tablespoons of the sugar, and the lukewarm water. Stir and set aside. In a large bowl or in the bowl of a stand mixer, combine the remaining ⅔ cup sugar, the coffee, oil, caraway seeds, cocoa, and salt. Stir until the sugar has dissolved. Add the beaten eggs (reserve about 1 tablespoon of the eggs for coating the loaves at the end), pour in the yeast mixture, and stir to combine.

2. Stir together the all-purpose and rye flours, then add the flours 1 cup at a time to the rest of the ingredients. Start by stirring in the first 4 cups flour with a fork, then switch to kneading by hand

or using the stand mixer fitted with the dough hook. Don't be afraid to add more bread flour as needed. You do not want sticky dough. Knead the dough until it is soft and pliable and bounces back when you poke it with your finger, about 12 minutes if kneading by hand. If you're using a stand mixer, you'll want to let it run on speed one or two until it forms a ball of dough and pulls off the sides of the bowl, about 7 minutes. Note that the rye dough is much less pliable than the classic white flour dough and will never achieve the same texture—that's okay. The key is to knead it for enough time for it to become smooth and pliable.

3. Transfer the dough to a clean bowl and cover with a kitchen towel or plastic wrap. Let rise in a warm place for at least 2 hours, or until the dough has doubled in size. Do not rush this first rising. The rye dough may need up to 4 hours to properly rise.

4. While the rye dough rises, make the classic challah dough following the instructions (see pages 88 and 90).

5. When the rye dough has risen, punch it down and lightly knead it on a floured surface. Repeat with the classic challah dough. Separate the rye dough into 12 pieces, about the size of golf balls. Repeat with the classic challah dough. Roll each piece into a ball and then roll each ball into a long rope. Each rope should be about 8 inches long. Braid the ropes into four challahs using the six-braid method (see page 91). Each loaf will be made up of 3 rye ropes and 3 classic challah ropes. For beautiful marbling, alternate rye and white ropes at the outset. Place the braided loaves on two baking sheets lined with parchment paper. Using a pastry brush or your fingers, coat each loaf with the reserved egg and sprinkle with caraway seeds. Set aside to rise for 45 minutes, until they are puffy.

6. Preheat the oven to 350°F. Bake the challah for 30 minutes, switching the loaves on the top rack to the bottom rack and vice versa halfway through the baking time. At 30 minutes, check the challah by (carefully) lifting each one up and tapping the bottom with a knuckle. If it sounds hollow and the outside of the challah has a hard and browned crust, the challah is ready. If it sounds completely solid or is still pale in color or doughy in the places where the braids meet, bake for 5 to 10 minutes more and test again.

7. Remove from the oven and let cool on a wire rack. Serve warm or at room temperature. Challah freezes well and can be thawed and reheated before serving.

MAKE-AT-HOME MATZO

JEFFREY

Unlike the mass-produced squares usually found on your seder table, homemade matzo is actually something you'll want to snack on all holiday. If you're trying to follow the letter of Jewish dietary law, you have to be quick. From flour and water being mixed to completion, the whole process should take no more than 18 minutes according to kosher rules. You can do it, we promise—but no dillydallying. That's why we made this a small recipe. Feel free to double or triple it. Also, a warning: When we bake at very high temperatures in our small apartments, our ovens get smoky, so keep the windows wide open and the exhaust fans blasting.

MAKES ABOUT 4 MATZOS

1½ cups all-purpose flour (or 1 cup all-purpose flour plus	½ cup rye or whole wheat flour), plus more for dusting	½ teaspoon kosher salt (optional)	½ cup plus 2 table-spoons warm water

1. Preheat the oven to 475°F. If you have a convection oven, use the convection setting for even browning. Place a sturdy baking sheet on each rack of the oven, or use a pizza stone if you have it.

2. In a large bowl, combine the flour and salt (if using), then add the warm water. Note that for kosher matzos, the moment the water is added, the 18-minute clock will begin counting down. Stir with a fork to form a sticky dough. Remove the dough from the bowl and quickly knead it on a well-floured surface, adding more flour if needed until it forms a pliable, nonsticky dough.

3. Separate the dough into 4 golf ball–size pieces using a sharp knife or a bench scraper. Working with one at a time, roll each piece as thin as possible with a flour-dusted rolling pin.

4. With a sharp knife, cut off the edges of the rolled-out dough to form square matzos. Using a fork, poke holes all over each matzo to keep the dough from puffing up.

5. Carefully transfer the matzos to the hot baking sheets or pizza stone in the preheated oven. Bake for about 3 minutes, flip the matzos over, using tongs, switch the baking sheets from the top rack to the bottom rack, and bake for 3 to 4 minutes more. Keep the oven light on to keep an eye on the matzos. Every oven is different, so your matzos may bake more quickly or may take longer.

6. Remove the matzos from the oven and carefully transfer to a wire rack to cool. Once at room temperature, store in an airtight plastic bag for up to a week.

PICKLE BRINE BREAD

 When my friend's mom sent me a recipe for "Unusual Pickle or Olive Juice Bread" from *Recipes for a Small Planet* by Ellen Buchman Ewald, published in 1973, I was thrilled at the possibility of clearing my fridge of some of the excess containers of pickle brine I had accumulated. I started with the original recipe and came out with a super-dense bread that tasted really "healthy," like one of those foods from the era when nutrition was more glorified than flavor. I saw its potential, though, so I *potchkied* around and made a few sample versions. Eventually, I was able to get it more "pickly" and a whole lot lighter.

This bread slices really well, so top it with Pickled Trout (page 160) or Spiced Herring in Oil (page 161). Or do what I do: slice it, toast it, then spread it with Everything Bagel Butter (page 18) and sprinkle with Sauerruben (page 65). Now *that* is the kind of "healthy" snack I'm into.

**MAKES 2
9 X 5-INCH LOAVES**

---

3 tablespoons warm water

1 tablespoon active dry yeast (1 [¼-ounce] packet plus a little more)

½ teaspoon sugar

2 cups leftover pickle brine from Classic Sour Dills (page 50) or Crisp Garlic Dilly Beans (page 56), or from store-bought salt-water pickles

⅓ cup vegetable oil, plus more as needed

⅓ cup honey

1½ teaspoons kosher salt

2½ cups all-purpose or bread flour, plus more as needed

3½ cups whole wheat flour

---

1. Pour the water into a large bowl or the bowl of a stand mixer, fitted with the dough hook, and sprinkle in the yeast and sugar. Mix to incorporate and let sit for 5 minutes. Stir in the pickle brine, oil, honey, and salt. Slowly incorporate the all-purpose and whole wheat flours 1 cup at a time, stirring the mixture with either a fork or the dough hook.

2. Knead until the dough is smooth and elastic, about 12 minutes by hand or about 7 minutes using the stand mixer,

incorporating more flour as needed so the dough is not too sticky. Transfer to a bowl. Cover the bowl with a kitchen towel or plastic wrap and set it somewhere warm and draft-free to rise for at least 2 hours, or until doubled in size. Do not rush this first rising.

3. When the dough has doubled in size, punch it down, remove it from the bowl, knead it for another minute on a flour-dusted surface, and divide it in half.

4. Grease two 9 x 5-inch metal loaf pans with oil. Place one half of the dough into each pan. Let the dough rise in the pans for about 1 hour.

5. Preheat the oven to 350°F. Bake the loaves for 45 to 50 minutes. To check if the loaves are ready, lift up carefully and tap with a knuckle. If they sound hollow, and the top is crusty and hard to the touch, the bread is ready. Let cool for at least a half hour before slicing and serving.

SEEDED HONEY RYE PULL-APART ROLLS

This is a semisweet, crumbly bread that's easy for the amateur baker and perfect for a communal meal like brunch. It was inspired by a trip to New York Bread, a famous Russian bakery in Coney Island whose pièce de résistance is its coriander-crusted Borodinsky. While we could never claim to replicate the rich heftiness of that loaf, the coriander seeds were irresistible, and I knew they'd be the perfect addition to the caraway rolls Jeffrey and I were working on at the time. These rolls are the perfect vessel for Everything Bagel Butter (page 18) or pickled fish.

MAKES 14 ROLLS OR 1 LOAF

---

1 cup warm water

1 (¼-ounce) packet active dry yeast (2¼ teaspoons)

1 tablespoon sugar

3 tablespoons vegetable oil, plus more for greasing the bowl and the pan

2 large eggs

1½ teaspoons kosher salt

2 cups rye flour

2½ cups all-purpose flour, plus more for kneading

⅓ cup honey

2 tablespoons ground coriander

1 tablespoon plus ½ teaspoon caraway seeds

1½ tablespoons crushed coriander seeds

1. In a large bowl or in the bowl of a stand mixer fitted with the dough hook, combine the warm water, yeast, sugar, oil, and 1 egg. Beat with a fork or using the dough hook until combined. Let sit for 5 minutes, or until the yeast bubbles slightly. Add the salt, flours, honey, ground coriander, and 1 tablespoon of the caraway seeds. Knead the dough by hand or on medium speed until it comes together into a smooth but still slightly sticky ball, about 10 minutes.

2. Place the dough in an oiled bowl, turning to coat. Cover with a kitchen towel or plastic wrap and let sit in a warm, draft-free place to rise for about 2 hours, until it has doubled in size. Do not rush this first rising.

3. Preheat the oven to 350°F. Lightly grease a 9-inch round springform or cake pan. Remove the dough from the bowl and divide it into 14 equal pieces. Roll each piece into a ball and place them all in the greased pan, squeezed in tightly next to one another. Cover with plastic wrap and set aside in a warm, draft-free place for about 45 minutes, or until doubled in size again.

4. Lightly beat the remaining egg. Using a pastry brush, lightly brush the beaten egg over the top of the dough and sprinkle with the crushed coriander and remaining ½ teaspoon caraway seeds. Bake until lightly brown on top, 35 to 40 minutes. Remove from the oven and let cool slightly on a wire rack.

JEWISH RYE

JEFFREY

In eastern Europe, the common cereal grain was rye, which makes for a gummier dough than the more expensive wheat, which holds its shape nicely. Naturally leavened bread had the advantage, however, of lasting an entire week or more before going stale. The long shelf life made rye doughs practically indispensable back in the day. Styles of rye bread varied by region in eastern Europe, and the American version of Jewish rye bread is mostly associated with the Polish Jewish baking tradition.

Our recipe for Jewish Rye bread utilizes both active dry yeast and wild yeast in the form of a rye starter for leavening. Rye starter is made from fermenting flour and water, which produces a live cultured mixture of natural airborne yeasts and *Lactobacillus* that help leaven rye bread and give it a distinct flavor and texture. "The old style Jewish rye starter is made by taking the previous day's fully baked rye bread . . . and cutting it up and using that to feed your starter culture," writes Ari Weinzweig of Zingerman's in Ann Arbor, Michigan, whose rye bread was an inspiration to me and Liz. Our recipe calls for the optional addition of older rye or pumpernickel bread for flavor. Pumpernickel adds nice color.

If you can get your hands on a rye starter from a friend or a bakeshop, you'll be a step ahead in this recipe. If you don't have access to a starter, carefully follow the rye starter recipe on page 102 to make your own. Liz thinks it's peculiar that I find the sweet smell of bubbling rye starters intoxicating, especially since the stronger notes of cantaloupe and plum that emerge could mean that the starter may have turned more acidic than is ideal. It's best when the fruity smell is somewhat muted. If you're having trouble getting your starter to bubble, switch from filtered water to distilled bottled water, as some filters do not clear out all the chlorine, and starters are particularly sensitive to the chemical. Note that making traditional rye bread from scratch (from starter to finish) is a lengthy process but a rewarding one, and it's the perfect bread for your evening of deli specialties. You can even use your rye starter in our Żurek (page 124) and Russian Rye Kvass (page 293).

MAKES 1 MEDIUM LOAF

1 (¼-ounce) packet active dry yeast (2¼ teaspoons)

½ teaspoon sugar

2½ tablespoons lukewarm water, plus more if using bread

1 or 2 slices rye or pumpernickel bread (about 2 ounces; optional)

2½ cups bread flour, plus more as needed

½ cup rye flour, plus more as needed

1½ teaspoons kosher salt

1½ teaspoons caraway seeds (optional)

¾ cup rye starter, homemade (page 102) or from a friend

½ cup filtered water

1. In a small bowl, combine the yeast, sugar, and 2½ tablespoons lukewarm water. Stir and set aside for a couple of minutes until the yeast blooms. In another small bowl, rip up your slices of bread (if using) and mix with 2 tablespoons of lukewarm water. Press it together with your hands to make a bread mash. In a medium bowl, combine the flours, salt, and caraway seeds (if using) and mix to distribute the salt evenly. Add the rye starter, yeast mixture, bread mash (if using), and filtered water. Mix roughly with a large wooden spoon, then moisten your hands with water and begin kneading to form a dough, about 10 minutes, adding more bread flour as necessary to reduce any stickiness. When finished kneading, the dough should be pliable and smooth but will remain quite dense.

2. Transfer the dough to a clean bowl. Cover the bowl with a kitchen towel or plastic wrap and let rise for at least 2 hours in a warm place, or until the dough has doubled in size. Remove the dough from the bowl and shape it into a long oval. Place the loaf on a parchment paper–lined baking sheet or a pizza stone and let rise for 2 hours more.

3. Preheat the oven to 450°F. Using a knife or a single edge razor dusted with rye flour, cut five crosswise ¼-inch slashes onto the top of the loaf and lightly dust the loaf with some additional rye flour. Toss a few ice cubes onto a baking sheet and place at the bottom of the oven to create steam. Immediately slide the baking sheet or pizza stone with the shaped loaf on it into the oven as well and close the oven door, trapping the steam inside. After 5 minutes of baking time, reduce the oven temperature to 400°F and bake for 25 to 30 minutes more until the crust turns a shade darker than golden brown and the bottom of the loaf, when tapped, sounds hollow.

4. Let the bread cool for about 15 minutes before serving. Enjoy with Home-Cured Pastrami (page 210), Grandpa Joe's Famous Chicken Salad (page 192), Cultured Cream Cheese (page 25), or Everything Bagel Butter (page 18). Stored in a paper bag at room temperature, the bread will stay fresh for 5 to 7 days.

(continued) ▶

▶ (Jewish Rye, *continued*)

For the rye starter:

Filtered water

Rye flour

1. TO MAKE THE RYE STARTER: Into a clean quart-size glass jar, measure out ⅓ cup rye flour and ⅓ cup filtered water. Stir vigorously to incorporate and cover the jar with the lid, but don't screw it on tightly. Leave this mixture on your counter at room temperature for 24 hours. Bubbles should begin to form in the mixture. If it's particularly cold, this may take longer. On day 2, repeat the process, stirring in an additional ⅓ cup rye flour and ⅓ cup filtered water. Let sit for 24 hours more.

2. On day 3, the mixture should have nearly doubled in size and begun to smell fruity, with bubbles continuing to form. Discard about half the mixture and then "feed" it with an additional ⅓ cup rye flour and ⅓ cup filtered water. Let sit for 24 hours. On day 4, repeat the process, discarding half the mixture and feeding it ⅓ cup rye flour and ⅓ cup filtered water.

3. On day 5, you can begin maintaining your starter culture by regularly feeding it ¼ cup rye flour and ⅓ cup filtered water. The additional water helps cut the acidity of the starter and makes it a bit looser than a conventional wheat-based sourdough starter—a tip we learned from a pro. You should keep feeding your starter for at least 2 additional days, for a total of 7 days sitting time. It's kind of like having a pet, except not at all. It will continue to bubble. It is now ready to be used for baking or stored in the fridge.

4. TO MAINTAIN THE RYE STARTER: Store the jar in the fridge, covered with lid on and sealed, and refresh it weekly by bringing to room temperature, disposing of about one-third to half of it, then stirring in ¼ cup rye flour and ⅓ cup filtered water. Let the mixture sit for 3 hours or until bubbles form. You can use it to bake at this point, or you can return it to the fridge and refresh it again in a week's time. If left in your fridge long enough, a dark liquid will form on the surface. It's perfectly safe. Simply pour it off, discard a portion of the starter, and refresh accordingly. If you need more starter to make a big batch of bread, double the amount of water and flour during the feeding; just allow more time for the mixture to turn active and bubbly. Note that a warm kitchen is an ideal place for a starter to thrive.

RACHEL'S BUCKWHEAT BREAD

JEFFREY

Once I finally put my gluten-free lifestyle behind me, I began dating a woman who was gluten-free. I worried about Rachel constantly. Was she ever full? How did she feel at Shabbat dinner in the presence of all that challah? I became fixated on baking gluten-free bread with a Jewish character that would satisfy those cravings I knew all too well. Gluten-free breads on the market are often made with tapioca starch or xanthan gum and other hard-to-pronounce ingredients. This recipe, made with whole buckwheat, is a much cleaner alternative. It makes a great sandwich bread, too. It's no challah, but it's an option I would have savored during those breadless years.

This recipe is fairly easy, but does require letting the grains ferment for some time. Note that this recipe calls for plain buckwheat groats, which means kasha (roasted buckwheat) won't work. Whole unroasted buckwheat groats can be found in various health food stores (see Resources, page 327). Note that this recipe has a quick prep time but an extended wait time.

MAKES 1
9 X 5-INCH LOAF

2½ cups whole unroasted buckwheat groats (not kasha)

1 cup filtered water

Unsalted butter or grapeseed oil, for the pan

1½ tablespoons sesame seeds, plus more for the pan

2 teaspoons kosher salt

1 tablespoon honey

2½ tablespoons sunflower seeds

1 tablespoon pepitas (pumpkin seeds)

---

1. Rinse the groats thoroughly with cold running water and place in a bowl. Fill the bowl with enough cold water to cover the groats and let them soak for at least 2 hours.

2. Drain the groats in a fine-mesh strainer, then rinse and drain them thoroughly to wash away the sliminess that may develop from soaking. Place the groats in a ceramic, wooden, or glass bowl (avoid plastic or metal) along with the filtered water. Blend using an immersion blender until the mixture is liquefied to a paste. It will be thick and grainy. (Alternatively, blend in a standing blender and then pour the mixture into a bowl.)

3. Place a kitchen towel over the bowl and let sit on the counter at least overnight or for up to 24 hours. The longer the mixture sits, the sourer the bread will be

(continued) ▶

▶ (Rachel's Buckwheat Bread, *continued*)

once baked. (You can wait longer than a full day if you prefer a sourer flavor.) The buckwheat paste will ferment, and bubbles may develop.

4. When ready to bake, preheat the oven to 350ºF. Position a rack in the middle of the oven. Grease a 9 x 5-inch loaf pan well with butter or oil or line it with parchment paper and sprinkle the bottom of the pan with a thin layer of sesame seeds.

5. Uncover the buckwheat paste and stir in the salt, honey, 2 tablespoons of the sunflower seeds, 1 tablespoon of the sesame seeds, and ½ tablespoon of the pepitas. Pour the mixture into the prepared loaf pan and sprinkle the top with the remaining ½ tablespoon sesame seeds, ½ tablespoon sunflower seeds, and ½ tablespoon pepitas.

6. Bake the bread for 50 to 55 minutes. The top will turn white and the sides will brown a bit. It may look like the bread is getting dry, but that's normal—don't worry, it'll be moist inside. Remove from the oven and let cool completely before turning out of the pan and slicing.

7. Store in an airtight container on the counter or in the fridge for up to 5 days. After the first 2 days, it's best toasted.

BAGELS AT HOME

LIZ

As any New Yorker or former New Yorker knows, bagels are something you crave from a place deep inside. When you want a bagel, nothing else will do. But the quality of most bagels outside of the New York or Montreal area can be pretty dismal. Consider this recipe anytime you can't get the bagels you crave. And frankly, it's easy enough that it's worth making them even if you live in Brooklyn! And be sure to schmear with Cultured Cream Cheese (page 25). For an everything bagel, mix together all the optional seasonings (except for the cinnamon and raisins). For a Montreal-style seasoning, dip each bagel to cover fully with sesame seeds.

MAKES 10 BAGELS

FOR THE DOUGH:

1½ cups lukewarm water

1 (¼-ounce) packet active dry yeast (2¼ teaspoons)

½ teaspoon sugar

1 large egg

¼ cup honey (or barley malt syrup)

3¾ cups bread flour, plus more as needed

¼ cup whole wheat flour

2 teaspoons kosher salt

Vegetable oil, for oiling the bowl

FOR THE BOILING BATH:

2 teaspoons baking soda

2 teaspoons kosher salt

OPTIONAL SEASONINGS:

Sesame seeds

Poppy seeds

Coarse salt

Dried minced onion

Ground cinnamon

Raisins

1. TO MAKE THE DOUGH: In a small bowl, combine the lukewarm water, yeast, and sugar and let stand for 5 minutes. Whisk the egg and honey into the yeast mixture. In a large bowl, mix together the bread flour, whole wheat flour, and salt.

2. Add the wet mixture to the bowl with the flour mixture and stir until the dough comes together. Turn the dough out onto a liberally floured surface and knead for about 10 minutes until the dough is firm yet supple and smooth, working in additional bread flour as needed. Form the dough into a ball.

Place the dough ball into an oiled bowl, turning to coat. Cover with a kitchen towel and allow the dough to rest in the bowl for 1 hour, or until it doubles in size.

3. Divide the dough into 10 equal portions. At this point, if you're planning to make cinnamon-raisin bagels, work the cinnamon and raisins into the portions of dough you'd like to be sweet (a little bit of both goes a long way). Roll each portion out into an 8-inch strand—just long enough to wrap around your four fingers, then connect the ends (see

illustration below). Place the bagels on a greased baking sheet, cover with plastic wrap, and let rest in the fridge for at least 2 hours (or, for best results, overnight).

4.   TO MAKE THE BOILING BATH: While the bagels are in the fridge, bring a stockpot filled with about 3 quarts water to a boil and stir in the baking soda and salt.

5.   Preheat the oven to 500°F. Line at least two baking sheets with parchment paper and keep your optional seasonings nearby.

6.   Remove the bagels from the fridge and boil in batches for 1½ to 2 minutes, flipping halfway through. Do not crowd the pot. After a few seconds in the water, the bagels will expand and float to the surface. Remove with a slotted spoon, and let them drain well. Sprinkle the bagels with the desired toppings and place on the prepared baking sheets.

7.   Slide one baking sheet at a time onto the middle rack of the oven and bake for 5 minutes. Reduce the oven temperature to 450°F and bake for an additional 5 to 7 minutes until golden brown and a bit crisp on the outside. Remove and let cool slightly before slicing and serving. Store any leftover bagels in an airtight plastic bag. They will keep for about 5 days, but may need to be toasted for maximum enjoyment after day 2. Bagels can also be kept in the freezer, wrapped individually in aluminum foil and then stored in an airtight plastic bag. To defrost, simply leave at room temperature for 1 hour and then toast before serving.

Roll dough into a strand.

Press the ends of the dough strand together securely.

DEBATE: THE BIALY VS. THE BAGEL

JEFFREY Liz didn't want to include a bialy recipe in this book. "No one even eats bialys anymore," she said. "People want bagels." As far as I'm concerned, a bagel is just overhyped Jewish bread with fantastic PR. That's how I tried to explain it to her anyway, but she didn't want to hear it. I swear, if she cared about baseball even remotely (which she doesn't), she'd probably be a fan of the Yankees, the bagel of baseball. I'm more of a Mets fan myself, clearly the bialy of the sport. Once every few decades, the bialy gets its moment in the sun, but there's always a risk of it being lost forever.

The great thing about bialys is that they've resisted assimilation. In their lack of notoriety, and their elusiveness, they've remained untainted by the forces of mass production and consumption. They're an underappreciated, underloved type of *bulke* (Yiddish for "bread roll"), always just the right size, and punctuated with savory onions and poppy seeds. My mouth is watering just thinking about them. Bagels, on the other hand, have gone mainstream, and they frequently disappoint me. Most bagel bakeries these days buy mass-produced bagel dough, mix in scandalous flavors like blueberry and jalapeño-cheddar, and then schmear those same bagels with "contemporary" cream cheeses like honey-walnut or sun-dried tomato.

Sure, I can admit that there has been a bagel renaissance in our midst, in New York City and cities as unlikely as Denver and Philadelphia, where bakers are turning out really terrific old-school bagels. And in learning to bake my own, I've also rediscovered how good they can be, which is why we decided to include recipes for both bagels and bialys in this book. Liz still thinks bialys are more complicated than bagels to turn into a sandwich, which doesn't really matter to me. When baked fresh, bialys can be eaten on their own or slathered with salted butter or cream cheese, and thus merit a place in these pages, and in your home.

>⟨

BIALYS

JEFFREY

Every so often at a brunch spread or a Kiddush luncheon, where the bagel usually holds court, a bialy makes an appearance. It's a moment worth celebrating. I've never understood why the bialy remains so elusive and why it's always unfairly compared to the bagel. It's really more like a roll in that it's softer to eat, toasts exceptionally well, and is practically begging to be slathered with salted butter. Not to mention its amazing onion-poppy center. Thankfully, the bialy has its die-hard advocates. Mimi Sheraton, a former *New York Times* food critic, may be the most famous. She documented her search for the bialy and its Polish origins in her book *The Bialy Eaters*, a moving tribute to the old country bread. And while bialys were hard to track down, even in Bialystok, the bialy's namesake city, Sheraton found important traces of the bread in communities around the world and, through her book, inspired a new generation of bialy eaters.

When making your own bialys, be sure not to let the dough rise for too long, since it will puff up and won't hold its shape well. If it does happen to puff up, then you'll have delicious onion rolls. It happens to the best of us. Our caramelized onion and poppy mixture for the center may be a bit unorthodox, so feel free to swap in traditional raw minced onion and poppy seeds instead.

MAKES 10 BIALYS

FOR THE DOUGH:

3 cups unbleached bread flour or all-purpose flour, plus more as needed

½ cup whole wheat flour

2 teaspoons kosher salt

1 (¼-ounce) packet active dry yeast (2¼ teaspoons)

1½ cups lukewarm water

FOR THE ONION FILLING:

2 tablespoons olive oil

1 medium yellow onion, minced (about 1½ cups)

½ teaspoon kosher salt

2 teaspoons poppy seeds

---

1. TO MAKE THE DOUGH: In a large bowl or in the bowl of a stand mixer fitted with the dough hook, combine the bread flour, whole wheat flour, salt, and yeast. Stir gently using a fork or with the mixer on low, adding the lukewarm water little by little to form a dough. Knead the dough until it comes together and the texture is smooth, about 10 minutes by hand or about 5 minutes on medium speed using the stand mixer. Place the ball of dough in a greased bowl and cover with plastic wrap. Let rise in a

(continued) ▶

draft-free area for about 1½ hours, or until the dough has doubled in size.

2. TO MAKE THE ONION FILLING: In a small saucepan, heat the oil over medium-high heat. Add the onion and salt. Cook, stirring often, until the onions are shrunken and caramelized, 10 to 15 minutes. Remove from the heat, stir in the poppy seeds, and set aside.

3. Turn the dough out onto a floured work surface, punching it down and kneading it for a minute or two.

4. Preheat the oven to 475°F. Position a baking sheet on the floor of the oven and a second baking sheet on the middle rack.

5. Divide the dough into 10 equal portions. Form each portion into a bialy by working the dough ball into a flat disk. Stretch out the middle of the disk, leaving a thicker outer ring and a paper-thin 1- to 2-inch indentation in the middle. Fill the center

of each bialy with about 1 teaspoon of the onion filling. Work quickly to get them into the oven.

6. Carefully slide the bialys onto the heated baking sheet on the middle rack of the oven. Toss a few ice cubes onto the baking sheet at the bottom of the oven to create steam, which helps the bread to expand. Immediately close the oven door, trapping the steam inside. Bake for 10 to 12 minutes, until the bialys are golden brown. Remove from the oven and let cool. Bialys are best eaten straight up, fresh from the oven, with fresh Everything Bagel Butter (page 18), Cultured Cream Cheese (page 25), pickled fish, and a full appetizing spread (see page 146). Store leftover bialys in an airtight plastic bag. They will keep for 4 to 5 days, but need to be toasted for maximum enjoyment after day 1. You could freeze bialys according to the instructions for freezing bagels on page 107, but let's face it, there won't be any left over.

Form a well in the bialy by stretching the dough with your thumbs.

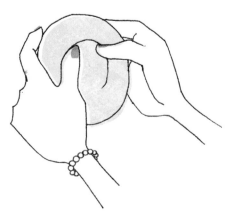

~~ FOUR ~~

SOUPS AND DUMPLINGS

LIZ Maybe I was just a picky eater, but as a child all I ever wanted to eat was soup. Every Saturday after Shabbat services, my brother, dad, and I walked across the street from the synagogue to the Lido Kosher Deli. It was our family ritual. Wally, the owner, would greet us warmly, and without skipping a beat, I would order matzo ball soup—the kind served with a fluffy matzo ball the size of my face in a shallow pool of chicken broth with eyes of fat on the surface. To the surprise of most waiters, I would finish every last drop. They didn't understand what I did: that the fluffy matzo ball was the pinnacle of soup transcendence, which I could never, and would never, take for granted. Soup continues to enchant me just as much as it did was when I was a kid. It's still primarily what I want to cook and eat, especially in the winter.

In the frigid winters of central and eastern Europe, hot soup is the key to staying warm and nourished. "Poor people cook with a lot of water," goes the Yiddish proverb, which was as relevant to life in the United States for poor Jewish immigrants as it was in the Old World, where simple soups of cabbage and water could constitute an entire meal for poverty-stricken Jewish families. In *97 Orchard*, Jane Ziegelman writes of Jewish immigrants living in the tenement buildings on the Lower East Side, "The truth of the proverb was borne out on a daily basis in the immigrant soup pot." In fact, most of the vegetables eaten by eastern European Jewish immigrants in New York at the turn of the century were in the form of soup, odds and ends transformed into rich and nutritious concoctions.

One winter, Jeffrey and I sourced a pasture-raised goose from Yiddish Farm, a farm located in upstate New York with the dual mission of expanding the use of the Yiddish language and promoting environmental stewardship. We hosted an epic dinner in the goose's honor, roasting it carefully with onions and apples. The most exciting part of that culinary adventure for me, however, was the next day, when I turned the goose carcass into stock. I didn't follow a recipe. I did what I've done many times before with chickens, turkeys, and ducks: I simmered the goose bones and remains in water all day with onions and bay leaves and carrots and peppercorns. The minerals and collagen from the bones turned into a flavorful stock. The aroma filled the kitchen so intoxicatingly that after four hours, I began lifting the pot lid to scoop out cups of deeply rich consommé, which I sipped as I continued other kitchen projects. The roasted dark meat had been absolutely delicious, but in the simple broth, I tasted the life of the bird.

Soup is an ideal way for the Ashkenazi cook to practice spicing, salting, and waiting while using everything you have in your pantry. The soups and dumplings in this chapter are classics with some contemporary flair, but not too much. Feel free to riff on them and improvise as you see fit. Let soup be your canvas and your inspiration, just as it's been mine. And remember that you can make stock from just about anything, whether it's old goose carcasses, onion skins, and carrot peels, or chicken and beef bones.

JEFFREY

When Liz and I first began cooking for New York's gourmet flea markets, we served cups of beet borscht, one of the few traditional eastern European soups that made it into my family's weekday repertoire. Inevitably, customers would reveal their own family histories to us as they sipped their beet soup garnished with sour cream and dill. As we served up different soups throughout the seasons, we found that hot—and sometimes chilled—soup broth almost always triggered nostalgia, connecting flavors with comfort and memory. Like borscht, soups like chicken soup, matzo ball soup, and mushroom and barley seem to exist on an ethereal plane, possessing magical healing properties. These salty, fatty fluids tap into a deep-seated feeling of being nourished and cared for.

But the true essence of soup will always come back to the stories and memories that emerge from the bowl. My great-aunt Rachel, for example, who lives in Israel, makes chicken soup with kreplach every year during the holiday of Sukkot, as is customary. She had grown up with my grandpa Julius before the war, in Wyszków, Poland, and she knew how to make kreplach just as his mother had. Kreplach are labor-intensive dumplings that play second fiddle to the matzo ball in many American Jewish households, but Rachel's kreplach were so delicious that the entire family patiently awaited this soup all year long. Rachel's children, born in Israel, have mostly abandoned eastern European traditions for modern Israeli ones. Eating kreplach in the autumn is their major tie to the family's European roots and the tragic circumstances that relocated them to the Middle East.

My father tasted Rachel's kreplach on a visit to Israel in the 1960s. "They're the best kreplach in the world," he gushed, and recounted to me how much his own father, Grandpa Julius, had thought so, too. When I visited Israel a decade ago, my father insisted that I do whatever I had to do to eat at Rachel's for Sukkot.

When I finally tasted Rachel's soup, I was taken aback by the folded white dumplings, which looked like royal crowns floating in golden broth. As I ate krepl after delicious krepl, I realized that for once, my father had not been exaggerating even a little. I then thought of my grandfather, and imagined him eating those soft pouches of juicy beef and onion one by one, the flavors transporting him to his mother's cooking from before the war, warmed and comforted as if still a child in his family kitchen, delighting in a bowl of this nourishing soup.

SOUPS AND DUMPLINGS
≥ RECIPES ≥

LILYA'S SUMMER BEET BORSCHT

LIZ →

One summer day, Jeffrey and I headed to Little Odessa in Brighton Beach, Brooklyn. We were visiting our business partner Jackie's ninety-two-year-old Russian-born great-aunt, Lilya. She had immigrated to Brighton Beach from the Soviet Union in 1989. Lilya was known for her borscht, and she'd invited us to spend time with her while she salted and seasoned three varieties of the soup. At ninety-two, she was extraordinary, foisting shots of vodka on us and showering us with words of wisdom. We left Brighton Beach inspired and feeling lucky to have met her. She passed away a couple of years later. We developed this recipe with her in mind.

This beet borscht is perfect served chilled on summer days or served hot in the colder months. The ideal borscht, writes Aleksandar Hemon in the *New Yorker* of his Bosnian family traditions "contains everything . . . and it can be refrigerated and reheated in perpetuity, always better the next day . . . The crucial ingredient . . . is a large, hungry family, surviving together."

Jeffrey thinks that this recipe should utilize *rossel* (the brine from fermented beets, otherwise known as beet kvass) instead of vinegar to add tang, since traditionally borscht's coveted sour flavor was cultivated by first fermenting the beets. But I disagree. I like the flavor that vinegar adds, even if it isn't as Old World. This recipe uses vinegar (I won!), but if you'd like to be more old school and first wait a week to ferment your beets, follow the Beet and Ginger Kvass recipe (page 290) but omit the ginger. And while this recipe calls for roasting beets and adding them to the soup, it also tastes great without roasted beets. Just cut the beet amount to 1 pound if omitting the roasting step.

SERVES 6 TO 8

---

2 pounds whole beets, scrubbed but unpeeled

2 carrots, unpeeled and coarsely chopped

2 celery stalks with leaves, coarsely chopped

2 medium onions: 1 quartered, 1 diced

5 garlic cloves: 2 left whole, 3 minced

2 dried bay leaves

2 tablespoons kosher salt

2 tablespoons whole black peppercorns

2 tablespoons caraway seeds

9 cups cold water

2 tablespoons olive oil

3 tablespoons honey

3 tablespoons apple cider vinegar

Sour cream, store-bought or homemade (page 24), or crème fraîche, for garnish

Chopped fresh dill, for garnish

(continued) ▶

1. Preheat the oven to 400°F. Wrap 1 pound of the beets individually in aluminum foil and set on a baking sheet. Roast until they can be easily pierced with a fork, 40 minutes to 1 hour, depending on the size of the beets (larger beets take longer). The skin should peel off easily under cold running water. Dice the beets into bite-size pieces and refrigerate until serving.

2. While the beets are roasting, in a large soup pot, combine the remaining 1 pound beets, the carrots, celery, quartered onion, whole garlic cloves, bay leaves, salt, peppercorns, caraway seeds, and 9 cups water. Bring to a boil, then reduce the heat to low and simmer for 1 hour. Remove from the heat.

3. Fill a large bowl with water and ice. Remove the boiled beets from the pot and place them in the ice-water bath. When cool, peel and coarsely chop them. Strain the broth through a fine-mesh strainer into a large bowl, discarding the solids.

4. Rinse and dry the soup pot and set it over medium heat. Add the olive oil and diced onion and sauté until the onion is fragrant, about 3 minutes.

Add the minced garlic and sauté for 3 to 5 minutes more, until the onion begins to turn golden. Add the beet broth and coarsely chopped boiled beets to the pot and simmer over low heat, covered, for about 20 minutes.

5. Remove from the heat and puree the soup in the pot using an immersion blender. (Alternatively, transfer it in small batches to a standing blender and puree—just be careful!) Add the honey and vinegar and simmer over very low heat for 5 minutes.

6. If serving hot, place 2 tablespoons of diced roasted beets in the bottom of each bowl and then ladle the hot soup over them. Garnish with sour cream and chopped fresh dill. If serving chilled, remove from the heat and let the soup cool completely and then refrigerate overnight. Be sure to stir the soup well and taste immediately before serving. Once cooled, many soups require a touch more salt. If necessary, add more salt, a teaspoon at a time. As with hot borscht, place 2 tablespoons of the roasted beets at the bottom of the bowl and ladle the soup on top. Serve garnished with sour cream and chopped fresh dill.

SPICED BLUEBERRY SOUP

JEFFREY

There's an intriguing tradition of fruit-based soups in Ashkenazi cooking, much as there is in Scandinavian cuisine. Growing up, I was familiar with sour cherry soup, but I hadn't heard of blueberry soup until I began reviewing old Jewish cookbooks. I'm glad I found it.

Many old recipes call for straining out the blueberries, but Liz and I prefer the texture that the stewed fruit adds to the soup. This recipe is a great way to highlight the berry harvest in early summer or a delicious way to utilize frozen berries when the weather turns cold. Also, it is a very quick recipe. You can serve it hot right after it's finished cooking, but the flavor develops nicely after a day. Once cooled, you can refrigerate the soup and serve it cold (our preference) or at room temperature.

SERVES 4 TO 6

2 cinnamon sticks

2 teaspoons whole cloves

1 tablespoon coriander seeds

2 teaspoons whole black peppercorns

6 cups fresh or frozen blueberries

¼ cup honey

¼ cup fresh lemon juice

1 cup cold water

2 egg yolks, lightly beaten

2 teaspoons lemon zest, plus more for garnish

Sour cream, store-bought or homemade (page 24), or plain yogurt, for serving

1. Tie the cinnamon sticks, cloves, coriander seeds, and peppercorns in a square of cheesecloth for easy removal later.

2. In a medium saucepan, combine the blueberries, honey, lemon juice, spice bundle, and cold water. Bring to a boil over medium-high heat, then reduce the heat to maintain a simmer and cook for about 8 minutes. The berries will break down quite quickly and release a good deal of liquid.

3. Remove the pot from the heat. Very slowly spoon 3 tablespoons of the hot blueberry liquid into the egg yolks (1 tablespoon at a time to avoid curdling the egg yolks). Whisk with a fork until thick, 1 to 2 minutes, then return the blueberry-egg mixture to the pot and return the soup just to a boil. Immediately reduce the heat to maintain a simmer and cook for 3 minutes more, until the soup has thickened. Remove from the heat, and immediately mix in the 2 teaspoons of lemon zest.

4. Remove the spice bundle before serving hot, cold, or at room temperature, garnished with sour cream and remaining lemon zest.

LEEK SOUP WITH BEET GREENS

JEFFREY

Whenever I visit my octogenarian Jewish friend Celia who grew up in prewar Poland, she ladles out a bowl of hot leek soup for me. Her soup inspired this recipe, which also pays homage to the classic spring soup *schav*, a sour sorrel soup. Since sorrel can be tough to source, the combination of leeks and beet greens in this version will satisfy your craving for a light, springtime soup. We add lemon to give the soup some brightness. Adding acidity is common with Ashkenazi soups, as it balances out some of the heavier flavors in the diet. This soup gets better each day, so make a big pot and eat it throughout the week. If the soup sits with the beet greens, you may see some pink splotches develop in the broth. That's what beet greens do, so just give it a stir.

SERVES 8

¼ cup grapeseed oil, light olive oil, or unsalted butter

1 large onion, coarsely chopped

4 pounds leeks (about 8 small), white and light-green parts only, rinsed thoroughly to remove grit, thinly sliced

7 cups vegetable broth, homemade (page 123, made with white wine) or store-bought

5 teaspoons kosher salt

¾ teaspoon freshly ground white pepper

2 tablespoons fresh lemon juice

1 cup stemmed beet greens (from 1 small bunch beets), shredded (optional)

2 lemons, quartered, for serving (optional)

Seasoned croutons (page 38), for garnish

Chopped fresh parsley, for garnish

---

1. In a large saucepan, heat the oil or butter over medium heat. Add the onion and sauté for about 5 minutes, or until translucent. Add the leeks and sauté over low heat, stirring frequently, until the leeks are soft and lightly caramel in color, about 25 minutes.

2. Add the broth, salt, and white pepper. Cover and simmer for about 20 minutes, or until the leeks are limp and completely cooked through. Puree the soup using an immersion blender. (Alternatively, transfer it in small batches to a standing blender and puree—just be careful!) Add the lemon juice, taste, and adjust the seasoning. If using beet greens, toss them into the pot and simmer for 15 minutes more before serving.

3. Serve hot, with a wedge of lemon for squeezing over the top, if desired. Garnish with seasoned croutons and parsley.

FULL-BODIED VEGETABLE BROTH

Making a rich and flavorful vegetarian broth is not always easy. Without bones and fat, veggie broth can often feel flat. Red wine adds depth when making a broth for a richer, heavier soup like Mushroom and Barley (page 127). White wine is good for broths in lighter soups such as Leek Soup with Beet Greens (page 122) or as a vegetarian base for Beef Kreplach (page 135) or Rustic Matzo Balls (page 133).

One of the best aspects of making stock and broth is how forgiving they are. While the wine is key in this recipe, the vegetable quantities do not need to be precise. I always keep at least two quarts of broth in the freezer, and it always comes in handy.

MAKES 1½ TO 2 QUARTS RICH VEGETABLE BROTH; SERVES 6 TO 8

3 tablespoons olive oil

2 medium onions, unpeeled, cut into eighths

3 celery stalks with leaves, coarsely chopped

½ fennel bulb with fronds, coarsely chopped

6 carrots, unpeeled and coarsely chopped

5 garlic cloves, crushed

3 sprigs fresh parsley

6 sprigs fresh thyme

1½ tablespoons whole black peppercorns

1½ teaspoons fennel seeds

4 dried bay leaves

1½ cups red or white wine

9 cups water

2 tablespoons kosher salt

1. In a large stockpot, heat the oil over medium heat. Add the onions, celery, fennel, carrots, and garlic and cook, stirring frequently, until the vegetables are slightly browned and very aromatic, about 20 minutes. Add the parsley, thyme, peppercorns, fennel seeds, and bay leaves and cook, stirring, for 5 minutes more.

2. Increase the heat slightly and pour in the wine, scraping up any vegetables stuck to the bottom of the pot using a wooden spoon. Reduce the heat to low and simmer, stirring occasionally while the alcohol cooks off, about 5 minutes.

3. Add the water and reduce the heat to very low. Cover and cook for 1½ hours. After about 45 minutes, stir in the salt—no need to stir otherwise.

4. Strain the broth through a fine-mesh strainer into a large vessel, taking care to press on the vegetables with a ladle to squeeze out all the flavorful liquid. Discard the solids. Let the broth cool, then cover and refrigerate. It tastes best the next day, but will keep in the refrigerator for up to 5 days or in the freezer for months.

ŻUREK (SOUR RYE SOUP)

JEFFREY

You won't find too many *Żurek* recipes in Jewish cookbooks, since it's one of those places where Ashkenazi and Polish cuisines diverge. The base—potatoes and cream—could easily be found in either kitchen, but Polish *Żurek* is generally flavored with sausage or bacon. Liz and I were nevertheless attracted to this soup (sans sausage) because of its peasant roots, the potato's prominence in it, and its sourness from rye starter, which we often have on hand. We decided to make a vegetarian-friendly version.

If you're keeping a rye starter (see page 102) in your kitchen, you can use it in this soup (just add the garlic and bay leaves and let sit for two days), or you can follow the recipe for a quick-and-easy sour rye ferment below. You'll want to plan ahead when making this soup, since it requires a couple of days of sitting for the starter to develop. If you do not eat gluten (or even if you do), sauerkraut brine makes a great substitute for the rye starter and requires less preparation than the quick rye ferment. Just add the same quantity of sauerkraut brine to the soup in place of the quick rye ferment.

SERVES 4 TO 6

FOR THE QUICK RYE FERMENT:

¾ cup rye flour

2 dried bay leaves

1 large garlic clove, crushed

1¾ cups filtered water

FOR THE SOUP:

3 tablespoons unsalted butter

1 medium onion, diced

2½ cups coarsely chopped scallions (from about 1½ bunches)

¾ pound russet potatoes, peeled and coarsely chopped

4 cups vegetable broth

2½ teaspoons kosher salt

1½ teaspoons freshly ground black pepper

¾ cup heavy cream or half-and-half (if you want the soup to be a little lighter)

½ cup whole milk

4 to 6 tablespoons rye starter (page 102) or sauerkraut brine (if not using the quick rye ferment)

3 room-temperature hard-boiled eggs, quartered lengthwise

Minced fresh chives, for garnish

---

1. TO MAKE THE QUICK RYE FERMENT: Two days before you'd like to serve this soup, combine the rye flour, bay leaves, and garlic in a clean glass jar and pour in the water. Seal the jar and shake to combine.

Let the starter sit at room temperature, sealed, for 2 days. After 2 days, shake and then taste it. It should be earthy and sour and garlicky, but not pungent.

(continued) ▶

If it's not yet sour, wait another day. Once you've reached the desired level of sourness, place the jar in the fridge. It will last, refrigerated, for up to 2 weeks.

2. TO MAKE THE SOUP: In a large pot, melt the butter over medium heat. Add the onion and sauté until slightly browned, about 10 minutes. Add the scallions and sauté for 5 minutes more, or until the scallions are soft and wilted but not browned.

3. Add the potatoes, broth, salt, and pepper, cover, and simmer until the potatoes are soft, about 25 minutes. Puree the soup using an immersion blender, adding the cream and milk as you do so. Taste and adjust the seasoning.

4. When ready to serve, remove the soup pot from the heat. Remove the bay leaf and garlic from the rye ferment and shake the jar to evenly distribute the contents. Slowly add 4 to 6 tablespoons of the rye ferment to the soup, tasting every 2 tablespoons until the desired level of sourness is reached. The more ferment you add, the more intense the flavor. (The rye ferment can also be spooned into each bowl separately, about 1 tablespoon per serving.)

5. Ladle the soup into bowls and garnish with the hard-boiled eggs and chives.

MUSHROOM AND BARLEY SOUP

LIZ →

Part of what made mushrooms—one of the primary flavoring agents of Ashkenazi cuisine—so popular was the fact that they could be foraged from the forests, free of charge. They also possess a meaty, umami character. The best foragers, often peasant women, would gather extras after a rain spell and sell them at markets.

Among the types of mushrooms eaten by Jews in Europe, porcinis (often referred to as cèpes, from the French) were quite common. Even after Jews immigrated to North America, where they relied mostly on North American ingredients for cooking, there was a robust mushroom trade for imported porcinis from the Old World. "Mushrooms were one of the few things they [Jews] bothered to bring in from the Old Country," explains food historian Jane Ziegelman. "There was even a little mushroom wholesale district on Houston Street."

This recipe is best made with porcinis, both dried and fresh, but a variety of mushrooms, including shiitakes and even portobellos, will taste great. The dried mushrooms give this soup particular depth. Also note that the barley is cooked separately from the broth, to ensure a soup that isn't gummy or porridge-like, as mushroom barley can sometimes be.

SERVES 8

2½ tablespoons vegetable oil

½ cup pearl barley

8 cups vegetable broth, store-bought or homemade (page 123, made with red wine)

4 sprigs fresh dill, plus chopped fresh dill for garnish

½ ounce dried mushrooms (about ¾ cup loosely packed)

½ cup boiling water

1 large carrot, peeled and diced

1 celery stalk, diced

1 small onion, diced

1 pound fresh porcini mushrooms, stems removed, quartered

1 teaspoon kosher salt

1 teaspoon freshly ground black pepper

1. In a small nonstick saucepan, heat ½ tablespoon of the oil over medium heat. Add the barley and toast it, stirring frequently, until it becomes fragrant and flecked with dark brown spots, about 7 minutes. Pour in 1 cup of the broth and add 1 sprig of the dill. Bring to a boil, then cover and simmer over medium heat until the barley is

(continued) ▶

▶ (Mushroom and Barley Soup, *continued*)

cooked through but not soft, about 25 minutes. Remove from the heat, discard the dill sprig, and drain any remaining liquid from the grain. Set aside.

2. While the barley is cooking, place the dried mushrooms in a small bowl and pour the boiling water over them. Let them rehydrate for about 25 minutes, then strain through a fine-mesh strainer into a bowl, reserving the liquid and slicing the reconstituted mushrooms into small pieces.

3. In a large stockpot, heat the remaining 2 tablespoons oil over medium heat. Add the carrot, celery, onion, and porcinis. Sauté, stirring frequently, until the onion starts to brown, about 10 minutes. Add the rehydrated mushrooms, reserved mushroom soaking liquid, remaining 7 cups broth, the salt, pepper, and remaining 3 sprigs dill and simmer until the vegetables are soft, 25 to 30 minutes. Remove and discard the dill sprigs. Stir in the barley. Salt to taste.

4. Serve the soup garnished with chopped fresh dill. It tastes best when reheated the next day.

CLASSIC CHICKEN SOUP

LIZ

The smell of chicken soup—the undeniable scent of *bubbes* (grandmothers) and Friday night dinners—is the backdrop to the Ashkenazi kitchen. "How could one greet so important a guest as the Holy Sabbath with only *borscht* or barley soup?" asks Hirsz Abramowicz, explaining the importance of chicken soup for the Sabbath from his days as a Jewish villager in prewar Lithuania. "That would be a profanation."

Let the chicken, vegetables, spices, and water simmer slowly, for hours, as you *potchkie* around the house. Once the broth is sufficiently cooked, let it cool, then leave it in the fridge overnight. It only gets better with time. If you're serving your soup right away, pull out the carrots and celery before straining, and chop them into small pieces to serve in the soup. Since I always make my chicken soup in advance, I strain out all the vegetables and then toss in diced fresh carrots and celery the next day when reheating. It only takes about 20 minutes at a simmer for them to cook through. Be sure to always salt to taste, no matter what chicken you're using. And don't worry too much in general about the exact measurements in the recipe below. If you only have three celery stalks, you'll be fine. Also, dill is an optional ingredient, as it can sometimes dominate the flavor of the broth, and not everyone loves a strong dill flavor. Chicken soup is forgiving, as long as you give its broth the time it deserves.

MAKES ABOUT 2 QUARTS SOUP; SERVES 6 TO 8

---

2 tablespoons vegetable oil or schmaltz (page 35)

3 pounds chicken parts, pieces, or whole carcass

3 medium onions, washed and quartered

4 carrots, peeled and halved lengthwise

4 celery stalks with leaves, halved lengthwise

4 garlic cloves, crushed

9 to 10 cups cold water

3 dried bay leaves

1½ tablespoons whole black peppercorns

4 sprigs fresh parsley

4 sprigs fresh thyme

3 sprigs fresh dill (optional)

1½ to 3 tablespoons kosher salt

---

1. If desired, remove excess fat and skin from the chicken and reserve for making schmaltz (page 35).

2. In a large, heavy-bottomed soup pot, heat the oil over medium heat. Add the chicken, skin-side down (working in

(continued) ▶

the meat into smaller chunks and place in a food processor, along with the onion from the pot, the egg, schmaltz or oil, salt, and pepper. Pulse the ingredients to form a loose paste.

2. TO MAKE THE DOUGH: In a large bowl, whisk together the flour and salt. Add the oil and hot water and stir gently to form a dough. Using your hands, knead to form a soft, smooth ball. If the dough is sticky, add a bit more flour.

3. TO ASSEMBLE THE KREPLACH, take half the dough and roll it out on a well-floured surface; keep the other half covered to avoid drying. The dough should be rolled out as thin as possible, or your kreplach will be tough and doughy. Cut the dough into 2½-inch squares. If you do not have a square cookie cutter, cut out rounds instead using a glass. Keep your surface well floured to prevent the kreplach from sticking.

4. Place ½ teaspoon of the filling in the center of each krepl (yes, that's the singular). Work quickly or the dough will dry out. Do not overstuff. You will be tempted to do so, but we cannot stress enough that overfilling will not end well. Fold the dough over into a triangle, pressing the edges together and sealing them, applying water at the seams if necessary. Fold again to connect the two ends of the triangle (see photos page 138). Repeat the process with the remaining dough, putting the finished kreplach on a baking sheet and keeping them in the freezer while you work on the second half.

5. Meanwhile, fill a large pot with water, add salt (the ratio should be 1 tablespoon salt for every 1 quart water), and bring to a boil. Drop the kreplach into the boiling water and cook for 15 minutes. Remove one krepl with a slotted spoon and taste to ensure that the dough is fully cooked, just like you would with pasta. If they need more time, boil for 5 minutes more, then remove, drain, and place in hot broth just before serving.

(*continued*) ▶

▶ (Beef Kreplach, *continued*)

SPINACH AND LEEK FILLING

1 tablespoon olive oil

1 large leek, white and light-green parts only, rinsed thoroughly to remove grit, sliced (about 1 cup)

5 ounces spinach, stems removed, leaves coarsely chopped (about 6 cups loosely packed)

1 large egg

1 tablespoon fresh lemon juice

½ teaspoon kosher salt

In a medium saucepan, heat the oil over medium heat. Add the leek and sauté until the leek is soft and caramel in color, about 15 minutes. Add the spinach in batches and cook until it has wilted, about 5 minutes. Let the spinach-leek mixture cool slightly, then transfer it to a food processor and add the egg, lemon juice, and salt. Process until a smooth paste is formed. Form the kreplach as directed, using the spinach-leek filling in place of the meat filling.

PIEROGI

LIZ →

Pierogi are just one of a wide array of eastern European dumplings, which include *vareniki* (often fruit filled), *pelmeni* (smaller and usually meat filled), and, of course, Beef Kreplach (page 135). We love pierogi for their ubiquity at Jewish dairy restaurants such as B&H in the East Village and the now-defunct Ratner's on the Lower East Side, and also because of their everyday nature. Whereas kreplach for me hold an elevated status, floating daintily as they do in holiday chicken soups, I prefer my pierogi quickly boiled, pan-fried, and devoured for a hearty lunch or a weeknight meal.

In addition to a few fillings we have scattered throughout the book, we've also included a satisfying lentil and chard filling here. If you're making a double batch and want to freeze some for later, simply boil the pierogi, then place them on a baking sheet, freeze, and transfer to an airtight container once they are frozen. To reheat, let thaw slightly and fry according to the instructions in step 5.

**MAKES ABOUT
48 SMALL PIEROGI**

FOR THE DOUGH:

4½ cups all-purpose flour, plus more as needed

1 tablespoon kosher salt

3 large eggs

½ cup warm water, plus more as needed

FILLING OPTIONS:

Quick and Creamy Farmer's Cheese (page 21)

Savory Mushroom-Potato Filling (page 228)

Spinach and Leek Filling (page 139)

Wine-Braised Sauerkraut and Mushrooms (page 64)

Lentil and Chard Filling (recipe follows)

Kosher salt, as needed

2–4 tablespoons unsalted butter or vegetable oil, for frying

Sour cream, store-bought or homemade (page 24), for serving

Chopped fresh parsley, for garnish

---

1. TO MAKE THE DOUGH: Sift together the flour and salt into a large bowl. Form a well in the center of the flour and pour the eggs and warm water into the well. Stir with a fork to incorporate, adding more warm water by the tablespoon until a soft, sticky but pliable dough is formed (you should need no more than 4 tablespoons additional water). Do not knead the dough any more once it comes together. You want to minimize the amount you handle it. Wrap the dough in plastic wrap or cover with a moist towel and let sit for at least 30 minutes while you prepare your filling of choice.

2. Cut the ball of dough into 3 separate pieces. Using a rolling pin, flatten out

(continued) ▶

▶ (Pierogi, *continued*)

a piece of dough on a lightly floured surface and roll it very thin, to about ⅛-inch thickness. Using the top of a glass, cut out 3½-inch-diameter circles as close together as possible, minimizing the amount of wasted dough between pieces. In the center of each circle, place about 1½ teaspoons of filling. Fold the edge over to form a half-moon and seal the ends together, making sure the seal is as tight as possible and any air bubbles that form around the filling are released. If needed, use a bit of water to seal the edges together. For a decorative flair, press down on the edge of each dumpling with the tines of a fork, creating lines around the edges of the dumplings. Work quickly, keeping the filled pierogi under a damp kitchen towel to prevent drying out. Keep working until you run out of dough or filling, whichever comes first.

3. Bring a large pot of heavily salted water (the ratio should be 1 tablespoon salt for every 1 quart water) to a low boil. Drop several pierogi into the pot. Once

they rise to the top, boil for 3 minutes more, then remove with a slotted spoon. Do not overcrowd the pot, and be sure to drain them thoroughly once they are done. Repeat until all the pierogi have been boiled and drained.

4. You can eat them then and there with sour cream, or continue to step 5 to fry. You can also freeze them now for frying later (see the headnote).

5. In a large skillet, melt the butter or oil over medium heat. Add a few pierogi to the pan, being sure not to crowd them. Fry until both sides are golden brown, about 1½ minutes on each side. (If frying frozen pierogi, thaw them slightly before frying.)

6. Remove from the heat and serve immediately with sour cream and parsley, preferably accompanied by a fresh salad.

(continued) ▶

▶ (Pierogi, *continued*)

LENTIL AND CHARD FILLING

½ cup brown lentils, rinsed well

1½ cups water or vegetable broth (page 123)

1 small sweet potato, peeled and finely diced

1 celery stalk, halved

1 small onion, finely diced

2 dried bay leaves

½ teaspoon kosher salt

⅛ teaspoon freshly ground black pepper

Pinch of red pepper flakes (optional)

1 teaspoon fresh marjoram or oregano (optional)

1 small bunch Swiss chard, stemmed and finely chopped

Place the lentils in a pot with cold water to cover. Bring to a boil and boil for 2 minutes. Drain in a colander, rinse the lentils and the pot, and return the lentils to the pot. Add the 1½ cups water or broth, sweet potato, celery, onion, bay leaves, salt, black pepper, and red pepper flakes and marjoram (if using). Bring to a boil over medium heat, then reduce the heat to maintain a simmer and cook for 20 minutes, or until the lentils are totally cooked through. Remove the bay leaves and celery from the pot and discard them. Add the Swiss chard and cook for 2 to 3 minutes. The Swiss chard will be fully cooked but still vibrant green in color. Remove from the heat and drain any stock or water from the lentil-chard mixture. Mash the mixture with a fork, creating a paste for easy filling.

EGG LOKSHEN "NOODLES"

JEFFREY

These aren't actually noodles at all, but gluten-free crepe strips that my great-aunt Yetta used to make for Passover. When made with dill or marjoram, the "noodles" add spice and a soft, light texture to your chicken or vegetable soup—even when it's not Passover. Plus, making these noodles is fast and easy. And if you're looking for a simple gluten-free or Passover blintz recipe, you can use the crepe before cutting it into strips. Just stuff it with Sweet or Savory Blintz fillings (page 224). This is a super-quick recipe.

SERVES 3 OR 4

---

3 large eggs, beaten

3 tablespoons potato starch

¼ teaspoon kosher salt

1 teaspoon dried dill, thyme, or marjoram (optional)

½ to 1 tablespoon unsalted butter, grapeseed oil, or vegetable oil, for greasing the pan

---

1. In a medium bowl, combine the eggs, potato starch, salt, and dried dill (if using) and whisk with a fork until the potato starch is evenly distributed.

2. Grease a nonstick skillet with the butter and set it over low heat. Pour a very thin layer of the egg batter into the pan (about 3 tablespoons of batter if using an 8-inch-diameter pan; about 2 tablespoons of batter if using a 6-inch-diameter pan) and cook until set in the middle, about 1 minute. Flip with a spatula and cook the other side until golden, about 30 seconds.

3. Remove the egg pancake from the pan and set it on a plate. Continue to make crepes, stacking them on the plate and lightly greasing the pan between rounds if it looks dry.

4. When all the batter has been used up and the crepes have cooled slightly, slice each individually by rolling it up into a log and slicing it crosswise into thin strips (about the thickness of fettuccine). You may then also wish to cut them in half lengthwise if they seem too long. Use these "noodles" immediately, placing them in individual bowls of soup, or prepare them in advance and refrigerate in an airtight container until ready to use. They will last for about 5 days. If preparing them in advance, refrigerate, then toss into hot soup a few minutes before serving.

~~ FIVE ~~

APPETIZING AND LIGHTER SIDES

LIZ⟩ One hot day at the end of August a few years back, Jeffrey and I invited a food journalist friend over for a nosh and a hang. Lunch was typical of what Jeffrey and I eat on the regular: gefilte fish, homemade pickled vegetables and trout, a light cabbage slaw with caraway and mustard seeds, and slices of freshly baked bread, all washed down with some refreshing beet and lettuce kvass. When she saw our spread, she lit up. "It's like a Latvian picnic," she said, "straight out of the Old World."

The idea of the Latvian picnic stuck with us. Most friends would probably have declined an invitation to eat Ashkenazi foods on a hot summer day, assuming that it would mean fatty smoked meats and other heavy, stick-to-your-ribs delicacies. Our friend, however, was all too aware that such a perception was way too limiting.

At the root of Ashkenazi cuisine is an entirely seasonal cycle, yet too often when we talk about Jewish foods, at least here in the United States, the warmer months are forgotten. Light, fresh foods represented a reprieve from the harshness of winter and the repetitive staples that were pulled from the root cellar during the colder months. Meat and potatoes weren't absent in the summer, but Jews of central and eastern Europe were prioritizing feasting on—and preserving—the limited-availability fresh fruits, vegetables, dairy, and fish. Warmer weather meant that wild mushrooms, young greens, and horseradish roots could be foraged from the wild, as lakes thawed and fish could be caught more easily. Precious fats like butter and schmaltz were used sparingly, and instead, flavor came from onions, garlic, and fresh herbs. As memoirist Abe Rosenberg from Brzeziny, Poland, recalled at the turn of the twentieth century, "After the harsh winter's groats, and bread and garlic *borscht*, it was a delight to eat *schav* [sorrel] *borscht* with new potatoes, crumbled farmer's cheese with green onions, and the early summer vegetables and fruit."

Jeffrey and I constantly refer to the Latvian picnic for inspiration. It is our framework for honoring the lighter side of our food tradition. We like to imagine that if we were guests at such a picnic, we'd be feasting on a crisp Sunflower Salad (page 152), fresh gooseberries, Sweet Vinegar–Brine Pickled Trout (page 160), Lewando's Leek Frittata (page 159), and, of course, slices of Herbed Gefilte Fish (page 162) with Carrot-Citrus Horseradish Relish (page 176).

~~~

JEFFREY One of my most prized books as a child was Barbara Cohen's classic *The Carp in the Bathtub*, which tells the story of a mother who brings a live carp from the fishmonger in Brooklyn to spend the week in her family's bathtub until it's time to make gefilte fish. With no refrigeration, the best way to ensure the freshest gefilte fish was to pick up the fish in advance and keep it alive in the tub at home. Often that fish would have been carp, and keeping the fish in water reduced its muddy flavor. An unforeseen problem arises when her children fall in love with their new "pet." The children name the fish Joe and sneakily relocate him to a neighbor's tub, but his fate is all but certain. The story of the carp in the tub resonated deeply with me, and with Liz. That a family would sacrifice its only bathtub for a week in pursuit of the freshest fish was a testament to the importance of the dish—and to the outsized role that appetizing foods play in the Yiddish kitchen.

Smoked, salted, and pickled fish were staples of the European diet from the Middle Ages on. The methods of preservation, from pickling to curing to smoking, allowed the fish to be transported over long distances. Jewish merchants became heavily involved with importing fish from the Middle and Far East since they were, for the most part, not allowed to own land or join guilds, which excluded them from the most common professions. Like their neighbors, Jews were eating preserved fish as a protein source, and since the Jewish community had the inside track, fish became an even bigger part of their diet. Also, kosher dietary laws classified fish as pareve—neither meat nor dairy—so fish were among the most versatile foods available to observant Jews. "It could be claimed that each Jew eats a herring a day," wrote Édouard de Pomiane, a French food writer who traveled through Poland in 1929 to document its Jewish culture. "It is the food of the poor, but it is also the delicacy of the rich."

Fish was so central to Ashkenazi life that Jewish immigrants in North America established the appetizing shop as a place where cured, salted, and pickled fish were served with cream cheese, dairy kugels, and all sorts of buttery pastries. Whereas kosher delis kept dairy foods off their menus out of deference to the dietary laws, appetizing shops embraced them. Jews were also active in the fruit trade in Europe, leasing plum, apple, and pear orchards from non-Jewish neighbors to sell the fruit abroad, which explains why you can find plenty of dried fruit in appetizing shops today. Also common in the anti-deli are imported treats like halvah, which similarly has its roots in the Jewish importing of exotics, even in small villages. My great-aunt's parents in Wyszków, Poland, for instance, owned the only shop selling oranges and lemons in town.

To this day in North America, the foods of the appetizing shops—think bagels and lox—have continued to dominate major life events, whether a bris, a shiva, or a bar mitzvah. When Liz and I reflect on the Jewish foods that were the most a part of our everyday lives in New York, these foods keep coming up. Gefilte fish tells the story of Ashkenazi life—in both Europe and North America—so well. As we made plans to breathe new life into Ashkenazi cuisine, we began with gefilte fish, to honor that piece of our history.

APPETIZING AND LIGHTER SIDES
=RECISES=

SUNFLOWER SALAD

LIZ

SERVES 6

I love how this salad evokes the brightness of a sunflower. It pairs some of the most seasonal items you can find at the farmers' market with a sweet and tangy dressing we make from shallot brine. Feel free to modify the recipe based on what is available at the market. We used French breakfast radishes, in season during the summer.

1 head butter lettuce, washed, dried, and torn into large pieces

½ Persian cucumber, thinly sliced

5 radishes, halved and thinly sliced

1 cup pea shoots, sunflower sprouts, or other sprouts

Shallot Brine Salad Dressing (page 80)

¼ cup unsalted hulled sunflower seeds, toasted

About 6 squash blossoms, coarsely shredded

1. In a large bowl, toss together the lettuce, cucumber, radishes, and pea shoots. Pour the dressing over the mixture and gently toss again to coat the vegetables.

2. Place a handful of salad on each serving plate. Sprinkle with the toasted sunflower seeds and squash blossoms.

AUTUMN KALE SALAD

LIZ

While kale was not, by any accounts, as widely eaten by Ashkenazi Jews as it is now by residents of Brooklyn, the leafy green fits easily into the pages of this book for both its lineage and its overall heartiness. Kale is a close cousin to many of the star vegetables in this book, such as cabbage, turnips, brussels sprouts, and cauliflower. These vegetables, all part of the cruciferous family in the genus *Brassica*, are highly nutrient-rich and easily cultivated in colder climates like northern and eastern Europe.

The salad below celebrates the colors and flavors of fall, adding a hint of sweet raisins to contrast the slightly bitter kale greens. If you can't source delicata squash, a small butternut squash can work in its place. Be sure to peel the butternut squash before roasting. Pair this salad with a bowl of hot Leek Soup with Beet Greens (page 122) and Seeded Honey Rye Pull-Apart Rolls (page 98) for one of my favorite meals.

SERVES 4 TO 6

½ head garlic

6 tablespoons extra-virgin olive oil, plus 1 teaspoon for roasting garlic

1 small delicata squash, unpeeled and thinly sliced, seeds removed

1 teaspoon kosher salt

Pinch of freshly ground black pepper

2 tablespoons apple cider vinegar

2 tablespoons fresh lemon juice

1 teaspoon honey

Pinch of cayenne pepper or hot paprika (optional)

1 large head lacinato kale, thickest ribs removed

½ cup golden raisins

½ cup hazelnuts or almonds, toasted and chopped

Shaved Parmesan cheese (optional)

1. Preheat the oven to 400°F. Trim about ¼ inch off the head of the garlic, exposing the cloves. Drizzle 1 teaspoon of the olive oil on the garlic skins and rub it in. Wrap the garlic in aluminum foil and place on a baking sheet in the oven. Roast for 30 to 40 minutes, or until the individual cloves are completely soft. Remove from the oven and set aside.

2. At the same time as you roast the garlic, roast the squash. Place the squash pieces in a small bowl and coat with 2 tablespoons of the oil, ½ teaspoon of the salt, and the black pepper. Spread out the squash on a large baking sheet and roast for about 20 minutes, flipping halfway through, until the pieces are browned and cooked through. Set aside to cool to room temperature.

3. TO MAKE THE DRESSING: In a small bowl, stir together the remaining 4 tablespoons oil, vinegar, lemon juice, honey, remaining ½ teaspoon salt, and the cayenne (if using). Squeeze out the roasted garlic into the dressing. Stir well, breaking up the garlic. Set aside.

4. Wash and dry the kale thoroughly and slice it into thin strips. Place it in a large bowl and add the dressing a bit at a time, using your hands to massage the kale leaves gently until the volume is reduced and they look softened and shiny. You may have leftover dressing. Add the raisins, nuts, and squash pieces and toss.

5. Serve the salad at room temperature. Top with shaved Parmesan, if desired.

SWEET LOKSHEN KUGEL WITH PLUMS

Adapted from Jayne Cohen's *Jewish Holiday Cooking*

JEFFREY

My non-Jewish friends find this sweet noodle dish a bit confusing. When should it be eaten? Is it an entrée or a dessert? Don't worry too much about fitting this dish into a box. It's sweet, rich, and cinnamon-y in all the right ways.

While noodle kugel has a centuries-old provenance, the rich cheese-and-egg version is supremely North American. It's an almost absurd showcasing of abundance, as in the United States and Canada, cheese, milk, and eggs were available on the cheap. We knew from the start that we had to include noodle kugel in this book, since it's one of those recipes that defines both of our American Jewish childhoods, especially Sunday brunches and Yom Kippur fast breaking. The plums on top add a tartness and sweetness that complement the creamy kugel and give this classic casserole an elegant flourish. If planning to serve this for a party or a brunch, prep the dish up to a day in advance and refrigerate, then bake it right before your guests arrive.

SERVES 12 AS
AN APPETIZER

---

8 ounces egg noodles

½ cup (1 stick) unsalted butter, at room temperature, plus more for greasing the pan

1 cup small-curd cottage cheese

8 ounces cream cheese, store-bought or homemade (page 25), cut into pieces, at room temperature

2 cups whole milk

¼ cup sour cream, store-bought or homemade (page 24)

3 large eggs

½ cup pure maple syrup or granulated sugar

2 teaspoons pure vanilla extract

About 1½ pounds plums, pitted and sliced

1 teaspoon ground cinnamon

6 tablespoons light brown sugar

---

1. Bring a large pot of salted water to a boil. Cook the noodles just until tender, about 5 minutes. Drain and transfer to a bowl. Add the butter and stir gently to coat the noodles. Set aside.

2. In a large bowl with high sides, whisk together the cottage cheese and cream cheese until fluffy. (Alternatively, use a hand mixer.) One at a time, add the milk, sour cream, eggs, maple syrup or sugar, and vanilla, whisking to incorporate after adding each ingredient.

3. Add the cottage cheese mixture to the bowl with the egg noodles and gently

(continued) ▶

▶ (Sweet Lokshen Kugel with Plums, *continued*)

combine. Pour the mixture into a greased 9 x 13-inch baking pan. Cover the pan and refrigerate for at least 1 hour and up to overnight.

4. Preheat the oven to 350°F. Bake the kugel, uncovered, for 45 minutes, then top decoratively with the plums and sprinkle with the cinnamon and brown sugar. Bake for 30 minutes more, until the fruit has softened and released its juices. Remove from the oven and let sit for at least 30 minutes before slicing and serving. Eat the kugel warm or at room temperature.

LEWANDO'S LEEK FRITTATA

Inspired by *The Vilna Vegetarian Cookbook*

JEFFREY

I loved reading through the 400 or so recipes in *The Vilna Vegetarian Cookbook* by Fania Lewando, originally published in the 1930s but only recently translated from Yiddish to English. The recipes provide a window into the kitchen wisdom of a master Jewish cook of a different era. Many of the recipes are super simple and take for granted how familiar the reader will be with the methods and ingredients outlined. Fania's leek frittata recipe, for example, reads as follows: "Beat 3 eggs with some salt, pour over the leeks and cook like a frittata." This leek frittata recipe is inspired by hers, but with a few more details. It's a perfect main dish for a brunch spread and pairs well with bagels (page 106) and lox. If you want to make it without bread crumbs, no problem—the frittata will just have a looser texture.

SERVES 6 AS AN APPETIZER

---

2 tablespoons grapeseed or vegetable oil

4 medium leeks (about 2 pounds), white and light-green parts only, rinsed thoroughly to remove grit, thinly sliced

2 medium onions, thinly sliced

6 large eggs

3 tablespoons olive oil

¼ cup bread crumbs

4 scallions, thinly sliced

¼ cup chopped fresh dill, plus more for garnish

2½ teaspoons kosher salt

½ teaspoon freshly ground white pepper

Sour cream, store-bought or homemade (page 24), or plain yogurt, for garnish

---

1. Preheat the oven to 350°F.

2. In a large skillet, heat the oil over low heat. Add the leeks and onions and sauté slowly until they are sweet and golden in color, about 20 minutes. Remove from the heat and set aside to cool slightly.

3. In a large bowl, whisk the eggs, then stir in the olive oil, bread crumbs, scallions, dill, salt, and white pepper. Add the leeks

and onions to the egg mixture and stir to incorporate. Pour the mixture into a very well-greased 8-inch square nonstick baking pan or 8-inch round cast-iron skillet (you can also use muffin tins for making individual frittatas—just grease them well). Bake for 15 to 20 minutes, or until the frittata is puffy, set in the middle, and lightly browned on top. Serve warm or at room temperature with a dollop of sour cream and some dill.

SWEET VINEGAR–BRINE PICKLED TROUT

JEFFREY

My grandfather was a herring-in-cream-sauce kind of guy, but I prefer my fish pickled in vinegar. It makes a great picnic dish or a brunch (or dinner) appetizer to serve with our warm buttered Jewish Rye (pages 100 and *150*). Bring some of this sweet pickled trout to your next after-services Kiddush luncheon and you'll be a rock star. Herring fillets work for this recipe, too, and if you are working with herring fillets that have already been salted, start the recipe with step 2. Note that this recipe has extended wait times.

SERVES 10 AS
AN APPETIZER

1 cup kosher salt

1 pound trout fillets, skin removed, flesh cut into 2-inch pieces, or 1 pound salted herring fillets

1 quart white vinegar

½ cup water

1 cup sugar

2 teaspoons whole allspice berries

2 teaspoons yellow mustard seeds

½ teaspoon whole black peppercorns

4 garlic cloves, crushed

3 dried bay leaves

1 carrot, thinly sliced

1 large red onion, thinly sliced

3 sprigs fresh dill

1. Pour 1 quart of water into a jar. Add the salt and stir until as much salt as possible has dissolved. Add the trout to the jar, cover, and soak for 24 hours in the refrigerator. Drain the fish, but don't rinse it, and return it to the jar. (If using salted herring, skip this step.)

2. Add the vinegar to the fish and soak for 24 hours in the refrigerator. Drain, reserving 1 cup of the vinegar, and rinse the fish under cold running water. Clean the jar thoroughly and set aside.

3. In a small saucepan, combine the reserved 1 cup vinegar, the water, and sugar. Bring to a boil, stirring to dissolve the sugar, then remove from the heat and let cool to room temperature.

4. Add about one-third of the fish to the jar, then top with about one-third of the spices and vegetables. Repeat twice more with the remainder of the fish, spices, and vegetables so that the ingredients are layered and evenly dispersed. Pour the cooled vinegar mixture into the jar. Cover tightly and refrigerate for at least 1 week to allow the flavors to develop.

5. Serve the fish and vegetables directly out of the jar or display decoratively on a platter. The fish will keep in the refrigerator for about 2 months.

SPICED HERRING IN OIL

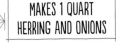

LIZ →

Traditionally, the best-quality and fattiest herrings were cured in oil and flavored with warming spices such as cloves, juniper berries, allspice, and cinnamon—spices that complement rather than mask the fish's natural flavors. Poorer-quality herrings, by contrast, are often doused in harsh vinegars and cream sauces to cover up their fishiness.

You may find herring packed in oil referred to as schmaltz herring. The word *schmaltz* in this context doesn't refer to rendered chicken fat (page 35), but to the fat content of the fish itself, which should be at least 18 percent to qualify as "schmaltz." While it can be pretty tough to find fresh, whole herring in the States, we've found very good-quality herring fillets at Jewish and Russian markets. This recipe features herring that has already been packed in oil or salty brine. I learned to eat this on a thick slice of bread (page *150*) with a shot of vodka, and now I don't want it any other way.

MAKES 1 QUART
HERRING AND ONIONS

16 ounces herring fillets, packed in oil or salt brine (a 16-ounce package will generally contain about 6 ounces oil and 10 ounces fillets)

About 2 cups flaxseed, grapeseed, or vegetable oil, or as needed

1½ teaspoons juniper berries

1½ teaspoons whole allspice berries

1½ teaspoons coriander seeds

½ teaspoon whole cloves

¼ cup fresh lemon juice

2 teaspoons kosher salt

1 large onion, halved and thinly sliced into half-moons

1. If you are working with herring in oil, drain the herring, reserving the oil, set aside the fish fillets, and proceed with step 2. If you are working with salt-brined herring, simply drain the fish and soak the fillets in water in the refrigerator for 4 to 6 hours, drain again, then proceed with step 2.

2. Pour the oil (including the reserved oil from draining the fish, about 6 ounces) into a small saucepan and heat it over medium heat. Toss in the juniper berries, allspice, coriander, and cloves, allowing them to infuse in the hot oil for no more than 1 minute. Pour the oil and spices into a quart-size jar and let cool. Stir in the lemon juice and salt.

3. Add half the fish and a layer of onions to the jar. Repeat with another layer of fish and onions. Seal the jar and refrigerate for 1 week before eating. Herring will keep in the refrigerator for about 2 months.

HERBED GEFILTE FISH

JEFFREY

At its most basic, gefilte is a cold fish appetizer served before Ashkenazi holiday and Sabbath meals, and is made by mixing freshwater fish with eggs, onions, and spices. One of the things that drew us to gefilte fish was that it stood as a symbol of resourcefulness—how far a single fish could be stretched to feed an entire family. It had a practical aspect, too. On the Sabbath, Jews are prohibited from separating bones from flesh, so by finely grinding the fish, the proscription was circumvented.

We love thinking of ways to restore gefilte to its rightful place on the table, especially for the Passover seder, when gefilte is often front and center. This recipe has a classic base, but we've added herbs to give it a taste of spring and a touch of color. There is also no matzo meal or bread crumbs in this recipe, giving it a lighter texture and removing any gluten. You have two options for how to cook and serve your gefilte fish. Poaching quenelles in a fish broth is a classic method used by generations of Jewish cooks, and baking the fish in a terrine is a quick and contemporary approach that will slice and plate beautifully. Liz and I both prefer the baked terrine, but enough friends and family members request the poached option that we couldn't ignore the pull of tradition.

The first stage of the process for this gefilte fish is nearly identical to the Smoked Whitefish Gefilte Terrine (page 172) and the Old World Stuffed Gefilte Fish (page 169) (until it gets stuffed into the skin).

Note   The whitefish we use here refers to the species *Coregonus clupeaformis* from the Great Lakes. If you can't find whitefish, substitute any one of the following: hake, sole, flounder, whiting, tilapia, or halibut.

(continued) ▶

Baked Terrine

⟩⟩ MAKES 1 SMALL TERRINE; SERVES 8 TO 10 ⟨⟨

1 small onion,
coarsely chopped

12 ounces whitefish
fillet, skin removed,
flesh coarsely
chopped

1¼ tablespoons
vegetable or
grapeseed oil

1 large egg

2 tablespoons
coarsely chopped
fresh watercress
(or spinach)

2 tablespoons
coarsely chopped
fresh dill

1 teaspoon
kosher salt

⅛ teaspoon freshly
ground white pepper

1 tablespoon sugar

Horseradish relish,
store-bought or
homemade (page 174
or 176), for serving

1. If there are any bones left in your fillets, remove the larger ones by hand, but don't fret about the smaller ones since they'll be pulverized in the food processor. You can buy your fish preground from a fishmonger (usually a Jewish fishmonger) to ensure all the bones are removed, but try to cook your fish that day since ground fish loses its freshness faster.

2. Place the onion in the bowl of a large food processor and process until finely ground and mostly liquefied. Add the fish fillets to the food processor along with the rest of the ingredients, except for the horseradish. Pulse in the food processor until the mixture is light-colored and evenly textured throughout. Scoop into a bowl and give it an additional stir to ensure that all the ingredients are evenly distributed throughout.

3. Preheat the oven to 350°F. Line an 8 x 3-inch loaf pan with parchment paper and fill the pan with the fish mixture. Smooth out with a spatula.

4. Place the loaf pan on a baking sheet on the middle rack of the oven and bake for 40 to 45 minutes. The terrine is finished when the corners and ends begin to brown. The loaf will give off some liquid. Cool to room temperature before removing from the pan and slicing. Serve with horseradish relish.

Poached Gefilte Quenelles

⇥| MAKES 10 2-OUNCE QUENELLES |⇤

Heads, bones, and tails from a fish (see Note)

4 quarts water

1 tablespoon kosher salt

2 onions, coarsely chopped

4 medium carrots

3 tablespoons sugar

Gefilte terrine mixture from Baked Terrine recipe (see steps 1 and 2)

Horseradish relish, store-bought or homemade (page 174 or 176), for serving

1. Place the fish parts, salt, onions, carrots, sugar, and water in a large stockpot and bring to a boil. Reduce the heat to maintain a simmer, cover, and simmer for at least 45 minutes before poaching the quenelles. Skim off any foam that rises to the surface.

2. Wet your hands and form the gefilte fish mixture into about 10 quenelles the size of an egg, with a similarly oblong shape. They will expand as they cook.

3. Place them one by one into the poaching liquid. When all the servings are in the pot, make sure the heat is on low and cover the pot. Poach for 30 minutes. Remove the quenelles with a slotted spoon and place them in a bowl or deep serving dish. Spoon enough poaching liquid over to cover the quenelles and let cool slightly before refrigerating. The poaching liquid will gel slightly as it chills.

4. To serve, remove the carrots and cut them into ¾-inch-thick rounds. Serve the quenelles chilled, with the carrot pieces and fresh horseradish relish. If you're old-school or adventurous, serve with spoonfuls of the poaching gel alongside.

Note If poaching, a fishmonger can save the head, bones, and tail for you if he/she sells you the fillet—just ask. The poaching liquid can be made without these fish parts, but the gefilte quenelles will be slightly less flavorful.

OLD WORLD STUFFED GEFILTE FISH

LIZ →

Gefilte is actually Yiddish for "stuffed." Back in Old World Europe, the fish mixture would have been stuffed back into the fish skins, then baked. Over time, the stuffing process has fallen out of fashion, which is too bad. Stuffed gefilte fish is delicious and dramatic, and hearkens back to a time when gefilte received the place of honor that it deserves on the table. Ask your local fishmonger to save the fish skins and heads for you. It's always best to call in the morning and ask them to set the scaled skins aside, as fish skins get discarded later in the day. If you are working with a fishmonger who isn't familiar with gefilte fish, simply ask him or her to scale and fillet two whole fish for you and to save the skins and heads. Pike skin has a particularly beautiful yellow hue, but most fish skins will do. The length of skins will vary depending on the species, but an 8-inch length is preferable.

Note The whitefish we use here refers to the species *Coregonus clupeaformis* from the Great Lakes. If you can't find whitefish, substitute any one of the following: hake, sole, flounder, whiting, tilapia, or halibut.

MAKES 2 STUFFED FISH

---

2 medium onions, coarsely chopped, plus 4 medium onions, sliced into thick rounds

1 pound whitefish fillet, skin removed, flesh coarsely chopped

2 tablespoons vegetable or grapeseed oil

1 large egg

1½ teaspoons kosher salt

¼ teaspoon freshly ground white pepper

2 tablespoons sugar

3 tablespoons matzo meal

2 sets of fish skins and heads

Horseradish relish (page 174 or 176), for serving

---

1. If there are any bones left in your fillets, remove the larger ones by hand, but don't fret about the smaller ones since they'll be pulverized in the food processor. In a food processor, pulse the 2 coarsely chopped onions until completely ground and mostly liquefied.

2. Add the whitefish fillets, oil, egg, salt, white pepper, sugar, and matzo meal and continue to pulse until the mixture is light colored and evenly textured throughout, scraping down the bowl with a rubber spatula or spoon between pulses to make sure the ingredients are

(continued) ▶

evenly distributed. Scoop the mixture into a bowl and give it an additional stir.

3. Preheat the oven to 350°F. In a long, oven-safe dish (a 9 x 13-inch baking pan will fit both sets of skin), make a bed of onion slices. Then take 3 pieces of twine, about 1 foot long each, and lay them on top of the onions crosswise, evenly spaced, followed by a long piece of parchment paper. Place one fish skin on the parchment paper, outside facing down, and scoop 1½ to 2 cups of the fish mixture onto the skin. (Quantities vary slightly with the size of the skin, but no need to overstuff.) Place the other piece of skin, outside facing up, on top of the fish and place a fish head where the skin would have met the head to replicate the look of a whole fish. Wrap the stuffed fish in the parchment paper, tying it with the twine tightly enough to create a bundle. Repeat the process with the second set of skins.

4. Pour about ¼ inch of water into the bottom of the pan. Cover the pan with aluminum foil. Bake for 40 to 45 minutes, until the fish is firm and cooked through to the middle; pressing on it should feel like touching the fleshy base of your thumb. Remove from the oven, let cool to room temperature, and refrigerate. If desired, after the gefilte fish has finished cooking, continue to roast the onions, uncovered, until they are browned. When the gefilte is completely chilled, remove from the parchment and serve atop a bed of roasted onions with plenty of horseradish relish.

SMOKED WHITEFISH GEFILTE TERRINE

Adapted from Jayne Cohen's *Jewish Holiday Cooking*

Smoked whitefish adds a rich flavor and delightful creaminess to the dish we love to reclaim. Though the technique is quite similar to the Herbed Gefilte Fish (page 162) and Old World Stuffed Gefilte Fish (page 167), this recipe is incredible on toasted rye bread and will make a believer out of even the most stubborn gefilte skeptics. We find that this gefilte fish is best served chilled with a simple Carrot-Citrus Horseradish Relish (page 176) or even a plain white horseradish relish.

MAKES 2 LOAVES OF GEFILTE (ABOUT 24 SLICES)

3½ tablespoons olive oil

1 medium onion, coarsely chopped

1 cup coarsely chopped scallions

2 large eggs

2 tablespoons fresh lemon juice

1½ pounds flounder or sole fillet, coarsely chopped

10 ounces smoked whitefish fillets, or

flesh cut from the whole fish (bones and skin removed)

1¾ teaspoons kosher salt

¼ teaspoon white pepper

3 tablespoons matzo meal (optional)

Horseradish relish, homemade (page 174 or 176), or store-bought, for serving

---

1. In a skillet, heat the olive oil over medium-low heat. Add the onion and sauté until soft, about 5 minutes. Add the scallions and cook, stirring, for 1 minute. Remove from the heat.

2. If there are any bones left in your whitefish, remove the larger ones by hand, but don't fret about the smaller ones since they'll be pulverized in the food processor. In a food processor, combine the eggs and lemon juice and process for a few seconds. Add the flounder, smoked whitefish, salt, white pepper, and matzo meal (if using). Process until the fish is well ground and pastelike. Add the onion and scallions and pulse to further grind, stirring between pulses. Once you've reached a consistent texture with no clumps, transfer the mixture to a bowl and give another stir to ensure that the ingredients are evenly distributed. Cover and refrigerate for about 1 hour, until cold.

3. Preheat the oven to 375°F. Grease two 8 x 3-inch loaf pans or line with parchment paper. Place the chilled mixture in the loaf pans, cover with aluminum foil, and bake for 25 minutes. Remove the foil and bake for 10 minutes more. Remove the gefilte from the oven and let cool completely before slicing and serving. Serve cold or at room temperature.

THE GEFILTE LINE

LIZ I can practically see the question coming from a mile away. As soon it comes up at a dinner party that I'm, among other things, a gefiltemonger, someone will inevitably ask, "So . . . do your make your gefilte sweet or peppery?" It's the question Jeffrey and I have wrestled with since day one of cooking together. He pushed me to decide which way I liked my gefilte, and I pushed him right back.

We'd both grown up with sweet gefilte but flip-flopped constantly over where we wanted our recipes to fall on the "Gefilte Line." It's kind of like the geographic wine-beer line that separates warm southern Europe (wine drinkers) from cool northern Europe (beer drinkers). In Galicia, modern-day southern Poland, where sugar beet factories were common, Polish Jews added sugar to everything, including gefilte. North of Galicia, Lithuanians, Latvians, and some Russians spiced gefilte fish with pepper. There was even a third camp, those who lived even farther south of Galicia, in Hungary, for example, and preferred not to spice gefilte with anything at all.

I can remember one particular incident when some guy cornered me at a party and wouldn't stop telling me how sugar is a corruption of the sacred dish. The way I see it, both sides of the line have merit. Gefilte fish can often be too sweet, or too peppery, but plain gefilte always feels like it's missing something.

Luckily, Jeffrey and I found a hedge. Our Herbed Gefilte Fish (page 162) and Old World Stuffed Gefilte Fish (page 167) feature both sweet and peppery flavors but not too much of either. The Smoked Whitefish Gefilte Terrine (page 172) is savory through and through. Whatever your affiliation, try them out and serve them to guests. If an argument over sweetness levels ensues, consider it a success.

Also, I discovered something that Litvaks, Hungarians, and Galicians can all agree on: horseradish relish, or *chrain* in Yiddish, is the only acceptable condiment to serve atop gefilte fish. There's even a Yiddish proverb that says, "Gefilte fish without *chrain* is punishment enough."

SWEET BEET HORSERADISH RELISH

JEFFREY

Horseradish grew wild outside of the cities in eastern Europe, and foragers would gather their own. The root thrives in cool soil, which is why its harvest schedule of early spring and fall lines up with prime gefilte fish holidays (Passover and Rosh Hashanah). There's a wider culinary wisdom to it, however, similar to the Japanese practice of eating wasabi with sushi. Wasabi and horseradish root both contain antimicrobial properties that kill off any bad bacteria.

When grating or processing horseradish, you should know that the fumes released when the skin is pierced are, well, intense, to say the least. The gas released by horseradish is actually the same used to make mustard gas. When we prepared horseradish during The Gefilteria's first holiday run, we resorted to tried-and-true protest tactics—wearing bandannas dipped in vinegar over our mouths and noses, and snorkel goggles to protect our eyes. There are countless stories and pictures of old *bubbes* wearing gas masks. It's eerie.

Generally speaking, making horseradish in small quantities doesn't need to be this dramatic. Just make sure to keep your windows open, and when first opening the food processor, definitely look away. If you don't have a food processor, don't be deterred. You can make this recipe by grating the horseradish and beets on the small or medium holes of a box grater and mixing it with the other ingredients in a large bowl. Also, feel free to play with the ratio of beets to horseradish for a milder or spicier final product. Godspeed.

MAKES ABOUT 1 QUART RELISH

12 ounces beets (about 4 small to medium beets), scrubbed well	½ pound coarsely chopped peeled horseradish root	¼ cup distilled white vinegar	3½ tablespoons fresh lemon juice
	¼ cup sugar	1 cup cold water	½ teaspoon kosher salt

1. Place the beets in a small saucepan and add water to cover. Bring to a boil over high heat. Boil for about 10 minutes, until the beets are fork-tender. Drain, then place in a bowl of ice and water. When cool enough to handle, peel and quarter the beets and transfer them to a food processor along with the horseradish pieces.

2. Meanwhile, in a small saucepan, combine the sugar, vinegar, and cold water and bring to a slow boil over medium-high heat. Cook, stirring

occasionally to dissolve the sugar, for 3 minutes, then remove from the heat.

3. Add the lemon juice and salt to the food processor. With the motor running, slowly pour in the vinegar-sugar mixture. You do not want the relish to be soupy, so add the liquid a bit at a time and stop at the point when the beets and horseradish are fully coated, shiny, and moist. You may need to stop and stir a few times to ensure that the horseradish

is fully ground. Run the processor until the horseradish and beets are evenly ground and as fine as your processor can get them.

4. Transfer the relish to an airtight container and refrigerate for at least 24 hours before serving with homemade (pages 162, 167, 172) or store-bought gefilte fish. Horseradish relish will keep in the refrigerator for about 3 months.

CARROT-CITRUS HORSERADISH RELISH

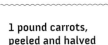

The carrot served on top of gefilte fish is sometimes called the yarmulke, but it always looks so limp and sad, and it really has no flavor. This recipe combines the carrot's color with the classic gefilte condiment, horseradish relish.

Each holiday, we've given out a version of this recipe, and many devoted fans have been making it every year. It's also delicious in a Pickle Brine Bloody Mary (page 305). Feel free to play with the ratio of carrots to horseradish for a milder or spicier final product.

If you don't have a food processor, don't be deterred. You can make this recipe by finely chopping the carrots, grating the horseradish on the small or medium holes of a box grater, and mixing it all together in a large bowl with the other ingredients.

**MAKES ABOUT
1 QUART RELISH**

---

1 pound carrots, peeled and halved

½ pound coarsely chopped peeled horseradish root

¼ cup sugar

¼ cup distilled white vinegar

1 cup cold water

1 tablespoon grated lemon zest

3¼ tablespoons fresh lemon juice

½ teaspoon kosher salt

---

1. Place the carrots in a saucepan and add water to cover. Bring to a boil over high heat. Boil for about 5 minutes, until the carrots are cooked through but not soft. Drain the carrots and place them in a food processor along with the horseradish pieces.

2. Meanwhile, in a small saucepan, combine the sugar, vinegar, and cold water and bring to a slow boil over medium-high heat. Cook, stirring occasionally to dissolve the sugar, for 3 minutes, then remove from the heat.

3. Add the lemon zest, lemon juice, and salt to the food processor. With the motor running, slowly pour in the vinegar-sugar mixture. You do not want the relish to be soupy, so add the liquid a bit at a time and stop at the point when the carrots and horseradish are fully coated, shiny, and moist. You may need to stop and stir a few times to ensure that the horseradish is fully ground. Run the processor until the horseradish and carrots are evenly ground and as fine as your processor can get them.

4. Transfer the relish to an airtight container and refrigerate for at least 24 hours before serving with homemade (pages 162, 167, 172) or store-bought gefilte fish. Horseradish relish will keep in the refrigerator for about 3 months.

~~~ SIX ~~~

DELI SIDES AND SPECIALTIES

| JEFFREY | My religious education may have been outsourced to our synagogue, but my father took it upon himself to impart upon me a spiritual relationship to pastrami, potato knishes, and kasha *varnishkes*. Being a kid from Brooklyn, he wanted to make sure that I loved the deli as much as he did.

His mother, my grandma Lily, suffered from colitis, so in the fifties and sixties, she attempted to treat her illness with a healthy vegetarian diet. At first she cooked meat just for my father and grandfather, but that only lasted so long. In short time, my father was living in a schmaltz-less home. Chicken soup was replaced by vegetable broth, stuffed cabbage by vegetable kugel, and so on and so forth.

When he was about ten, my father hit a breaking point. The story goes that while he and his extended family were vacationing for two weeks at a Jewish vegetarian hotel in the Catskills, he was forced to eat the same foods every day: vegetarian chopped liver, blueberries and sour cream, radishes and vegetables from the garden, and freshly baked bread (all of which sound pretty good to me). But my father was a kid who didn't want vegetables, and being away from Brooklyn only intensified his cravings for salty, garlicky, and fatty meats. He cried and threw tantrums at the resort, begging for chicken or cold cuts. Relatives were shocked by his behavior and put pressure on my grandmother, pleading with her to "let the boy have some deli."

One afternoon, my grandfather couldn't take it any longer, so he and my father snuck away to Monticello, to the once-famous Kaplan's Deli. My father joyously devoured two kosher hot dogs with Gulden's mustard and sauerkraut. Grandpa Julius apparently didn't touch the meats, afraid that my father would tattle on him, but he did treat himself to a knish. "Of course she knew," my father says when asked if Grandma Lily was aware of their clandestine deli outing. "Believe me, she could smell the deli all over us."

The Jewish deli was simultaneously my father's rebellion from his mother's vegetarian clutches and the fulcrum of his New York Jewish identity. To this day, when I join my father at a classic deli, he behaves like an overenthusiastic child at Disney World, unable to decide whether he should begin at Space Mountain or Epcot. Once, at the Mill Basin Kosher Deli in Brooklyn, he was literally shaking while he held the menu, filled with the wonderment of possibility. He instilled in me a love of deli so strong, so powerful, that I feel guilt when I pass by Katz's or 2nd Ave Deli without stopping.

Despite what some tourists might think, the deli is by no means the be-all and end-all of Ashkenazi Jewish food. In fact, in many ways it's an aberration—a peculiar American development. Most Jewish immigrants from central and eastern Europe knew nothing of pastrami unless they were from Romania, and even then, Romanian Jews just knew that pastrami was cured goose meat served cold, certainly not on rye bread.

The first delis opened in the mid-nineteenth century by non-Jewish German immigrants. Eventually, German Jews began opening their own establishments in New York and adapting the *treyf* dishes of their neighbors' delis to kosher standards. By the late nineteenth century, eastern European Jewish immigrants began frequenting the delis, and then they started opening their own. It's been said that the deli, an institution created by American Jewish immigrants, essentially played a role in the assimilation of future Jewish immigrants.

The deli menu evolved significantly as Jews from Romania, Hungary, Russia, Latvia, and Poland all imbued their own establishments with dishes from their homelands. While Italian American immigrants could visit "back home" to remind themselves of the traditional Italian cuisine, Jews from central and eastern Europe had no such option after the Second World War. As David Sax lays out brilliantly in *Save the Deli*, Jewish deli owners were cooking from memories of a world that no longer existed, and were basing their recipes on a culture that had been transplanted from the Old World to the New. The deli became a mishmash of different cultural forces blended into one. It was particular in its evolution and took on some of the most comical American characteristics, like its gargantuan portions and its reverence of celebrities (many New York delis decorate with signed celebrity photos).

Still, despite some of the schmaltziness, a classic deli meal—pastrami sandwiches, pickles, matzo ball soup, coleslaw, and kasha *varnishkes*—would without a doubt be my last meal if I were ever forced to choose. My father may have rebelled against his mother with deli, but for me, deli is the best way I know of to connect with my father.

~~~

LIZ

The smell of smoked meat emanating from Schwartz's deli on Boulevard Saint-Laurent in Montreal stretched for at least two blocks in both directions. There was a continuous line out the door, even during the frigid winter. I salivated whenever I passed through that stretch of spice mixed with the cool Quebecois air. The tricky part was that for most of my years living in Montreal, I was vegetarian. It was a complicated time when I was negotiating my adult relationship to food. Schwartz's was a Jewish deli through and through, but it had little to offer me as a Jewish non-meat eater. Each time I walked by, despite being drawn to the smell, I felt too conflicted to even walk in.

After I'd been living in Montreal for about three years, Schwartz's was calling. It seemed to taunt me each time I walked by. It reminded me of my weekly childhood outings to the deli with my dad, but there was also something that went beyond nostalgia. Schwartz's smelled like the most Jewish place I could imagine.

One random spring day, I woke up with a thought I couldn't get out of my mind: if there was ever anything worth breaking my vegetarianism for, it was a smoked meat sandwich from Schwartz's. I walked to Boulevard Saint-Laurent from my apartment with singular focus. There was no turning back. I could feel it. When I arrived, I took a seat at the counter and asked for the fattiest smoked meat sandwich. If I was going to do it, I was going to do it right. The smell of the restaurant alone nearly sated me. That first bite, though. Wow. The smokiness and the spiciness of the rub hit the back of my throat and warmed my whole body. I chewed slowly, intently, with my eyes closed, concentrating on the spices and the layers of flavor. I took my time with it. And while I went back to vegetarianism the next day, at least for one more year, I never regretted that digression.

The key to good deli is also the right bread (rye) and the precise condiments (spicy mustard). Slaw and pickles should be placed on a patron's table immediately in a proper deli establishment. There should be absolutely no white bread or mayonnaise served, unless the mayo is in the coleslaw. And kasha *varnishkes* must be slathered in schmaltz, not oil.

With the recipes in this chapter, you can replicate your own deli experience however you like. If you start with your own rendered schmaltz (page 35), the possibilities are endless. And there are some vegetarian recipes, since, well, there's still quite a bit of my older self in me, and I'd want her to eat at my deli.

DELI SIDES AND SPECIALTIES
≡ RECIPES ≡

MUSTARD SLAW

LIZ

Over the years, I started to get turned off by the typical mayo-drenched slaw found at most delis. As my palate matured, I learned to prefer the crunchiness and earthiness of fresh cabbage. I no longer wanted the scoopable version.

That's why Jeffrey and I worked on this fresh mustard slaw. It's quick to prepare, goes perfectly with a deli spread, and the flavor deepens as it sits, so make sure to prepare it at least an hour or up to half a day in advance to really bring out the flavor by the time you serve it. Be sure to shred your cabbage as thinly as possible—it makes a big difference. Red and green cabbage both work fine, though the red is more striking in color. Note that after sitting for a couple of days, the mustard seeds turn a bit spicy.

SERVES 6 TO 8

---

1 small head red or green cabbage (2 to 3 pounds), cleaned and cored

1 small red onion, thinly sliced

1 tablespoon yellow mustard seeds

1 tablespoon caraway seeds

2 teaspoons kosher salt

3 tablespoons distilled white vinegar

3 tablespoons apple cider vinegar

¼ cup fresh lemon juice

1 tablespoon grapeseed or canola oil

2 to 3 tablespoons honey

¼ cup chopped fresh dill

---

1. Finely shred the cabbage with a knife or mandoline on the thinnest setting and place in a large bowl with the red onion.

2. In a small jar, combine the mustard seeds, caraway seeds, salt, vinegars, lemon juice, oil, and honey. Let sit for 5 minutes, until the mustard seeds plump up.

3. Stir the dressing well (or cover and shake) until the honey has dissolved, then pour it over the cabbage and onion and mix well with a wooden spoon or your hands. Sprinkle the dill into the mixture and stir. Let sit at room temperature for at least 1 hour in its juices before serving so the flavors have time to meld. The longer it sits, the better. It will keep in the refrigerator for up to 1 week. The flavors intensify over time.

CHOLENT DEVILED EGGS

Usually, home cooks toss a few eggs into the cholent (slow-cooked Sabbath stew, page 239 or page 242) so they can enjoy hard-boiled eggs with a deep, almost roasted flavor. We take this brown-colored stew egg (similar to a Chinese tea egg) and add a deviled twist, with the help of mustard, dill, chives, and parsley. We like to serve these alongside deviled eggs filled with Chopped Liver Pâté (page 189). You could make this recipe using regular hard-boiled eggs, but they taste so much better when they've been slow cooked for at least eight hours. Cook them overnight (around twelve hours) for an even darker color and more intense flavor. You can cook the eggs in cholent or simply fill a slow cooker with water. Generally, it's easiest to peel the eggs after they've been thoroughly chilled because the structure of the egg becomes firmer and tighter as it cools, making it easier to separate the shell from the white. If making the slow-cooked eggs, be sure to plan ahead and leave enough time for them to cook. And be careful! Whenever you're using a slow cooker, be sure to monitor it and keep it away from anything flammable.

MAKES 12 DEVILED EGG HALVES

---

6 large eggs

2 tablespoons mayonnaise

2 to 3 teaspoons spicy Dijon mustard, store-bought or homemade (page 32)

1 teaspoon minced fresh parsley leaves, plus more for garnish

1 to 2 tablespoons chopped fresh dill

⅛ teaspoon kosher salt

Dash of freshly ground black pepper

Minced fresh chives, for garnish

---

1. Place the eggs in your cholent before it cooks, or place them in a slow cooker full of water and cook on Low for at least 8 hours or up to overnight. (If you don't have a slow cooker, place the eggs in a Dutch oven or oven-safe dish filled with water. Cover and place in the oven at 225°F for same amount of time.) Note that when cooked in a slow cooker, the smell of the eggs will be quite noticeable.

2. Drain the eggs and run them under cold water until they're cool enough to handle. Transfer them to the refrigerator or an ice-water bath until completely chilled.

3. Crack and peel each egg. Using a sharp knife, slice the eggs in half lengthwise. Scoop out the yolks and place them in a

(continued) ▶

Cholent Deviled Eggs and deviled eggs filled with **Chopped Liver Paté** (page 189)

▶ (Cholent Deviled Eggs, *continued*)

bowl; place the empty egg white halves on a serving tray.

4. In a food processor, combine the yolks, mayonnaise, 2 teaspoons of the mustard, the parsley, dill, salt, and pepper and process until very smooth. If you don't have a food processor, use a fork to mash and stir the ingredients until smooth. Adjust the mustard, salt, and pepper to taste.

5. Scoop 1 tablespoon of the egg yolk filling into each egg white half. If you'd like a more decorative-looking deviled egg, use a piping bag with a star tip to fill each half, swirling the mixture into the egg white like you are filling an ice cream cone with soft serve. If you do not have a piping bag and tip, you can still try piping. Simply take a zip-top bag, fill it with the egg yolk mixture (but leave room at the top), and cut off a tiny corner of the bag.

6. Garnish each egg with a sprinkling of minced chives and parsley.

CHOPPED LIVER PÂTÉ

JEFFREY

Chopped liver is one of those foods that I've always felt to be a litmus test of maturity. I didn't really like it as a child when it was served before holiday meals, and I was always shocked that my father would order it at the deli when there were pastrami and corned beef sandwiches to be enjoyed instead. Only when I hit my twenties, and my good friends launched Grow and Behold, a pasture-raised kosher meat company, did I try it in earnest. I learned to appreciate liver's rich flavor and velvety texture eating it at my friends' home for Shabbat dinner.

This chopped liver recipe can be served on its own like a liver pâté with crackers, or it can be piped into egg halves to make a classy deviled egg hors d'oeuvre. Hard-boiled egg yolks add richness to chopped liver, and we like to fill the resulting egg whites with liver pâté. The recipe makes enough for a dozen deviled egg halves as well as an extra serving bowl of liver pâté to spread on crackers. Garnish with chopped fresh parsley, salt, and *gribenes* for added flavor and effect. If you prefer your liver coarsely chopped and wish to forgo the food processor in this recipe, that works, too. Note that we've included instructions for kashering the livers, which is necessary if following Jewish dietary laws. If not kashering, you can begin this recipe with step 2.

*MAKES 2 CUPS PÂTÉ,
OR ENOUGH FOR
12 DEVILED EGG HALVES
PLUS 1 CUP PÂTÉ FOR
SERVING WITH CRACKERS*

½ pound raw chicken or turkey livers

1½ teaspoons kosher salt, or to taste, plus more for kashering livers

7 hard-boiled eggs, peeled

4 tablespoons schmaltz (page 35) or vegetable oil (but preferably schmaltz)

2 large onions, thinly sliced

3 tablespoons honey

Gribenes (page 35), for garnish

Chopped fresh parsley, for garnish

Crackers, for serving

1. If desired, kasher the livers: Preheat the broiler to high. Wash and clean the livers, removing the veins if there are any. Slice an X on one side of each liver, lay them out on a rimmed baking sheet, X-side down, and sprinkle with salt. Broil for 3 minutes, then flip the livers and broil for 3 minutes more. Remove from the oven and drain any blood that has gathered on the baking sheet. Rinse the livers and pat dry.

2. Place 1 hard-boiled egg in a food processor. Halve the remaining 6 eggs lengthwise and add 4 of the yolks to the

(continued) ▶

▶ (Chopped Liver Pâté, *continued*)

processor. Discard the remaining yolks or reserve them for another use; set aside the halved egg whites. Pulse the egg and egg yolks in the food processor until completely chopped.

3. In a large pan, heat 2 tablespoons of the schmaltz over medium heat. Add the onions and ½ teaspoon of the salt and sauté until golden, about 10 minutes. Add the whole livers and sauté until the livers are just cooked through and no longer pink inside, 3 to 5 minutes.

4. Transfer the livers and onion plus any schmaltz left in the pan to the food processor with the eggs. Add the remaining 1 teaspoon salt and pulse the mixture, slowly adding the remaining 2 tablespoons schmaltz and the honey until a smooth, velvety pâté is formed. The texture may be loose, but will firm up when cooled. Wait for the mixture to cool to room temperature (or refrigerate in an airtight container for later) before serving.

5. If desired, fill each of the egg halves (using a piping bag, a zip-top bag with one corner snipped, or simply a spoon). Garnish with gribenes, parsley, and a pinch of salt. Any extra pâté can be served on its own with crackers or Jewish Rye (page 100). Place it in a bowl and garnish with parsley and more gribenes. It will taste even better the next day, so feel free to make it a day ahead.

PEASANT POTATO SALAD

LIZ

I've never been one for mayo, so I usually steer clear of potato salad when it's part of the spread at a bar mitzvah or a Kiddush luncheon. I picture it sitting between the tuna and egg salad (which I also avoid), looking like it will soon be served with an ice cream scoop. Then I tried German-style potato salad, which is made without mayo, and something clicked. It had all the flavors I like—pickle brine, dill, and salt. This simple potato salad captures those flavors, and—bonus!—can be whipped up from ingredients you are likely to have around the house.

The sweet gherkins are what really set it apart. Store-bought sour pickles or Classic Sour Dills, page 50, are a fine substitute, but will make for a brinier salad. If you're prepping for an event, keep in mind that this potato salad tastes even better the next day.

SERVES 6 TO 8

---

2 pounds red potatoes, unpeeled and halved

2 tablespoons olive oil or grapeseed oil

1 tablespoon dill pickle brine, store-bought or homemade (page 50)

2 tablespoons apple cider vinegar

1 tablespoon honey

2 tablespoons mustard, store-bought Dijon or homemade (page 32)

½ small red onion, finely diced

½ cup sweet gherkins, chopped into bite-size pieces

3 tablespoons minced fresh dill, plus more as needed

¾ teaspoon kosher salt, plus more as needed

½ teaspoon freshly ground black pepper, plus more as needed

---

1. Bring a large pot of well-salted water to a boil (use about 1 tablespoon salt to every 1 quart water). Drop the potatoes into the pot and boil until cooked through but not mushy or soft, 18 to 20 minutes. Drain well, rinse with cold water, and dice into bite-size pieces. Transfer the potatoes to a large bowl.

2. In a small bowl, combine the oil, dill pickle brine, vinegar, honey, and mustard. Stir to incorporate. Pour the dressing over the potatoes and stir to coat them entirely. As you stir, gradually add the onion, gherkins, fresh dill, salt, and pepper.

3. Taste and adjust the salt, pepper, and dill as needed. Cover and refrigerate for at least 30 minutes before serving.

GRANDPA JOE'S FAMOUS CHICKEN SALAD

JEFFREY

When my grandpa Joe retired from Colonial Provisions, a meatpacker in Boston, he went to work part time at Michael's Deli in Marblehead, Massachusetts. My grandfather took on various tasks, but he was best known for his chicken salad, which he made from the cooked chicken from Michael's chicken soup.

There was nothing to the chicken salad, really, but my grandmother says the absolute secret was a healthy dash of white pepper. Customers lined up for it, or so the story is told in my family.

I never tasted my grandfather's chicken salad from the deli, but every Passover, he and my Grandma Ruth would stand together in the kitchen with a large metal bowl filled with the soup chicken from my mother's holiday soup, and together they'd pick the meat from the bones and place it in a separate bowl. They would speak in Yiddish if left alone, or they'd kibitz—chitchat—with the rest of us if we were around. It's one of my favorite memories of the two of them together. My grandfather passed away nearly a decade ago, but Grandma Ruth still makes the chicken salad each Passover for the whole family.

SERVES 4

½ pound leftover cooked soup chicken (see page 130), shredded (about 1½ cups, tightly packed)

2 tablespoons mayonnaise, plus more if needed

1 tablespoon schmaltz (page 35) or grapeseed oil

¼ cup minced red bell pepper (about ½ bell pepper)

¼ cup minced green bell pepper (about ½ bell pepper)

⅓ cup minced celery (about 1 stalk)

¼ to ½ teaspoon freshly ground white pepper, or to taste

¼ teaspoon celery seed

¼ to ½ teaspoon kosher salt, plus more as needed

1. Combine all the ingredients in a medium bowl. Stir with a large spoon to break down the chicken into smaller pieces and evenly distribute the vegetables and spices throughout. If it seems a bit dry, add an additional tablespoon of mayonnaise. Store in an airtight container in the refrigerator for 3 to 5 days and serve on Jewish Rye (page 100) or Make-at-Home Matzo (page 94) with lettuce.

ROASTED GARLIC POTATO KNISH

JEFFREY

Before the dawn of Tupperware, Jewish cooks would wrap leftovers in dough for an easy-to-carry package for a long day of work. Square, mass-manufactured fried knishes are now sold in most New York City hot dog carts. When I was thirteen, my father took me on a tour of Brooklyn centered on Coney Island amusements and Mrs. Stahl's, his favorite knishery, known for its iconic round knishes. I vaguely recall ordering both a kasha and a potato-broccoli knish while my father ordered his beloved cherry-cheese. I didn't know I had to savor those knishes, since they'd be the first and last I'd have from the iconic shop; it closed its doors for good back in 2005.

We use Mrs. Stahl's knish dough, a recipe developed by Toby Engelberg and Sara Spatz and adapted in Laura Silver's book on the topic, *Knish: In Search of the Jewish Soul Food*. A tip we learned from Mrs. Stahl's recipe is to bake the knishes in logs, rather than squares or rounds, and slice them—it's easier for serving to groups, as we often do. For a sweet dairy knish like my father prefers, take our sweet cheese blintz filling (page 224) and stir in ¼ cup cooked cherries and a little extra sugar. Note that the potato knish filling also tastes great stuffed inside savory blintzes (page 224).

MAKES ABOUT 15
SMALL KNISHES

FOR MRS. STAHL'S KNISH DOUGH:

1¾ cups all-purpose flour

1½ teaspoons sugar

1 teaspoon kosher salt

¼ cup vegetable or grapeseed oil, plus more as needed

½ cup lukewarm water

FOR THE MASHED POTATO FILLING:

1 head garlic

1 teaspoon extra-virgin olive oil

¼ cup schmaltz (page 35) or vegetable oil, plus more for the knishes

2 medium onions, diced

4 teaspoons kosher salt, plus more as needed

1½ pounds russet potatoes (about 4 medium), peeled and cut into 2-inch chunks

½ teaspoon freshly ground black pepper

TO ASSEMBLE:

¼ cup all-purpose flour, for dusting

Vegetable oil

1 egg, beaten

Mustard, for serving

---

1. TO MAKE THE DOUGH: In a medium bowl, stir together the flour, sugar, and salt. Pour in the oil and lukewarm water and knead lightly until a sticky dough is formed. Set aside, covered, for at least 1 hour while you prepare the filling.

(continued) ▶

▶ (Roasted Garlic Potato Knish, *continued*)

2. TO MAKE THE MASHED POTATO FILLING: Preheat the oven to 400ºF. Trim about ¼ inch off the head of garlic, exposing the cloves. Drizzle the olive oil on the garlic skins and rub it in. Wrap the head of garlic in aluminum foil and place on a baking sheet in the oven. Roast for 30 to 40 minutes, or until the individual cloves are completely soft.

3. In a medium saucepan, heat 2 tablespoons of the schmaltz or oil over medium heat. Add the onions and 2 teaspoons of the salt and sauté until golden, 5 to 7 minutes, then remove from the heat and set aside.

4. Bring a pot of salted water to a boil. Add the potatoes, reduce the heat to medium, and simmer until the potatoes are very tender and can be easily pierced with a fork, about 20 minutes. Drain the potatoes, then roughly mash with a fork or the bottom of a jar. Stir in the onions, remaining 2 tablespoons of schmaltz or oil, remaining 2 teaspoons of salt, and the pepper and squeeze the roasted garlic cloves from their skins into the potato mixture. Stir to incorporate and break up any large chunks of potato. Taste and adjust the salt levels to your preference.

5. TO ASSEMBLE THE KNISHES: Preheat the oven to 400ºF with a rack set in the center. Line a baking sheet with parchment paper.

6. Divide the dough into 3 balls and the filling into 3 equal portions of about ¾ cup each. Roll out the dough on a floured surface, one ball at a time, into a very thin square, about 10 inches on all sides. Place a 2-inch-wide line of filling along one end of the dough, leaving a border of about 1½ inches along the edge. Pick up the top edge and fold it over the filling. Brush schmaltz on the dough in a thin strip on the bottom edge of the filling. Pick up the filled dough and roll again, onto the oiled dough. Brush another line of schmaltz at the

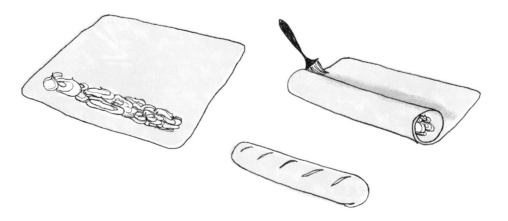

bottom edge of the filling and fold the filled dough over the oiled dough once again. Repeat the folding and brushing until you reach the end of the dough. Tuck the ends underneath the log.

7. Place the knishes on the prepared baking sheet, seam side down. Slash the top of the dough rolls with a knife every 3 inches or so. Coat the rolls with egg. Bake for 15 to 20 minutes. Keep an eye on the knishes while they bake to avoid overbrowning and drying out. The knishes are ready when they are soft and golden. Serve warm with mustard.

KASHA FILLING

ENOUGH FOR 15 SMALL KNISHES

¾ cup coarse or medium kasha

1½ cups hot chicken or vegetable broth (page 130 or 123) (or hot water)

2 tablespoons schmaltz (page 35) or vegetable oil, for sautéing

1 small onion, finely diced

1½ teaspoons kosher salt

2 large eggs, beaten

1. Pour the kasha into a small pan and toast the kernels over medium heat, stirring very frequently with a wooden spoon, until they are slightly aromatic, about 3 minutes. Reduce the heat to low and add the hot broth, then cover and simmer for 8 to 10 minutes, or until all the liquid has been absorbed. Set aside in a medium bowl.

2. In a medium saucepan, heat the schmaltz or oil over medium heat. Add the onion and sauté for 5 to 7 minutes, until translucent. Transfer the onion to the bowl with the kasha and stir in the salt and eggs, leaving a bit of egg aside for coating the dough later.

3. Fill and bake the knishes as directed in Roasted Garlic Potato Knish recipe.

CAULIFLOWER AND MUSHROOM KUGEL

JEFFREY

Kugel comes in many forms, not just noodles. Liz and I both love savory vegetable kugels, and this cauliflower-mushroom version is lighter and more refined than the ever-popular potato kugel. If you're lucky enough to live in a place where foraged mushrooms are accessible, get the best you can find. They will only enhance the dish. In Seattle, we made this dish with hedgehog and black trumpet mushrooms foraged from a nearby forest, and it was the best version of this kugel we've ever created.

Be aware that this kugel has a delicate consistency and serves more like an Italian *sformato* (vegetable soufflé) than the dense kugels you might be used to. Normally we like to make this dish in ramekins and serve it in individual portions, for an elegant look and feel. In Seattle, we found squat 8-ounce mason jars and baked individual kugels in those, but baking in a 9-inch square glass baking dish works well, too—just let the kugel cool slightly before slicing or scooping into individual portions. For Passover, you can swap out the bread crumbs for matzo meal. If you're making it a dairy kugel, you can use butter and sprinkle it with Parmesan cheese. Serve individual portions topped with crispy fried shallots and garnished with fresh parsley.

MAKES ABOUT 6
8-OUNCE SERVINGS

---

1 large head cauliflower (about 2 pounds), broken into florets

¼ cup vegetable oil or unsalted butter, plus more as needed

1 medium onion, diced

8 ounces fresh mushrooms, cleaned and chopped (porcinis, shiitakes and wild forest mushroom varieties are ideal, but any variety from the store is fine)

1¾ teaspoons kosher salt, plus more as needed

¼ teaspoon freshly ground black pepper

4 large eggs, plus 3 egg yolks

2 tablespoons bread crumbs, store-bought or homemade (page 38)

4 shallots, for topping (optional)

About ¼ cup grapeseed oil, for frying the shallots (optional)

Chopped fresh parsley, for garnish

---

1. Preheat the oven to 350°F. Bring a large pot of lightly salted water to a boil. Add the cauliflower and boil until the florets are tender but not mushy, 5 to 7 minutes. Drain the cauliflower thoroughly. Place it in a food processor.

(continued) ▶

▶ (Cauliflower and Mushroom Kugel, *continued*)

2. In a medium pan, heat the oil over medium heat. Add the onion and sauté until translucent and lightly golden, 7 to 10 minutes. Add the mushrooms, salt, and pepper and cook, undisturbed, for at least 1 minute to help the mushrooms darken. Cook, stirring occasionally, until the mushrooms are browned and their liquid has evaporated, 5 to 7 minutes more. Transfer the mushrooms and onion (and any extra oil from the pan) to the food processor with the cauliflower. Add the eggs and egg yolks and process until the mixture has a smooth consistency with minimal clumps. (If you do not have a food processor, mash the vegetables, eggs, and yolks together with a large fork or spoon until the mixture is as smooth as possible.) Transfer the mixture to a large bowl, stir in the bread crumbs, and mix well.

3. Grease six 8-ounce ramekins or a 9-inch glass baking dish. Fill with the cauliflower mixture. Each ramekin should hold a little under 1 cup of the filling. Tap the bottoms of the ramekins or baking dish against the counter so that the top of the kugel flattens out and you've released any air bubbles. If using individual ramekins, place them in a roasting pan with at least 3-inch-high sides. Pour boiling water into the pan to come about halfway up the sides of the ramekins (this will ensure that the kugel stays moist). Bake for 55 minutes to 1 hour. The kugel is done when a toothpick inserted into the center comes out clean and the kugel is lightly browned on top. Remove from the oven carefully, remove the ramekins from the water, and let cool slightly.

4. If using, while the kugel is baking, slice the shallots as thin as possible (if you have a mandoline, use it here on the thinnest setting). In a small nonstick pan, heat the grapeseed oil over medium heat. Immerse the shallots in the oil and fry them, stirring frequently, until they are crispy, crunchy, shrunken, and dark in color, 15 to 25 minutes. Keep an eye on them to make sure they don't burn. Transfer the shallots to a paper towel–lined plate to drain and sprinkle lightly with salt. Set aside until serving.

5. Garnish the kugel with the fried shallots (if using) and the chopped parsley. Store any leftover fried shallots in an airtight container.

CRISPY KASHA VARNISHKES WITH BRUSSELS SPROUTS

JEFFREY

To those who didn't grow up in a Jewish or eastern European home, kasha seems like an exotic grain, so in my early twenties, I turned to kasha when I needed to impress a friend or a date. Kasha *varnishkes*—essentially kasha with onions and noodles (usually farfalle, bow-tie pasta)—is kasha at its greatest. The addition here of brussels sprouts feels almost natural to us at this point, since the taste of the fried sprouts is so complementary to the grain.

The genius of this dish is that the kasha perfectly sops up the flavors of the caramelized onions, chicken broth, and schmaltz. Liz likes to make this dish a day in advance, then crisp it in the oven before serving. (See Note.) You can also serve it right out of the pan. If you don't have schmaltz or vegetable broth on hand, water and oil are good alternatives. Note that this version is a bit heavier on the kasha. Try it out, and if you prefer a more equal kasha-to-noodle ratio, simply decrease the amount of kasha to ½ cup and the hot broth to 1 cup.

SERVES 4 TO 6
AS AN APPETIZER

~~~~~~

1 cup uncooked
bow-tie pasta

3 tablespoons
schmaltz (page 35)
or olive oil

1 large onion, very
thinly sliced

½ pound brussels
sprouts, thinly sliced

1 teaspoon
kosher salt, plus
more as needed

1 tablespoon
light brown sugar
(optional)

¾ cup coarse or
medium kasha

1 large egg, beaten

1½ cups hot chicken
broth or vegetable
broth (page 130 or
123) or hot water

Chopped fresh
parsley, for garnish

1. Bring a medium pot of salted water to a boil and cook the pasta according to the package directions until al dente, usually 10 minutes. Drain the pasta and set aside in a large bowl.

2. In a nonstick medium pan, heat the schmaltz over medium heat. Add the onion and sauté, stirring occasionally, for about 10 minutes, until the onion is golden in color. Add the brussels sprouts, salt, and brown sugar (if using). Cook until the onion and brussels sprouts are brown and caramelized, 5 to 7 minutes. Remove and stir into the bowl with the pasta. Wipe the pan clean and set it over medium heat.

(continued) ▶

▶ (Crispy Kasha Varnishkes with Brussels Sprouts, *continued*)

3. In a small bowl, coat the kasha with the egg. Make sure that the kernels are well coated and have absorbed the egg. Pour the egg-coated kasha into the pan and toast the kasha kernels, stirring very frequently with a wooden spoon, until the individual groats no longer clump together, 3 to 4 minutes.

4. Reduce the heat to low and add the hot broth, then cover and simmer for 8 to 10 minutes, or until all the liquid has been absorbed.

5. Stir the kasha into the pasta mixture. Serve hot, with a heavy garnish of chopped parsley. Kasha *varnishkes* taste even better the next day, so make them in advance and reheat in the oven (see Note).

Note For extra crispness or reheating if made in advance, preheat the oven to 375°F. Transfer the kasha-pasta mixture (ungarnished), along with an additional ½ cup broth or water, to a rectangular oven-safe dish. Bake for 10 to 15 minutes until the tops of the pasta are visibly crisped.

ROOT VEGETABLE LATKES

 LIZ

Hanukkah is the time of year I feel the most Jewish. While the rest of New York is feverishly buying gifts and planning big family meals, I'm quietly grating potatoes by the light of the menorah. In contrast to so many other Jewish holidays, Hanukkah celebrations are relaxed and loose. It feels like all I need to do is fry up some latkes, and I'm in the perfect holiday spirit.

The latke as we know it took quite a culinary journey, beginning centuries ago in Italy as a cheese fritter fried in olive oil, then moving northeast, where it morphed into a buckwheat and rye pancake, and then a turnip fritter fried in schmaltz. Finally, in the mid-nineteenth century, the potato took over. This latke includes root vegetables alongside the classic potatoes, which lend extra color and flavor to the mix. Note that if you prefer a pure potato latke, simply substitute 6 small russet potatoes (about 3 pounds) for the veggies in this recipe. The root vegetable version is a bit lighter and more fragile than the purely potato version, so take care when forming into latkes for frying.

MAKES 18 TO 22 LATKES

---

4 russet potatoes (about 2 pounds), peeled

1 medium parsnip, peeled

1 medium turnip, peeled

1 small onion

4 scallions, finely chopped

3 large eggs, lightly beaten

1 tablespoon kosher salt

¼ teaspoon freshly ground black pepper

3 tablespoons all-purpose flour

⅓ cup bread crumbs or matzo meal

Schmaltz (page 35) or peanut, canola, or grapeseed oil, for frying

Apple-Pear Sauce (page 26), for serving (optional)

Sour cream, store-bought or homemade (page 24), for serving (optional)

---

1. Shred the potatoes, parsnip, turnip, and onion on the large holes of a box grater or in a food processor using the shredder plate. Place the grated vegetables in a large bowl and add cold water to cover. Let sit for about 5 minutes.

2. Drain the vegetables in a colander and squeeze out as much liquid as possible from the shreds into a bowl. It's helpful to take cheesecloth or a clean thin kitchen towel, drape in an empty bowl, then pour in the shredded vegetables. Wrap the cheesecloth or towel around the vegetables and squeeze tightly in the bowl. Repeat until as much liquid

(continued) ▶

▶ (Root Vegetable Latkes, *continued*)

as possible has been removed. White potato starch will collect at the bottom of the bowl. Carefully drain off the water, leaving the potato starch. Set aside.

3. Place the drained vegetable shreds in a large bowl. Add the scallions, eggs, salt, pepper, flour, bread crumbs, and the reserved potato starch. Mix well, preferably using your hands.

4. In a 9-inch nonstick or cast-iron skillet, heat a layer of schmaltz or oil, about ⅛ inch deep, over medium heat. Form the latke batter into thin patties, using about 2 tablespoons for each. As you form the patties, squeeze out and discard any excess liquid. Carefully slip the patties, about 4 at a time, into the

pan and fry for 2 to 3 minutes on each side, or until golden brown and crisp. Take care to flip them only once to avoid excess oil absorption. If the pan begins to smoke at all, add more schmaltz or oil and let it heat up again before frying another batch of latkes.

5. Remove the latkes from the pan and place on a baking sheet lined with paper towels to drain the excess fat. Latkes are best and crispiest when served right away. If serving later, transfer to a separate casserole dish or baking sheet and place in the oven at 200°F to keep warm until serving. Serve hot, topped with Apple-Pear Sauce and/ or sour cream.

HOME-CURED CORNED BEEF

Corned beef is a type of *pickelfleisch* (pickled meat), which was often eaten in Jewish homes, paired with potatoes and vegetables, since it was more economical than a fresh cut of meat.

Curing meat is a critical piece in the puzzle of Old World food preservation. The technique of wet curing, as this recipe outlines, transforms the flavor of the brisket while extending its shelf life significantly. We've made this easy for you, providing a step-by-step introduction to the process of curing beef at home. Note that the brining process is the same for corned beef and pastrami (page 210), so if you get a large enough cut of meat, you can split it up after the first half of recipe and try your hand at both. And while lots of folks will say that pastrami, with its smokiness and spicy rub, is the more exciting of the two, I say that the moist texture and pickled flavor of corned beef makes it just as thrilling. Note that this recipe requires some planning ahead and calls for 7 to 10 days of waiting time. If you're in a rush, however, you can purchase a prebrined brisket and skip to step 3. If you time it right, you can host your own artisanal deli night with Jewish Rye (page 100), knishes (page 192), Spicy Whole-Grain Mustard (page 32), and Classic Sour Dills (page 50).

MAKES 3 TO 4 POUNDS CORNED BEEF

---

3 to 4 pounds first-cut brisket

FOR CURING BRINE:

1 gallon cold water

5 ounces kosher salt

½ cup sugar

1½ teaspoons pink (curing) salt

2 tablespoons whole black peppercorns

1 tablespoon yellow mustard seeds

1 tablespoon juniper berries

3 tablespoons whole coriander seeds

5 dried bay leaves

3 garlic cloves, crushed

FOR COOKING LIQUID:

2 medium onions, halved

1 carrot

2 celery stalks

3 dried bay leaves

3 garlic cloves

2 tablespoons kosher salt

2 tablespoons whole black peppercorns

---

1. TO MAKE THE BRINE: In a ceramic, glass, or food-grade plastic vessel (see Resources, page 327), whisk together the water, kosher salt, sugar, and pink salt until the salts and sugar dissolve. Add the peppercorns, mustard seeds, juniper berries, coriander, bay leaves,

(continued) ▶

▶ (Home-Cured Corned Beef, *continued*)

and garlic and whisk. No need to heat the brine.

2. Rinse off the beef and place it in the brine. Cover and refrigerate for about 1 week for a typical 3-pound cut. For a larger 4-pound cut, brine for 8 to 10 days. Make sure the brisket stays in the brine, and turn over the brisket every day or two for even curing. Brining contributes both flavor and color. The brisket will turn gray on the outside, but that's natural. Note that if the brisket doesn't brine for long enough, you'll see brown spots on the meat where there should be red. No worries—it will still taste delicious.

3. Remove the meat from the brine and rinse it well under cold water. Pat dry with a clean kitchen towel or paper towels.

4. In a large pot or Dutch oven, combine the onions, carrot, celery, bay leaves, garlic, salt, and peppercorns. Place the rinsed brisket on top of the vegetables and add water to cover. If cooking in a pot, bring the liquid to a boil, then simmer over medium-low heat for about 3½ hours. If cooking in a Dutch oven, cook at 225°F in the oven for about 3½ hours. Using either method, the meat is ready when the brisket feels tender when pierced with a fork. Remove from

the pot and let rest for 45 minutes to 1 hour at room temperature so that it stays moist and tender.

5. To serve hot, place the rested meat in a steamer—either in a pot or a bamboo steamer, if you have one. Add 1 to 2 cups boiling water and steam for 5 to 7 minutes. For hot sandwiches, slice the beef against the grain, about ¼ inch thick, or thinner if that's your preference. You can also slice and serve the meat cold.

6. Eat on a sandwich with Jewish Rye (page 100) and apply Spicy Whole-Grain Mustard (page 32) liberally.

Note Two recipes in this book—corned beef and pastrami—call for curing meat. This refers to the process of placing your cuts of brisket in a highly concentrated brine of salt, nitrites, sugar, and spices. The nitrites help kill bad bacteria. Our recipes call for a wet brine. Dry curing is a great method, too, but note that our salt ratios and the quantity of pink (curing) salt (see the note on pink curing salt in Resources, page 327) apply to wet brining. It's important that you follow the recipe with the proportions and quantities as stated. As with most meat cures, if the meat you start out with is not good quality or fresh, your results will suffer.

HOME-CURED PASTRAMI

JEFFREY

While most Jews in Europe likely hadn't encountered pastrami, Romanian Jews applied a pepper-coriander dry rub on cured goose meat that they smoked and served cold. "When Romanian Jews settled on New York's Lower East Side," writes deli maven David Sax, "beef was more plentiful and replaced goose as the protein of choice, and pastrami started to be served hot, as a sandwich. . . ." I grew up eating those hot pastrami sandwiches as if they were part of my family's Jewish food tradition, and at this point, they are.

Brining and smoking pastrami is a long and involved process that can take upward of two weeks, but most of that time is just spent waiting. The brine infuses the meat with flavor, turns it that distinctive red color, helps the meat to retain moisture, and preserves it safely. The smoking process provides the meat with the necessary flavor to make it shine. Smoking pastrami while living in a small New York apartment with no backyard access can be challenging, so we provide a workaround (see page 214). Once your meat is smoked, you'll let it sit, then steam it, slice it, and eat it.

A few tips: You can buy a prebrined corned beef at the store and begin this recipe at step 3. If you want New York deli street cred, use beef navel for this recipe, but second-cut brisket (or deckle) is easier to source. Whatever cut of meat you use, tell your butcher what you're making and ask him or her to clean and trim it accordingly. The better quality and the fattier the cut, the moister and more flavorful the final product will be. The flip side is that a more tapered and leaner cut of brisket or navel will be easier to slice. Note that a meat thermometer is essential for this recipe and a digital thermometer is particularly helpful. Also, note that you lose about 1 pound of the original weight of the meat during the process.

> MAKES 2 TO
> 3 POUNDS PASTRAMI

---

3 to 4 pounds beef navel or second-cut brisket, cleaned and trimmed with fat cap in place

FOR THE BRINE:

1 gallon cold water

5 ounces kosher salt

½ cup sugar

1½ teaspoons pink (curing) salt

2 tablespoons whole black peppercorns

1 tablespoon yellow mustard seeds

1 tablespoon juniper berries

3 tablespoons whole coriander seeds

5 dried bay leaves

3 garlic cloves, crushed

FOR THE RUB:

¼ cup ground
coriander

¼ cup freshly ground
black pepper

4 teaspoons
smoked paprika

2 tablespoons plus
2 teaspoons light
brown sugar

2 teaspoons
mustard powder

1 tablespoon
onion powder

1 tablespoon
garlic powder

2 teaspoons whole
coriander seeds,
crushed (optional)

1 tablespoon
grapeseed or
vegetable oil

1 pound hickory,
oak, or cherrywood
chunks (about
8 cups), for smoking

1. TO MAKE THE BRINE: In a ceramic, glass, or food-grade plastic vessel (see Resources, page 327), whisk together the water, kosher salt, sugar, and pink salt until the salts and sugar dissolve. Add the peppercorns, mustard seeds, juniper berries, coriander, bay leaves, and garlic and whisk. No need to heat the brine.

2. Rinse off the beef and place it in the brine. Cover and refrigerate for about 1 week for thinner cuts and closer to 10 days for thicker cuts. Be sure to turn the meat every day for even brining. The meat will turn gray on the outside—this is normal. Note that if the meat doesn't brine for long enough, you'll see brown spots on the meat where there should be red. No worries—it will still taste delicious.

3. Remove the meat from the brine and rinse it well under cold water. Then, in a ceramic, glass, or food-grade plastic vessel, cover the meat with cold water and soak in the fridge to reduce the salt level. After 2 hours, repeat the process, draining the liquid and covering the meat with fresh water and soaking it in the fridge for 2 hours more. After the second soak, rinse the meat with cold water, rubbing the meat well. Pat dry with a clean kitchen towel or paper towels and place on a baking sheet lined with parchment paper.

4. TO MAKE THE SPICE RUB: In a medium bowl, mix all the spices together. Set aside.

5. Rub the meat well with oil, then coat with the spice rub, little by little, and begin rubbing it in. Coat the entire cut on all sides. Refrigerate, uncovered, overnight.

6. FOR SMOKING: Set your smoker to 225°F. If your smoker comes equipped with a smoker box, place the wood chips in the box according to the manufacturer's directions. If using a charcoal smoker, place the wood chips directly on the coals, pushing the coals and wood to one side of the bowl. If using a gas smoker, place the wood chunks on top of the outermost burner. Once the temperature remains steady at 225°F and there is a visible haze of smoke, place the meat, fat side up, on the top rack or away from the heat source so the meat is getting indirect smoke. Smoke until the internal temperature of the meat registers 155°F, 4 to 6 hours. Begin

(continued) ▶

checking the temperature of the meat at around 3 hours. Note that it is critical to keep the smoker at a steady 225°F during the entire process.

7. Once the meat registers 155°F, remove and place on a rack to cool for about 30 minutes, then place on a parchment paper–lined baking sheet and refrigerate, uncovered, overnight.

8. To steam and serve, place the whole pastrami in a steamer—either in a pot or a bamboo steamer, if you have one. Add boiling water to just below the steaming basket. Steam the pastrami for 1½ to 2 hours. Keep an eye on the water level in the steamer and add more boiling water as necessary. The pastrami is ready when a fork can be easily inserted into the meat, but is not so tender that a fork can no longer lift the meat out of the steamer.

9. To serve, slice the pastrami against the grain, about ¼ inch thick, or thinner if that's your preference. The meat can also be served and sliced at room temperature. Serve exclusively on Jewish Rye (page 100) and apply Spicy Whole-Grain Mustard (page 32) with reckless abandon. Pastrami will last stored in your refrigerator for at least a week. For more notes on curing meat, see below.

An Alternative to a Smoker

After step 5, preheat the oven to 225°F. Line an aluminum roasting pan with aluminum foil. Leave a foot or so of foil overhanging on either side of the pan (you'll use these long ends to create a pouch to seal in the smoke). Next, scatter ½ pound hickory, oak, or cherrywood chips (about 8 cups) along the bottom of the roasting pan and place a metal rack over them. Place the meat on the rack, then gather the long ends of the foil and crimp them together to create a pouch to seal in the smoke. Be sure no foil is touching the meat when you close up the pouch. Loop additional layers of foil over and around the roasting pan if necessary. Place the roasting pan on the stovetop over medium-high heat for 5 minutes, or until you begin to smell the faint smell of woodsmoke. Peel back some foil to make sure smoke is flowing if you're not sure. If there's no smoke, check again in 2 minutes. Once the smoke is flowing, place the roasting pan in the oven and bake for 2 hours. At this point, begin checking the internal temperature of the meat. Once it hits 155°F, after 2½ to 4 hours or longer, the meat is finished. Remove, let cool for 30 minutes, then place on a parchment paper–lined baking sheet and refrigerate, uncovered, overnight. Then it's time to steam and serve your pastrami, so pick things up from step 8 above.

~~ SEVEN ~~

MAINS

LIZ I lived for years in a frenetic Brooklyn apartment with at least

three roommates at any given time. Guests were constantly stopping by,

whether it was on their way home from the farmers' market, after work

on a Tuesday, or just in time for sundown on Shabbat. This meant that I

was always in the kitchen, throwing together meals on the fly like fish with

veggies, savory stews, and potato gratin.

When I moved to a new apartment, I thought I'd attempt a quieter

life. Turns out that I was the instigator of the craziness all along. My

new apartment took on the exact same rhythm as the old, so I decided

to accept and embrace my fate as a never-ending hostess and my natural

temperament to go with the flow. Jeffrey and I butt heads on this

sometimes. He prefers his kitchen to be orderly and neat, and for guests

to arrive at the appointed hour. He's careful about plating individual servings, and never forgets to garnish. I, on the other hand, prefer casual spontaneity, with guests arriving when they can and everyone lending a hand in the kitchen.

It turns out that a precedent exists in Ashkenazi culture for both a more formal and informal style, mine being more closely associated with the weekdays and his fitting more naturally with the rhythm of the holidays. In the shtetls and cities of eastern Europe, Jews generally didn't follow a set schedule of weekday meals. Eating happened organically. Women and children ate when they were hungry and men ate when they returned home from work. It was common for friends to drop by one another's homes, and guests were always given a bite to eat, no matter the time of day.

At formal holiday meals with multiple courses and richer foods, tables used to be set elaborately and dishes were presented on large platters, family style; however, the aesthetics of the foods themselves weren't terribly important. Roasted goose, hearty stews, and stuffed cabbages were transferred from the oven to the table without much flair. Focus was put on "taste, temperature and texture [rather] than the appearance of the food," write Mark Zborowski and Elizabeth Herzog in *Life Is with People*, their anthropological study of small-town Jewish life, "for eating is a gustatory rather than visual pleasure . . . and there is little effort to appeal to the eye with garnishes, color contrast or arrangement." While I can't say I don't care about aesthetics, I can understand why taste would trump presentation.

The recipes in this chapter offer a fun interplay between the formal and the informal, the organic flow and the appointed sit-down mealtime. Cholent, for example, can easily be added to a buffet and ladled by guests straight from the slow cooker. It can also serve as the centerpiece of a very special winter meal, with each guest receiving a beautifully plated bowl topped with a slow-cooked egg and a dusting of fresh herbs. Blintzes can be a simple and impromptu snack, made when friends come over on a Sunday afternoon. By contrast, they can also be the focus of an entire formal brunch, with homemade cheese stuffings and fresh fruit compote completing the rich display.

Whatever your style is, and whatever the occasion, cooking the main dishes in this chapter is a wonderful excuse to invite friends over for a meal, or to simply throw open your door and let the delicious smells wafting out of your home pull your neighbors in. As long as no one leaves hungry, our work here is done.

〰

JEFFREY The workweek at Adamah Farm, where I lived and worked as a farm fellow and a pickle apprentice in my early twenties, officially ended in the early afternoon on Friday. We'd eat a leisurely lunch in the field using cabbage leaves as plates and take a dip in the Housatonic River, which we treated as our mikveh—ritual bath. In the freezing water we shared the good and the bad from each of our weeks, to clear our minds and hearts before the Sabbath, which arrived at sundown.

I hadn't ever lived as in sync with the Jewish holidays as I did on the farm, where the Sabbath's promise of rest felt earned after a week of toiling in the field. The Sabbath set the structure for our weekly cooking rhythms on the farm, too, just as it had for centuries for Ashkenazi Jews in Europe.

Because Jewish holidays always begin at sundown and commence with a large meal, a practice developed among many observant Ashkenazi Jewish families to eat light meals on Fridays and the days before festivals began, as we did on the farm, to "heighten their enjoyment of their subsequent feasting," writes John Cooper in *Eat and Be Satisfied*.

All Jewish holidays fit into a rhythm and a structure, focused on work, followed by rest, and punctuated by seasonal celebrations. Sukkot provides a pause in the fall, as we fold kreplach, stir sweet-and-sour tomato sauce, and roll leaves of cabbage around ground meat. Passover heralds the start of spring, as we patiently wait for our brisket to braise. As centuries of Jews before me have known, and I only began to understand during my time on the farm, it is within this structure that life feels less chaotic. And it is within this structure that, ideally, we reconnect with what nourishes us most: family, community, and food. So indispensable was the Sabbath meal to the rhythm of Jewish life that if a family in a shtetl was unable to cobble together a meal, the Jewish community would intervene and provide enough food so that they could fulfill the religious and communal obligation to celebrate and enjoy the precious day.

I'll be the first to admit that living in the twenty-first century, in a place as hectic as New York City, I don't always tune in to this rhythm. But even as a child, generations removed from life in eastern Europe, I loved feasting on the seasonal classics for the Jewish holidays. Now, I turn to these recipes to ground me in who I am and where I come from, as I'm sure they did for my parents and grandparents. I think about those Jewish immigrants on the Lower East Side at the turn of the twentieth century who raised geese and chickens in the backyards of their tenements, rearing a taste of the Old World in the stark reality of the New. When I feel uprooted, these meals always bring me home again.

MAINS
≡ RECIPES ≡

BRAISED SAUERKRAUT
AND POTATO GRATIN

This braised sauerkraut gratin is a hearty vegetarian entrée with a flavor that hints at French onion soup and a surprising elegance for a dish made from such humble, quotidian ingredients. I love incorporating one of my favorite fermented foods into a main dish. The sourness works so well with the creaminess of the cheese, and the potatoes serve as the perfect base for all these elements. Note that this dish requires first making one full recipe of our Wine-Braised Sauerkraut and Mushrooms (page 64), so take a look at that recipe before you plan your shopping and cooking. Serve this dish with a fresh salad and a glass of wine.

SERVES 12

2½ pounds baking potatoes like russets (6 or 7 medium), quartered and thinly sliced (about ⅛ inch thick) using a box grater or a mandoline

1 recipe Wine-Braised Sauerkraut and Mushrooms (page 64)

1 pound Swiss or Gruyère cheese, shredded (about 4 cups loosely packed)

1. Preheat the oven to 400°F. Lightly grease a 9 x 13-inch casserole dish.

2. Arrange one-third of the potatoes on the bottom of the pan, followed by one-third of the sauerkraut and mushrooms, and then one-third of the cheese. Repeat the layering process twice more.

3. Cover the dish with aluminum foil and bake for 50 minutes. Remove the foil and turn on the broiler. Broil the gratin on low for about 15 minutes, or until the cheese on top is browned and bubbling. Serve hot out of the oven.

SWEET OR SAVORY BLINTZES

JEFFREY

I was only privy to homemade blintzes once in a blue moon when Grandma Ruth decided to make them. Hers were never too sweet, and they revealed their contents on the sides since she delicately sliced off the edges of each blintz, leaving the scraps for the children as a special treat. I feel every parent has to make at least one dish with ends to slice off for kids. It's not fair to make them wait until everything is finished. Blintz ends are a pretty solid way to go.

If necessary, you can make the blintzes in advance and store in the refrigerator or freezer until later. Just be sure to bring them up to room temperature before reheating so the insides don't remain cold. Note that the yield in this recipe is based on an 8-inch-diameter frying pan. If you have a different size pan, the yield will differ. The crepe recipe is adapted from Mitchell Davis's *The Mensch Chef* and works well with both our sweet cheese filling and savory mushroom-potato filling.

MAKES 16 BLINTZES

Sweet Cheese Blintzes

FOR THE CREPES:

4 tablespoons (½ stick) unsalted butter, melted and slightly cooled, plus more for frying

4 large eggs

1 cup whole milk

¾ cup cold water

½ teaspoon kosher salt

2 tablespoons sugar

2 cups all-purpose flour

FOR THE SWEET CHEESE FILLING:

3 cups farmer's cheese (about 1½ pounds), store-bought or homemade (page 21)

½ cup cream cheese (4 ounces), softened, store-bought or home-made (page 25)

¼ cup sugar

¼ teaspoon kosher salt

2 large eggs

2 tablespoons loosely packed lemon zest

Sour cream, store-bought or home-made (page 24), for serving

Fresh or macerated berries (optional), for garnish

1. TO MAKE THE CREPES: In a large bowl, food processor, or blender, mix together the melted butter, eggs, milk, cold water, salt, and sugar. Add the flour ½ cup at a time, mixing between each addition to remove as many lumps as possible.

2. In an 8-inch nonstick pan, melt a small pat of butter over medium heat. Pour about ⅓ cup of the batter into the center of the hot pan. Lift and rotate the pan

(continued) ▶

immediately so batter coats the bottom entirely, then place the pan back on the heat to cook. You'll get the hang of it after a couple of tries. At first, each crepe will take about 1 minute, but the process speeds up as the pan gets hotter, and each crepe should take 30 to 45 seconds. When the crepe is mostly cooked, the edges will lift up. With a spatula, check to make sure the crepe has splotches of brown on the bottom. When one side is fully cooked, flip the crepe onto a nearby plate lined with parchment paper so that the side that has not cooked is facing down. Repeat with the remaining batter, stacking each crepe on top of the others. No need to butter the pan between crepes—only add more butter about every fifth crepe. Note that the first crepe never comes out well. Don't despair.

3.   TO MAKE THE SWEET CHEESE FILLING: Combine all the ingredients in a bowl and mix well.

4.   TO FORM THE BLINTZES: Spoon about ¼ cup of the filling onto the cooked side of a crepe, in the middle of the lower half. Spread out the filling from side to side in a horizontal line. Fold the bottom of the crepe up to cover the filling, and then fold each end into the center to create a small package. Roll up the crepe tightly to form a compact blintz. It will be about 4 inches in length. Repeat with the remaining crepes and filling. At this point, you can fry them up now, or refrigerate or freeze the blintzes to eat later. To refrigerate, wrap each blintz individually in parchment paper (so they don't stick together) and store in an airtight plastic container for up to 5 days. To freeze, set the wrapped blintzes on a baking sheet in the freezer until they harden, then transfer to an airtight plastic container and freeze for up to 3 months.

5.   If you prepared your blintzes in advance, be sure to bring them up to room temperature before frying them (so the filling doesn't remain cold). Place a small pat of butter in a nonstick skillet over medium-low heat and place the blintzes in the pan, seam side down. If your blintz is cylindrical, flatten it slightly with a spatula for even cooking. Do not crowd the pan. Cook the blintzes until golden on the bottom, then flip to the other side and cook until golden brown and the sides are soft, 3 to 4 minutes total. You may need to flip each blintz multiple times to avoid them getting too brown.

6.   Serve the blintzes hot. Garnish with sour cream and berries. Keep just-fried blintzes warm in the oven at 250°F until ready to serve.

(*continued*) ▶

▶ (Sweet or Savory Blintzes, *continued*)

Savory Mushroom-Potato Filling

2 teaspoons kosher
salt, or to taste,
plus additional for
boiling water

2 pounds russet
potatoes (about
5 medium), peeled
and cut into
2-inch chunks

1 dried bay leaf

2 tablespoons
unsalted butter,
melted, plus more
for frying

8 ounces coarsely
chopped stemmed
fresh mushrooms
(chanterelles,
shiitakes,
porcini, etc.)

2½ tablespoons
chopped fresh sage,
plus more for garnish

2½ tablespoons
chopped fresh
tarragon, plus more
for garnish

½ cup whole milk,
warmed

2 large egg yolks,
lightly beaten

1 teaspoon freshly
ground black pepper

Sour cream, store-
bought or home-
made (page 24),
for serving

1. Bring a large pot of salted water to a
    boil. Add the potatoes and bay leaf.
    Reduce the heat to maintain a simmer
    and cook until the potatoes are very
    tender and can be easily pierced with
    a fork, 12 to 15 minutes.

2. While the potatoes are boiling, in
    a skillet, melt a pat of butter over
    medium-high heat. When the butter
    is just melted, add the mushrooms
    and 1 teaspoon of the salt and cook,
    undisturbed, for 1 minute to darken
    the mushrooms. Cook, stirring
    occasionally, until the mushrooms are
    lightly browned and their liquid has
    evaporated, 5 to 7 minutes. Remove
    from the heat and stir in the sage
    and tarragon.

3. Drain the potatoes, discarding the bay
    leaf. Roughly mash the potatoes with a
    fork, a potato masher, or the bottom of
    a jar, removing any lumps. Stir in the
    remaining 1 teaspoon salt, taste, and
    adjust the seasoning to your preference.
    This mixture should be saltier than
    what you're accustomed to, as the
    egg and the crepe itself will mute the
    saltiness significantly. Whisk in the
    2 tablespoons melted butter and the
    milk. Add the egg yolks, stirring quickly
    to avoid curdling. Fold in the mushroom
    mixture and the pepper.

4. Fill the blintzes and fry (or store for
    later) as directed in Sweet or Savory
    Blintzes recipe. Serve garnished
    with sour cream, chopped sage, and
    minced tarragon.

PAN-FRIED TROUT WITH HERBED MASHED POTATOES

JEFFREY

SERVES 4

My grandpa Joe went fishing in the waters of North Shore Boston in the warmer months and brought home fresh-caught flounder. He filleted the fish at home, then Grandma Ruth fried it up. She didn't add any salt since she said the ocean has plenty already. Rustle up a simple salad and you'll have a satisfying yet light dinner.

FOR THE HERBED MASHED POTATOES:

1½ pounds red potatoes

2 tablespoons unsalted butter

1 tablespoon olive oil

4 scallions, minced

1 teaspoon caraway seeds

1 bunch sorrel, spinach, or other leafy greens, coarsely chopped

3 tablespoons dried currants

⅓ cup sour cream, store-bought or homemade (page 24)

1 teaspoon kosher salt

½ teaspoon freshly ground black pepper

FOR THE PAN-FRIED TROUT:

2 tablespoons unsalted butter

1 tablespoon olive oil

4 trout fillets (about 5 ounces each)

Kosher salt and freshly ground black pepper

All-purpose flour, for coating

1 lemon, cut into wedges, for serving

1. TO MAKE THE HERBED MASHED POTATOES: Place the potatoes in a medium saucepan and add water to cover them fully. Bring to a boil and cook until fork-tender, about 25 minutes. Drain and transfer to a bowl. Mash the potatoes roughly with a fork or the bottom of a jar.

2. In a large skillet, melt the butter with the oil over medium-high heat. Stir in the scallions and caraway seeds and cook, stirring occasionally, for about 3 minutes, until fragrant and starting to brown. Add the mashed potatoes and cook, stirring, until the potatoes begin to color lightly, about 5 minutes. Stir in the greens, currants, sour cream, salt, and pepper. Remove from the heat, cover to keep warm, and set aside.

3. TO MAKE THE PAN-FRIED TROUT: In a separate pan, melt the butter with the oil over medium heat. Season the trout with salt and pepper and lightly coat with flour. Set the trout in the pan and cook, keeping a close watch to ensure that it doesn't stick to the bottom of the pan, for about 3 minutes on each side, or until the flesh is evenly white throughout. Serve the trout with the potatoes and a wedge of lemon for squeezing.

CRISPY CHICKEN WITH TSIMMES

LIZ

Tsimmes is a sweet Ashkenazi stew in which the ingredients vary depending on family origin and tradition. The dish is often eaten during the Jewish High Holidays to symbolically usher in a sweet new year. This sweet-and-savory chicken *tsimmes* is an easy dish with a built-in side. The juices of the chicken enhance the flavors of the carrots and prunes. It's filling when paired with rice or kasha, and it's colorful and complex enough to serve for the holidays.

SERVES 4

3 tablespoons grated peeled fresh ginger

3 tablespoons honey

2 tablespoons vegetable oil

2 teaspoons kosher salt, plus more as needed

½ teaspoon red pepper flakes, plus more as needed

1 teaspoon packed grated lemon zest

2 to 2½ pounds chicken pieces, bone-in with skin

1 medium onion, halved and thinly sliced into half-moons

1 pound carrots, cut into ½-inch rounds (about 3 cups)

½ pound pitted prunes, coarsely chopped (about 1½ cups)

½ cup water

Chopped fresh parsley, for garnish

1. Preheat the oven to 400°F. In a small bowl, mix together the ginger, honey, 1 tablespoon of the oil, the salt, red pepper flakes, and lemon zest to make a glaze. Set aside.

2. In a heavy-bottomed oven-safe skillet, heat the remaining 1 tablespoon oil over medium heat. Place the chicken in the pan, skin side down, and sear the pieces for 5 to 7 minutes until brown. Transfer the chicken pieces to a bowl, generously coat with the glaze, and set aside.

3. Add the onion to the pan and cook until it softens and becomes aromatic, about 3 minutes. Add the carrots and prunes and cook, stirring, for about 10 minutes, until the carrots are just beginning to soften, adding a pinch or two more salt and red pepper flakes. Add the water to the skillet, scraping up the bits of carrot, onion, and prune that have stuck to the bottom of the pan. Place the chicken, skin side up, on top of the tsimmes, drizzling any glaze in the bowl over the chicken.

4. Place the skillet in the oven, uncovered, and bake for 30 to 35 minutes, until the chicken is cooked through (the safe internal temperature for chicken is 165°F), its skin is crispy and browned, and the sauce looks thick and bubbly.

5. Serve the chicken with *tsimmes* and kasha or rice. Spoon over any pan juices and garnish with parsley.

ROAST CHICKEN WITH BARLEY AND VEGETABLES

LIZ

This dish makes for a fragrant meal that is unique enough for Friday night and simple enough for a weekday evening. While roast chicken is a classic centerpiece on the contemporary Jewish table, the earthiness of the mushrooms and barley in this recipe give it a decidedly Old World feel.

Note that this recipe highlights one of my favorite Ashkenazi ingredients: pearl barley, which is simply barley processed to remove the hull and bran. As a heavy, filling grain, barley is generally used in wintry Ashkenazi dishes like soups and stews, but it deserves wider use as a substitute for rice or kasha.

Using the technique in this recipe, the barley will soak up the savory flavors of the chicken and the mushrooms and remain silky, even when roasted in the oven. This dish is simple to execute but has a few components, so be sure to read through the entire recipe before you start.

SERVES 4 TO 6

¾ cup pearl barley

1 dried bay leaf

3½ teaspoons kosher salt, plus more as needed

4 scallions, coarsely chopped

1 pound mixed fresh mushrooms, coarsely chopped

3 tablespoons olive oil or schmaltz (page 35)

2 garlic cloves, minced

¼ teaspoon freshly ground black pepper

2½ to 3 pounds chicken pieces, cleaned and patted dry

¼ cup coarsely chopped fresh parsley, plus more for garnish

1 tablespoon apple cider vinegar

---

1. In a medium pot, combine the barley, bay leaf, and 1 teaspoon of the salt. Add enough water to cover the barley by 2 inches. Bring to a boil, then reduce the heat to low and simmer for 18 to 20 minutes, until the barley is half cooked but still al dente. Strain and remove the bay leaf. Toss the barley with the scallions, mushrooms, and 2 tablespoons of the olive oil or schmaltz. It may seem like too many mushrooms, but they will shrink in the oven.

2. Preheat oven to 425°F.

3. Combine the remaining 2½ teaspoons salt, the garlic, and the pepper. Rub the mixture on the chicken pieces, getting it between the skin and the flesh if

possible. Place the chicken pieces on a baking sheet, skin side up. Drizzle with the remaining 1 tablespoon oil or schmaltz. On a separate baking sheet, spread out the barley-mushroom mixture in an even layer.

4. Transfer both baking sheets to the preheated oven and roast for 25 to 30 minutes, until the barley is cooked through and the chicken is evenly colored when sliced in the thickest part. You can also test the internal temperature, which should register 165°F when done.

5. Transfer the chicken to a plate and pour any juices from the baking sheet onto the barley-mushroom mixture. Add the parsley and vinegar to the mixture and stir to combine. Taste and season with additional salt if necessary. Serve the chicken pieces with a heaping portion of the barley-mushroom mixture. Garnish with additional parsley.

ALSATIAN ROASTED GOOSE OR DUCK WITH APPLES AND ONIONS

JEFFREY

Roasting a goose is an epic undertaking that will whisk you back to the Ashkenazi holiday tables of the past. This recipe is our homage to Alsace-Lorraine, the region west of the Rhine River between Germany and France, considered to be the point of origin of Ashkenazi culture before it moved eastward. If you can't source a goose, duck works great. (Keep in mind duck can get a bit greasier.)

This recipe includes a guide for modifying your cooking time according to the size of the bird you procure (about 20 minutes per pound). For example, if roasting a 9-pound goose, your cooking time will be about 3 hours. When buying a raw duck or goose, you will want to plan for 1 to 1½ pounds per guest, so that 9-pound goose will feed 6 to 9 people. A goose will generally be available in a much larger size than a duck, but the ranges vary widely. In both cases, the key is to monitor the roasting so that the bird does not dry out.

This recipe calls for apples and onions stuffed inside the goose and placed underneath it in the roasting pan. Not only does cooking the bird with apples and onions make for a stunning presentation, but they soak up the richness of the drippings and make for a distinctive side. The ones stuffed inside the bird do not retain as much flavor, so serve or discard, depending on your preference.

MAKES 1 ROASTED GOOSE OR DUCK (EXACT YIELD WILL VARY DEPENDING ON SIZE OF BIRD)

---

1 goose or duck

Kosher salt

Freshly ground black pepper

4 to 6 baking apples (or more if serving a large crowd): 1 quartered, the rest left whole

1 or 2 large onions, quartered

---

1. Preheat the oven to 425°F. Boil a kettle of water to use for basting the bird.

2. Begin by trimming and removing excess fat from the bird, setting it aside to make schmaltz (page 35). Using your hands, carefully create space between the skin and the meat of the bird. Using a paring knife, carefully prick the skin of the bird all over. This will allow the fat to drain. Be careful not to prick the flesh, however.

(continued) ▶

▶ (Alsatian Roasted Goose or Duck with Apples and Onions, *continued*)

3.   Season the cavity generously with salt and pepper, then stuff it with as many of the apple and onion quarters as you can. The whole apples and remaining quartered onions should be placed in the bottom of the roasting pan. Secure the legs, wings, and neck tightly against the body with cooking twine (see illustrations on page 237).

4.   Place the bird in the roasting pan, breast side up, and roast for 15 minutes. Reduce the oven temperature to 350°F and turn the bird on its side. Baste with a couple of tablespoons of boiling water every 20 minutes or so to remove accumulated fat. As noted above, plan to roast your bird for 20 minutes per pound. Halfway through the roasting time, turn the bird onto the other side for even cooking.

5.   During the last 10 minutes of cooking, season the skin with salt and pepper, and increase the oven temperature to 425°F so that the skin browns. Roast until the thickest part of the bird reaches an internal temperature of 165°F.

6.   Let the bird sit for 15 minutes before removing the stuffing and carving. While carving, take the juices from the bottom of the roasting pan and place them in a small saucepan on the stovetop to reduce the liquid by at least one-third of its original volume. Serve the goose or duck on a platter, ladled with the reduced cooking liquid and surrounded by the apples and onions from the pan.

Note The technique outlined on the next page is one of the simplest and most straightforward methods for trussing poultry of all kinds, including goose, duck, turkey, and chicken. Trussing a bird before roasting it helps it remain moist and also holds in place any stuffing that may have been placed in the bird's breast cavity. While there are many different trussing methods used by chefs, we've found that the one included here is effective for all skill levels.

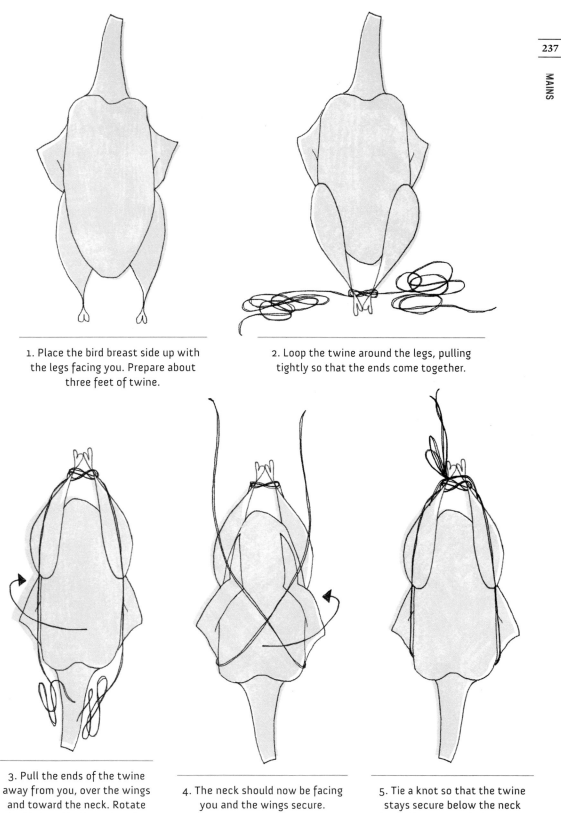

1. Place the bird breast side up with the legs facing you. Prepare about three feet of twine.

2. Loop the twine around the legs, pulling tightly so that the ends come together.

3. Pull the ends of the twine away from you, over the wings and toward the neck. Rotate the bird upside down, keeping the twine pulled tightly.

4. The neck should now be facing you and the wings secure.

5. Tie a knot so that the twine stays secure below the neck bone. You may tuck the goose neck next to the breast.

SPICY HUNGARIAN CHOLENT

LIZ →

In the shtetls of eastern Europe, cholent pots were handed down through generations and were sealed tightly, often with flour and water, before being placed in the communal oven on Friday before sundown. The cholent was retrieved on the way home from synagogue on Saturday, and the entire family waited in anticipation for the lid to be lifted and the delicious smell to fill the room. Historically, cholent contained a meat, a grain, and a vegetable, but variations abounded based on local flavors and economic status. In Poland, for example, potatoes were always included in the cholent, whereas in Germany, other root vegetables were used instead. Hungarian cholent, which inspired this recipe, is a bit soupier than other styles of cholent. Our version is spicier and more complex than what you might be used to, which I'd say is a good thing. Today, cholent is generally found in more observant Jewish homes, and is usually made in a slow cooker. Be sure to monitor the cooking and keep the slow cooker away from anything flammable.

SERVES 8 TO 10

---

2 pounds beef chuck roast, cut into cubes

2 tablespoons vegetable oil (or schmaltz, page 35)

2 medium onions, thinly sliced

4 large garlic cloves, minced

6 medium Yukon Gold or red potatoes, peeled and cubed

8 ounces fresh mushrooms, quartered

1 cup large dried lima beans, boiled, rinsed, and soaked for two hours, then drained and rinsed thoroughly

½ cup pearl barley (or rice)

4 cups beef, chicken, or vegetable broth, store-bought or homemade (page 130 or 123)

¼ cup tomato paste

2 tablespoons packed light brown sugar

2 tablespoons Hungarian sweet paprika

1½ tablespoons hot Hungarian paprika (optional)

2 teaspoons mustard powder

1 tablespoon kosher salt

1½ teaspoons freshly ground black pepper

3 cups water

4 large eggs, shells washed (optional)

Chopped fresh parsley, for garnish

---

1. Heat a nonstick pan over medium heat. Sear the beef on all sides until the pieces are lightly browned. Do not crowd the pan; sear in batches if your pan is small. Transfer to a plate.

2. Add the oil to the same pan and sauté the onions until they are lightly colored and fragrant, about 5 minutes, then transfer to a 5- to 7-quart slow cooker.

(continued) ▶

Place the meat in the slow cooker along with the garlic, potatoes, mushrooms, beans, and barley.

3. In a large bowl, mix together the broth, tomato paste, brown sugar, paprika, mustard powder, salt, pepper, and 3 cups water and pour the mixture into the slow cooker. Place the eggs (if using) in the slow cooker. Pour a bit more water in if more is needed to cover all the ingredients.

4. Set the slow cooker to low and cook overnight or up to 18 hours, until the beans and grains are soft and cooked through. The cholent will become thicker the longer it's cooked. Remove the eggs and cool. Add salt to taste and stir. Peel the eggs, then halve them lengthwise. Ladle the hot cholent into individual bowls. Place half an egg on top of each serving and garnish with parsley.

DEBATE: IS THERE AN AUTHENTIC JEWISH FOOD?

LIZ → Considering that Jews have always lived around the world and continually adapted local foods to Jewish dietary laws, there's an ongoing debate about whether there is such thing as an "authentic" Jewish food. Many writers and scholars have claimed Jewish ownership over a few particular items, and I feel strongly that two foods—cholent and matzo—have a Jewish character all their own. Jeffrey thinks it's a ridiculous line of reasoning, and we get into heated arguments on the topic, often when riding the subway.

Cholent, that delicious slow-cooked stew, exists in one form or another within Jewish communities around the world. It's a direct outgrowth of the Jewish prohibition against cooking on the Sabbath, and was developed precisely so that folks could enjoy a hot meal on Saturday afternoon. While the components of this stew vary across regions, the concept remains the same. And this, to me, makes cholent uniquely Jewish. Jeffrey claims that every culture has a slow-cooked stew and, Sabbath or not, a stew is a stew is a stew.

Regarding matzo, I know it's a flatbread made of flour and water, which are hardly uniquely Jewish ingredients. But matzo must be made in a precise manner in order to be considered kosher for Passover, the holiday during which matzo is central. As with cholent, this is a case of function over form, and to me, that makes it Jewish. Jeffrey, not surprisingly, points to traditional flatbreads around the world and says a flatbread is a flatbread is a flatbread. "Just because one is baked for a special holiday," he says, "doesn't make it Jewish."

We never get anywhere with this debate, and greater minds have also remained undecided. I leave it up to you. The good news is that recipes for Spicy Hungarian Cholent (page 239), Rice and Vegetable Cholent (page 242), and Make-At-Home Matzo (page 94) are all in this book, so you can taste the evidence and decide for yourself.

>←

RICE AND VEGETABLE CHOLENT

JEFFREY

Inspiration for this cholent struck when one of my best friends cooked Chinese congee for me. Congee is basically a slow-cooked rice porridge, in which the rice breaks down and thickens the liquid around it, sopping up flavor like crazy. While the dried mushrooms add a meaty flavor to this dish, the rice still manages to keep it nice and light. The result is a stew that's perfect for vegetarians and omnivores alike. Be sure to take precautions whenever using a slow cooker. Monitor the cooking and keep the slow cooker away from anything flammable.

SERVES 8 TO 10

---

1 large shallot, sliced

1 small onion, thinly sliced

2 garlic cloves, coarsely chopped

2 tablespoons vegetable oil

1 cup white, basmati, or jasmine rice

1 medium sweet potato, peeled and diced

8 dried porcini mushrooms

1 cup dried lima beans, soaked for at least 1 hour, then drained and rinsed

2 tablespoons plus 1 teaspoon kosher salt

6 cups vegetable broth, store-bought or homemade (page 123)

5 cups water

4 large eggs, shells washed (optional)

4 carrots

Olive oil

Chopped fresh parsley, for garnish

---

1. In a nonstick pan, sauté the shallot, onion, and garlic in the vegetable oil over medium heat until translucent, about 5 minutes. Transfer to a 5- to 7-quart slow cooker and add the rice, sweet potato, mushrooms, lima beans, 2 tablespoons of the salt, the broth, and water. Carefully place the eggs (if using) into the slow cooker. Cook on low overnight or for up to 16 hours.

2. At some point while the cholent cooks, preheat the oven to 400°F. Place the carrots in a roasting pan and coat them with olive oil. Sprinkle with the remaining 1 teaspoon salt, then roast for 20 minutes. Keep a close eye on them to make sure they don't burn. Slice each carrot into rounds, then refrigerate if roasting the day before, or set aside if roasting just before serving.

3. Toward the end of the cholent's cooking time, remove the eggs and let cool. Peel, then halve them lengthwise. Bring the carrots to room temperature, if necessary. Ladle the hot cholent into individual bowls. Garnish with the halved eggs, parsley, and carrots.

KIMCHI-STUFFED CABBAGE

Stuffed cabbage is traditionally associated with the holiday of Sukkot, which falls during the autumn harvest when cabbage is king. Because cabbage is so ubiquitous in the region, many Slavic cultures have a tradition of stuffing cabbage leaves. The Jewish version usually involves ground beef and rice, and sometimes sauerkraut, too.

We've included both a meat stuffing and a vegetarian lentil-mushroom variation in this recipe. Instead of kraut, we fold in our spicy Ashkenazi Kimchi (page 68) to add an extra kick. Both versions of this recipe work great with sauerkraut, so feel free to substitute it wherever kimchi is indicated as an ingredient. You may need to drain the kimchi or sauerkraut in order to chop it, but reserve any excess brine and stir it into the sauce and filling. If using store-bought kimchi, we caution against purchasing only the spicy variety, which can be very, very hot. A mix of mild and spicy kimchi will balance perfectly with the added spice in this recipe. Note that this is a longer, more involved recipe.

MAKES 12 LARGE CABBAGE ROLLS

FOR THE SAUCE:

Grapeseed or vegetable oil, for sautéing

2 medium onions, thinly sliced

¼ cup tomato paste

1 (28-ounce) can crushed tomatoes

½ teaspoon freshly ground black pepper

¼ cup packed dark brown sugar

2 teaspoons red wine vinegar

¼ teaspoon hot paprika (cayenne pepper is a fine substitute, but both are optional for extra spice)

2 cups finely chopped kimchi, store-bought or homemade (page 68)

¼ cup fresh lemon juice

Kosher salt

FOR THE MEAT FILLING:

¾ cup jasmine or basmati rice

2 cups water

2 teaspoons grapeseed or vegetable oil

1½ pounds ground beef chuck

1 teaspoon kosher salt

½ teaspoon freshly ground black pepper

½ teaspoon smoked paprika

1 cup finely chopped kimchi, store-bought or homemade (page 68)

1 large egg, lightly beaten

2 tablespoons bread crumbs

TO ASSEMBLE:

Kosher salt

1 head green cabbage

Fresh parsley and celery leaves, for garnish

---

1. TO MAKE THE SAUCE: In a medium saucepan over medium heat, heat enough oil to coat the bottom of the pan. Add the onions and sauté until they begin to turn translucent, about 5 minutes. Stir in the

(continued) ▶

tomato paste to coat the onions and cook for about 2 minutes. Add the crushed tomatoes, pepper, brown sugar, vinegar, and paprika (if using) and cook at a low simmer, covered, for about 20 minutes. Remove from the heat, stir in the kimchi and any reserved brine, the lemon juice, and salt to taste. Set aside.

2. TO MAKE THE MEAT FILLING: Pour the rice and water into a small saucepan and bring to a boil. Reduce the heat to maintain a simmer and cook for 5 minutes. Remove from the heat, drain through a fine-mesh strainer, and rinse with cold water. Set aside.

3. In a skillet, heat the oil over medium heat. Add the beef and sauté, turning the meat over with a wooden spoon until evenly browned. Add the cooked rice, salt, pepper, paprika, and kimchi to the pan. Sauté for 2 minutes more, then transfer the mixture to a large bowl. Stir in the egg, bread crumbs, and any reserved kimchi brine.

4. TO ASSEMBLE THE CABBAGE ROLLS: Bring a large soup pot of salted water to a boil. Remove the core of the cabbage with a long, sharp knife, very carefully cutting out a cone shape around the core and removing as large a chunk of the core as

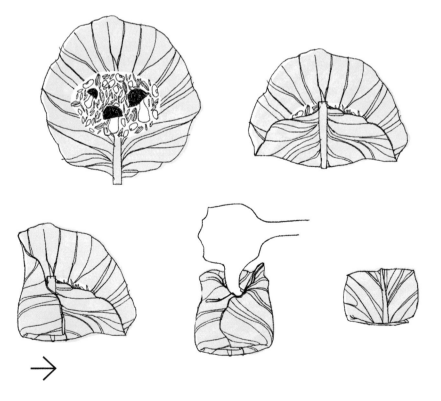

you can. This helps separate the leaves easily. Place the cabbage in the boiling water and cook for about 4 minutes.

5. Using tongs or two forks, remove the cabbage from the pot and carefully peel off any leaves that have become loose and translucent. Be careful and try to keep the leaves intact as best you can. Place the translucent leaves in a colander to drain, then return the cabbage to the pot and boil for 3 to 4 minutes more. Repeat the process until you have 12 large leaves. Pat the leaves dry with paper towels if still wet.

6. Preheat the oven to 300°F. Spread a layer of the sauce over the bottom of a large, high-walled oven-safe dish or a Dutch oven. Set aside.

7. Working with one leaf at a time, lay the leaf flat, rib side up, and use a paring knife to slice off the tough, raised part of the rib. Flip the leaf over and scoop ½ cup of the filling into the center. Try to keep the stuffing together in one clump.

8. Fold up the "bottom" of the leaf (where the core was attached) and lift it over the filling, about halfway up the cabbage leaf. While holding down the first fold with one hand, use the other to take the left side of the leaf and lay it over the first fold. Roll the leaf all the way to the right side and keep it tight. The top of the roll will be untucked. Push it down into the roll, forcing the top into the opening with your thumb or forefinger, which will form a tight little bundle. As you finish them, place the rolls into the baking dish, on top of the sauce.

9. Once all your rolls are in the baking dish, pour the remaining sauce over them. If there's not enough sauce to cover them entirely, add water until the rolls are covered. Cover the baking dish with a lid or aluminum foil and bake for 2½ to 3 hours. Check after 1 hour. If the rolls are no longer covered with liquid, add more water. Check again at the 2-hour mark and add more water, if necessary.

10. Stuffed cabbage is ready when the rolls feel completely soft when pressed with a finger (careful, they're hot). Remove from the oven and serve immediately, or prepare up to 2 days in advance and reheat in the oven before serving. If reheating, just be sure the cabbage rolls are covered with liquid and do not dry out. Serve the cabbage rolls hot, drizzled with extra sauce and garnished with parsley and celery leaves.

(continued) ▶

Lentil-Mushroom Filling

¾ cup jasmine or basmati rice

1 cup brown lentils

2 cups water

Grapeseed or vegetable oil, for sautéing

1 medium onion, diced

12 ounces fresh shiitake mushrooms, stems removed, caps quartered

1¼ cups finely chopped kimchi, store-bought or homemade (page 68)

1½ teaspoons kosher salt

½ teaspoon smoked paprika

2 large eggs, lightly beaten

1. Pour the rice, lentils, and water into a small saucepan, and bring to a boil. Reduce the heat to maintain a simmer and cook for 10 minutes. Remove from the heat, drain through a fine-mesh strainer, and rinse with cold water. Set aside.

2. In a skillet, heat enough oil to coat the bottom of the pan over medium heat. Add the onion and sauté, stirring frequently, until it starts to become translucent, about 5 minutes. Stir in the mushrooms and sauté until the mushrooms reabsorb some of their liquid, about 10 minutes. Add the cooked rice and lentils and stir in the kimchi, salt, paprika, eggs, and any reserved kimchi brine.

3. Assemble and bake the cabbage leaves as directed in Kimchi-Stuffed Cabbage recipe (page 245).

WINE-BRAISED BRISKET WITH BUTTERNUT SQUASH

LIZ

Brisket really gets Jews talking. The mere mention of the word brings up stories of holidays past, aunts who can't cook, aunts who can cook, grandmas force-feeding grandkids, etc. While beef was often very expensive in the old country, brisket became a symbol of plenty in North America, where it was more affordable but no less special.

This brisket is braised for hours, just as many Jewish briskets are, but we incorporate white wine instead of the more typical red, and butternut squash instead of potatoes. This makes for a lighter, brighter brisket, if such a thing exists, so it's a better fit for holiday meals served during the warmer months. Note that the second-cut brisket we recommend for this recipe will not slice as thinly as the first cut. It's softer and fattier. This doesn't bother us. The meat will be so tender you could cut it with a spoon—who needs a thin slice? Also note that if you'd like to make this a more wintry brisket, you can swap the squash for potatoes and/or turnips and put the veggies in an hour earlier than the recipe calls for. Jeffrey prefers it that way, and once again, we agree to disagree.

SERVES 6 TO 8

1½ cups canned diced tomatoes

4 cups beef, chicken, or vegetable broth, store-bought or homemade (page 130 or 123)

1 (750-mL) bottle white wine (pinot grigio, sauvignon blanc, etc.)

1 tablespoon kosher salt

1 teaspoon freshly ground black pepper

1 tablespoon vegetable oil

2½ pounds second-cut brisket (also called deckle)

1 large onion, sliced

Handful of fresh thyme sprigs

1 large butternut squash, peeled, seeded, and chopped into large chunks

Chopped fresh herbs, for serving

---

1. Preheat the oven to 300°F.

2. In a large bowl, mix together the tomatoes, broth, wine, salt, and pepper. In a large enameled Dutch oven (with a tight-fitting lid), heat the oil over medium heat. Place the meat in the pan

to sear, 2 to 3 minutes on each side, or until it is evenly browned.

3. Remove the meat and set aside. Line the bottom of the Dutch oven with onion slices. Place the brisket on top of the

(continued) ▶

▶ (Wine-Braised Brisket with Butternut Squash, *continued*)

onion and pour the tomato mixture over the meat, making sure that the liquid covers the meat entirely. If you are using a larger pot and the liquid does not cover the meat and vegetables, add water until it does. Add the thyme sprigs.

4. Cover and place in the oven for 3½ hours, checking every hour or so to make sure the liquid is still covering the meat. If at any point it isn't, pour hot water into the Dutch oven to make sure the meat remains covered. After 3½ hours, add the butternut squash, making sure to submerge it under the liquid. Cook for 1 hour more, then remove the pot from the oven. Let sit at least 45 minutes before slicing.

5. Brisket tastes even better the next day, reheated in the oven. To serve, scoop out about 3 cups of liquid from the Dutch oven and place in a small saucepot. Cook over medium-low heat until it has reduced into a sauce. Serve the brisket and squash on a platter, with the sauce ladled over the top, and garnish with fresh herbs.

EIGHT

DESSERTS

LIZ In my early twenties, I took a gig making pastries in a small café in Washington, D.C. I was sure that baking cakes and cookies day in and day out would give me just as much pleasure as eating sweets had when I was a kid. As a child, my parents took me to visit my local Jewish bakery every Friday and let me go wild. I ordered black-and-white cookies, hamantaschen, and rugelach for Friday night dessert. But the baker's life was not as sweet as I had hoped. The aroma of sugar-cinnamon mixtures and melted butter became sickening in no time. Surrounded by sweets all day, every day, I found they lost their appeal.

Perhaps unwittingly, perhaps intentionally, my mother imparted upon me a very Ashkenazi Jewish approach to dessert—it should separate holidays and special occasions from regular weeknights, the sacred from the profane (or simply the mundane). In a world of limited resources, cakes and cookies were reserved for times when eating rich food was practically a religious obligation. By indulging in extra sugar, eggs, and fruit, Ashkenazi Jews paid homage to the sacred nature of the day. I like that.

Ashkenazi desserts share a few common elements that come down to the dietary laws and availability of ingredients in central and eastern Europe. Because traditionally meat is often served at festive meals, and dietary laws prohibit dairy consumption following meat, cakes and cookies are generally made with oil instead of butter. Apples, pears, plums, and berries are prevalent since they were plentiful in eastern Europe. Walnuts were one of the most widely available nuts, so they were often incorporated into baked goods for their richness and flavor, and cinnamon was a common spice for cakes and cookies.

When Ashkenazi Jews immigrated to the United States in large numbers, they quickly set up bakeries that served their fellow newcomers. As with many other foods in this book, pastries became richer when they landed on this soil, particularly considering that eggs, flour, and sugar were available for cheap. Honey cake, babka, kichlach, and rugelach were available on a daily basis in America. For many immigrants, these kinds of treats would have been unimaginable back home.

Most desserts in this chapter aren't indulgent. Compotes are a wonderfully light Ashkenazi dessert. "The thought of cake or anything baked, except perhaps the lightest fruit tart, seems excessive after a full meal," writes Mimi Sheraton in her classic cookbook *From My Mother's Kitchen*. I feel exactly the same way after a Passover seder or a Friday night feast. And our Honey Sesame Chews (page 270) make the perfect post-meal snack. They are only slightly sweet, balanced with the savory flavor of sesame and the mild bitterness of poppy seed. And even though I feel strongly that desserts are for special occasions, somehow Bow-Tie Kichel (page 260) transcends the dessert category, and it's totally fine to enjoy it any day of the week.

JEFFREY

I don't have much of a sweet tooth. I tend to skip the dessert course at restaurants and turn down offers of fancy chocolate. And yet I absolutely love Jewish desserts. The way my Grandma Ruth taught me to see it, a proper dessert should never be too sweet and must pair well with herbal tea. It is to be eaten late at night over hushed conversation and then eaten again in the morning with breakfast. And when baking it, you should make an excessive amount so it lasts throughout a holiday or a visit.

Nothing exemplifies this take on dessert better than Grandma's strudel, which she made during early apple season for Rosh Hashanah. It was an approximate replica of the one that her mother made back in Poland. She used to climb her family's apple tree at the height of apple season and pick the fruit, which her mother would mix with homemade plum or strawberry jam. Whenever Grandma Ruth came to visit for the holidays, she'd bring her American version of the dessert. I'd sneak downstairs at midnight to snag a late-night strudel snack, only to find my sister Dahlia doing the same. Those midnight noshes became a family tradition.

Lots of desserts in this chapter follow Grandma's rules. Grandma Fay's Applesauce Cake (page 277), Anna's Passover Sponge Cake (page 280), and Orange-Spiced Rye Honey Cake (page 282) can all be baked in a loaf pan, and work well for any time of day, especially with a *glezel tei*—a glass of tea. I don't take compote with my tea, as is the Russian style, but I do love cooking the more textured Seasonal Fruit Compote (page 257), especially in the summer when there's an abundance of berries and stone fruits and in the fall and winter when apples and pears are always available.

And while I never cared much for sugar cookies, fortunately none of our cookies exactly fit into that category: our hamantaschen (page 264) and schnecken (page 268) are more like pastries; the Black-and-White Cookie Sticks (page 266) are more like cakes; the kichel (page 260) is more like a sweet biscuit; and the Honey Sesame Chews (page 270) are more like confections. Even the ice cream in this chapter—Dark Chocolate and Roasted Beet Ice Cream (page 275)—isn't too sweet. After all, its main ingredient is roasted beets. The ice cream may not pair well with tea on its own, but serve it with sponge cake or applesauce cake and you're in business.

DESSERTS
=RECIPES=

SEASONAL FRUIT COMPOTE

Compote is a stewed fruit dessert that's known for aiding in digestion, perfect for the generations of Jews who suffer from sensitive stomachs and holidays that feature many starchy dishes. "The compote that traditionally closes the seder meal," jokes Michael Wex in *Rhapsody in Schmaltz*, is "a last ditch attempt to counter the binding effects of the matzoh [*sic*]." I loved compote as a kid because it reminded me of a sweeter version of applesauce. Usually we ate compote in the winter with apples and stewed prunes, but sadly never in the early summer when rhubarb and strawberries were in season. Our Wintry Compote is more like the ones I ate as a kid. The variety of apple doesn't really matter. Just note that sweeter apples will lead to sweeter compote. The dried apricots will brighten it all up. The Strawberry-Rhubarb Compote is perfect to serve in little bowls after a meal, but it can also be used as a topping for a Sweet Cheese Blintz (page 224). It's a great way to use strawberries that may be just past their prime. Note that this is a super-quick recipe.

MAKES 3 TO
4 CUPS COMPOTE

Wintry Compote

2 tablespoons honey	½ cup quartered dried pitted prunes (about 4 ounces)	½ cup diced dried apricots (about 4 ounces)	2 teaspoons fresh lemon juice
2 cups water			
1 pound apples (about 3 medium), peeled, cored, and diced			

1. In a heavy-bottomed medium pot, combine the honey and water and bring to a rolling boil. Add the apples, prunes, and apricots and reduce the heat to low. Simmer, stirring regularly to break up the pieces of apple, until the apple pieces are completely softened and broken down, 25 to 30 minutes.

2. Remove the pot from the heat and stir in the lemon juice. Serve warm, at room temperature, or chilled, on its own or with cake and ice cream.

(continued) ▶

▶ (Seasonal Fruit Compote, *continued*)

~~~~~~

Summer Strawberry-Rhubarb Compote

¼ cup honey

1 cup water

1 pound fresh
rhubarb stalks, diced

8 ounces fresh
strawberries, hulled
and diced

1. In a heavy-bottomed medium pot, combine the honey and water and bring to a rolling boil. Add the rhubarb and cook for 5 to 7 minutes, until tender.

2. Remove the pot from the heat and add the strawberries. Stir and let sit for 10 minutes, or until the strawberries completely soften. Serve warm, at room temperature, or chilled, on its own or with cake and ice cream.

BOW-TIE KICHEL

LIZ

A *kichel* ("cookie" in Yiddish) is generally airy and light and not very sweet. Kichel can also refer to a savory cookie, like an onion or poppy seed kichel, which can be found in religious neighborhoods like Boro Park, Brooklyn. The kichlach (plural for kichel) in this recipe are about as simple as it gets and are vaguely reminiscent of a citrus fortune cookie. When kichlach are made fresh, they're nice and crunchy without being too dry, and we don't shy away from making them nice and sweet.

MAKES ABOUT 36 COOKIES

1¾ cups all-purpose flour, plus more as needed

½ teaspoon kosher salt

2 tablespoons sugar, plus ½ cup sugar for rolling out the dough

2 large eggs

4 egg yolks

6 tablespoons vegetable oil

2 tablespoons grated lemon zest

1. Preheat the oven to 350°F. Line a baking sheet with parchment paper.

2. In a medium bowl, mix together the flour, salt, and 2 tablespoons of the sugar. In a separate bowl, combine the eggs, egg yolks, oil, and lemon zest and stir to incorporate. Pour the wet mixture into the flour mixture and mix together swiftly with a fork to form a dough. Knead for about 10 minutes. Add a little bit of flour as needed, but expect the dough to be slightly sticky. After kneading, the dough should be smooth and pliable. Cover the dough with a clean kitchen towel or plastic wrap and let rest for 20 minutes.

3. On a lightly floured surface, sprinkle ¼ cup of the sugar, then roll out the dough to ⅛-inch thickness, pressing the sugar into the bottom of the dough with the rolling pin. Sprinkle the top of the dough with the remaining ¼ cup sugar.

4. Using a sharp paring knife, cut the dough into small rectangles, about 2 x 3 inches. Pinch each rectangle in the middle to form a bow-tie shape or half twist them into bow ties. Place the bow ties on the parchment paper–lined or greased baking sheet.

(continued) ▶

▶ (Bow-Tie Kichel, *continued*)

5. Bake for 15 to 18 minutes until the bottoms are dark and golden in color. If you are baking in multiple batches, let the baking sheet cool completely between batches. This is very important to avoid burnt kichlach.

6. Remove from the oven, let cool, and store in an airtight container. Kichlach are delicious served right out of the oven with tea, but will last for a few days when stored in a cool, dry place.

DEBATE: LATKES VS. HAMANTASCHEN

JEFFREY I can't believe I have to keep arguing with Liz over why her beloved hamantasch doesn't stack up to the latke. It's no debate, really. Starchy veggies fried in fat (and if you're lucky, goose fat) versus an oft-stale triangle with an overly sweet center? No contest. According to the story of Purim, hamantaschen represent the evil protagonist's ears or hat or something like that. Latkes don't purport to represent anything other than fried deliciousness to celebrate a military victory and the winter solstice.

Believe it or not, our argument is a rehashing of a decades-long tradition of faux-intellectual debates over which is the most perfect Jewish food, the latke or the hamantasch. The debates began at the University of Chicago as a means of lightening up the somber mood brought about by disturbing reports from Europe in the years immediately following the Second World War. The exercise quickly spread to other campuses. Professors staged the debates around Hanukkah-time, and each used his or her discipline to make a case for which food is better. These debates continue worldwide. I myself have taken part on two separate occasions, and have always rooted for Team Latke (even when moderating—shhh).

The good news is that the hamantasch recipe in this book is a pastry version that defies my perceptions of the dessert and gives Liz's side a little bit of clout. The way she sees it, freshly baked pastry filled with homemade jam is the pinnacle of Jewish dessert. And the tradition of giving hamantaschen to friends around Purim makes it even sweeter. But still, does this charade need to go on any longer? Let's all just agree that a great hamantasch can be satisfying at best, but a great latke can be transcendent.

PASTRY-STYLE HAMANTASCHEN

 LIZ

"It's hamantaschen time!" read the famous sign I used to see in Ratner's Restaurant on the Lower East Side for two weeks out of the year during the holiday of Purim, when families deliver gift packages called *mishloach manot*.

The predominant type of hamantaschen these days are made with a sugar cookie base, rather than yeast dough, which is how they used to be made. Jeffrey and I prefer these pastrylike versions and are yeast dough converts. Note that the dough can be made the day before you intend to bake it and refrigerated overnight. Give the dough a few minutes to come to room temperature before shaping and rolling. You can fill these pastries with the walnut filling or with jam. If you like a good Danish, try using the Sweet Blintz Filling (page 224).

MAKES ABOUT
16 PASTRIES

FOR THE DOUGH:

1 (¼-ounce) packet active dry yeast (2¼ teaspoons)

⅓ cup lukewarm whole milk

½ cup sugar

2½ cups all-purpose flour, plus more as needed

1 teaspoon kosher salt

1 cup (2 sticks) unsalted butter, chilled and cut into small chunks, about 16 pieces per stick

1 teaspoon pure vanilla extract

1 teaspoon grated lemon zest

¼ cup sour cream, store-bought or homemade (page 24)

1 large egg

1 egg yolk

FOR THE WALNUT FILLING:

¾ cup heavy cream

¼ cup sugar

⅓ cup light brown sugar

⅓ cup honey

2 teaspoons grated orange zest

1½ cups finely chopped walnuts

¼ teaspoon kosher salt

TO ASSEMBLE:

1 large egg

1 teaspoon water

1. TO MAKE THE DOUGH: In a small bowl, stir together the yeast, milk, and 1 teaspoon of the sugar. Set aside for about 5 minutes, until the yeast blooms.

2. In a large bowl, stir together the flour and the salt. Add the cold butter pieces to the flour mixture, rubbing the pieces of butter into the flour using your fingers, until pea-size clumps form. Add the remaining sugar, the vanilla, lemon zest, sour cream, egg, and egg yolk to the flour-butter mixture and whisk to combine. Slowly add the yeast mixture to the flour-butter mixture, stirring just until the dough comes together. Cover and refrigerate the dough for 15 minutes or up to 1 day before baking.

3. TO MAKE THE WALNUT FILLING: In a small saucepan, combine the cream, both sugars, honey, and orange zest and bring to a boil over medium-low heat. Cook until the mixture thickens and darkens, 5 to 7 minutes. Remove from the heat and stir in the nuts and salt. Set aside and let cool.

4. Preheat the oven to 375°F. Line two baking sheets with parchment paper.

5. Divide the dough into 16 equal-size balls, using additional flour to keep the dough from sticking while you work. On a lightly floured surface, roll each ball out to a ¼-inch-thick disk, 3 to 4 inches in diameter.

6. Fill each disk with a generous tablespoon of filling and fold up three sides of the hamantaschen toward the center, pinching the ends together to create a triangle. Set the formed hamantaschen on the lined baking sheets as you work.

7. Beat the egg with the water and coat the hamantaschen generously with egg mixture to seal the seams. Set aside to rise for 20 to 30 minutes.

8. Bake for 15 to 20 minutes until golden brown. Hamantaschen may be stored in an airtight container at room temperature for up to 2 days. They can also be frozen when completely cooled.

BLACK-AND-WHITE COOKIE STICKS

LIZ → Jeffrey and I assumed for decades that the black-and-white cookie, an iconic New York treat, had Jewish origins. We even served these black-and-whites at The Gefilteria's launch event and frosted matzos in this style for our first Passover production run. It turns out that we were wrong. Black-and-whites originated in upstate New York and were adopted by New York's Jewish bakeries as they increased their cookie inventories. The truth doesn't make us love these cookies any less.

"The thing about eating the black-and-white cookie," Jerry says to Elaine in a classic episode of *Seinfeld*, "is you want to get some black and some white in each bite." I agree. This black-and-white cookie stick is designed so each bite is the best bite. Note that making black-and-whites can be messy. Be sure to have plenty of wax paper available and ice your cookies on a wire rack to avoid them sticking to the paper.

MAKES 18 COOKIES

FOR THE COOKIES:

1¼ cups all-purpose flour

½ teaspoon baking soda

½ teaspoon kosher salt

⅓ cup well-shaken store-bought buttermilk

½ teaspoon vanilla extract

⅓ cup (about 5 tablespoons) unsalted butter, at room temperature

⅔ cup granulated sugar

1 large egg, at room temperature

FOR THE WHITE ICING:

2 cups confectioners' sugar

Pinch of salt

About 1 teaspoon fresh lemon juice

3 tablespoons warm water

FOR THE BLACK ICING:

3 ounces bitter or unsweetened chocolate, or ½ cup bittersweet chocolate chips

1 tablespoon unsweetened cocoa powder

2 cups confectioners' sugar

¼ cup boiling water

---

1. TO MAKE THE COOKIES: Preheat the oven to 350°F. Line two baking sheets with parchment paper.

2. In a medium bowl, whisk together the flour, baking soda, and salt. In a small bowl, stir together the buttermilk and vanilla.

3. In a large bowl using a hand mixer, or in the bowl of a stand mixer fitted with the paddle attachment, beat together the butter and granulated sugar, until the butter turns pale and becomes fluffy, about 4 minutes. Add the egg and continue to beat until incorporated.

4. Using a rubber spatula, gently stir one-third of the flour mixture into the butter mixture. Pour in half the buttermilk mixture. Add one-third of the flour mixture, then the remaining buttermilk mixture, and finally the remaining flour mixture. Be sure to scrape down the sides of the bowl between additions. Cover and refrigerate the resulting batter for at least 15 minutes before proceeding.

5. Fill a piping bag or a zip-top plastic bag with the batter, and pipe out strips of batter about 3 inches long and 1½ inches wide onto the lined baking sheets. Bake for about 10 minutes on the middle rack of the oven, until the cookies are lightly golden in color. If needed, bake for an additional minute or two. Remove from the oven, transfer to a wire rack, and let cool.

6. TO MAKE THE WHITE ICING: Place the confectioners' sugar in a bowl and stir in the salt, lemon juice, and warm water. The mixture should be loose. If needed, stir in another tablespoon of warm water. Place the wire rack over a sheet of parchment paper and ice half of each cookie with the white icing, gently spooning it onto the cookie. No need to be precise. Transfer the cookies to a clean wire rack set over a fresh sheet of parchment paper.

7. TO MAKE THE BLACK ICING: In the top of a double boiler or in a heatproof bowl set over a saucepan of simmering water, combine the chocolate, cocoa, and confectioners' sugar. Pour in the boiling water and stir well until the chocolate has melted and the icing is loose, dark, and liquid. The texture should be similar to a creamy soup.

8. Remove from the heat and keep stirring, then carefully ice the second half of each cookie. To make a clean line, cover the white half of the cookie with a bit of wax paper while spooning on the black icing, allowing excess icing to simply drip over the sides of the cookie. Let cool in the refrigerator for 5 minutes to set the icing, then store in a cool, dry place to prevent melting. The cookie sticks are best stored in a paper bag or an airtight container.

BESSIE WEINSTEIN'S SCHNECKEN

Adapted from Stephanie Levine via Joan Nathan

LIZ

Schnecken means "snails" in German and Yiddish. As a dessert, it's mostly known as a sweet cinnamon bun found in Germany and German enclaves in the United States. But Bessie Weinstein's schnecken are different. They're flaky, like dairy rugelach, sweetened with jam, and dusted with cinnamon-sugar. According to her family, Bessie Weinstein—whom I first learned about when recipe testing for Joan Nathan—was a sharp, wise, and classy woman who either got this recipe from a friend sometime in the 1940s or, more likely, found it on a cream cheese box.

Wherever it came from, schnecken were Bessie's signature recipe, and now they've become one of mine. They're delicate and easy to adapt. This recipe makes four separate logs that will make dozens of schnecken cookies when sliced. I often wrap two of the unbaked logs in plastic wrap, then aluminum foil, and freeze them for the future. When I want more schnecken, I let them thaw slightly while the oven heats up (not too long, or they'll get too soft) and bake them off. Sometimes I use different jams for each log to mix things up a bit. Note that the dough is delicate, so work quickly and carefully when rolling and wrapping for the freezer.

MAKES 48 TO 60 COOKIES (12 TO 15 COOKIES PER LOG)

8 ounces cream cheese, store-bought or homemade (page 25), at room temperature

8 ounces unsalted butter, store-bought or homemade (page 18), at room temperature

2 cups all-purpose flour, plus more for rolling out dough

1½ cups raisins, golden or otherwise

1½ cups walnuts

1 (12-ounce) jar apricot or raspberry jam (or whatever flavor you like best), store-bought or homemade (page 30)

2 teaspoons sugar

½ teaspoon ground cinnamon

1. In a large bowl using a hand mixer or spoon, mix the cream cheese and butter. Stir in the flour to form a dough. Form the dough into 4 equal balls. Wrap the dough balls in plastic wrap and refrigerate for about 5 hours, until the dough is firm to the touch.

2. Preheat the oven to 375°F. Line two baking sheets with parchment paper.

3. Pulse the raisins and walnuts together in a food processor until coarsely chopped.

4. Generously flour your work surface and roll out one ball of dough into a thin rectangle, about 8 x 12 inches. Note that the dough will be hard when it first comes out of the fridge but will soften as you roll it. The dough can become delicate as it softens, so work quickly but gently to avoid tearing. Using one-quarter of the jam (about 3 tablespoons), coat the dough, leaving a ½-inch border all around the edges, then spread a layer of the raisins and walnuts

(about 6 tablespoons) over the jam. Carefully roll up the rectangle from one of the longer sides like a jelly roll and tuck the ends underneath the log. Repeat with the remaining balls of dough.

5. In a small bowl, mix together the sugar and cinnamon. Using your hands, coat each schnecken log with cinnamon-sugar mix, rubbing it on the top and the sides. Place the logs, seam side down, on the lined baking sheets.

6. Bake the logs for 30 to 35 minutes. Your schnecken are ready when they are ever-so-slightly browned and crisp on top and on the sides without being dry. It's best to keep an eye on the baking, starting at the 30-minute mark. Once out of the oven and slightly cooled, gently slice the logs with a serrated knife into 2-inch pieces (any smaller and they will crumble). Nosh on the end pieces while slicing and display each whole piece sideways to show off the snail-like swirl of the cookie.

HONEY SESAME CHEWS

JEFFREY

Sesame chews appeared around the Jewish holidays during my childhood and I'd snack on them incessantly in the weeks that followed. We added poppy seeds to this version to give them some extra color and flavor. This is a great project to do with the whole family, and the chews are a fun giveaway for parties and special occasions. For a more fanciful presentation, wrap each candy in a piece of parchment paper and twist the ends, like saltwater taffy.

MAKES ABOUT 32
1-INCH CANDIES

Vegetable oil or unsalted butter, for greasing the pan

1¼ cups sesame seeds

5½ tablespoons poppy seeds

⅓ cup honey

⅓ cup packed light brown sugar

Generous pinch of salt

½ teaspoon fresh lemon juice

---

1. Grease a baking sheet.

2. In a small skillet, toast the sesame seeds over medium-low heat, stirring continuously, until lightly golden and fragrant, 8 to 10 minutes. Remove from the pan and place in a large bowl with the poppy seeds. Stir to combine and set aside.

3. In the same skillet, over medium heat, stir together the honey, brown sugar, and generous pinch of salt. Bring to a boil and cook for 2 minutes without stirring. Stir in the lemon juice and remove the skillet from the heat. Pour the mixture into the bowl with the sesame and poppy seeds and, using a rubber spatula, stir to incorporate. Using greased hands, spread the sesame mixture onto the prepared baking sheet, creating an even 1-inch-thick layer. Pressing the mixture into a rectangle will help you get the cleanest lines when cutting later. Wait for it to cool slightly, about 2 minutes, then score the candy into 1-inch squares using a sharp knife.

4. Let the mixture cool completely, about 30 minutes, then break into individual pieces along the scored lines. Store in an airtight container with the layers of candies separated by sheets of parchment paper, or wrap them individually in parchment paper. They will stay crunchy for up to 1 week.

CHEESECAKE WITH CURRANT GLAZE AND CARAWAY CRUST

This cheesecake incorporates farmer's cheese, cream cheese, and sour cream, a hybrid of the German and New York styles. Cheesecake went mainstream in the United States in the 1930s, when a baker in Chicago, the founder of Sara Lee, brought it to national acclaim by freezing and selling the cakes nationwide.

My father was always known for his cheesecake. He was given the recipe in the early 1970s by an older Jewish colleague who was trying to fix him up with her daughter. "I looked like Charles Manson at the time," he said, "but I was Jewish so I guess she was able to overlook certain red flags." There's a lot of cream cheese, sugar, and sour cream in this cake, but it's sort of Jewish, and it's amazing, so I'm willing to overlook certain red flags.

Farmer's cheese gives the cake a lighter texture and caraway seeds in the crust add a savory note. If you can't find graham cracker crumbs in the store, just purchase graham crackers and crush them in a food processor. You'll need 10 to 12 full graham crackers. Substituting gluten-free bread crumbs for graham crackers (or simply forgoing the crust altogether) will make this a gluten-free dessert.

MAKES 1 9-INCH CHEESECAKE

FOR THE CRUST:

1½ cups graham cracker crumbs

4 tablespoons (½ stick) unsalted butter, melted

3 tablespoons sugar

4 teaspoons caraway seeds

FOR THE CAKE:

12 ounces cream cheese, store-bought or homemade (page 25), at room temperature

12 ounces farmer's cheese, store-bought or homemade (page 21), at room temperature

1½ cups sugar

4 large eggs, at room temperature

1½ teaspoons vanilla extract

16 ounces sour cream, store-bought or homemade (page 24), at room temperature

FOR THE RED CURRANT GLAZE:

1 teaspoon cornstarch

2 tablespoons sugar

2 teaspoons fresh lemon juice

2 tablespoons water

2 cups fresh or frozen red currants

1. Preheat the oven to 375°F. Grease a 9-inch springform pan.

2. TO MAKE THE CRUST: Combine the crust ingredients in a small bowl and pack the

(continued) ▶

► (Cheesecake with Currant Glaze and Caraway Crust, *continued*)

crust mixture firmly into the bottom of the prepared pan.

3. TO MAKE THE CAKE: In the bowl of a stand mixer fitted with the paddle attachment, or in a large bowl using a hand mixer, beat together the cream cheese and farmer's cheese until fluffy, gradually adding the sugar in increments, then adding the eggs one by one. Add the vanilla and sour cream and beat until incorporated. Pour the mixture into the pan over the crust. Bake for 30 minutes. Turn off the oven and let the cheesecake sit inside, undisturbed, for at least 2 hours so it sets properly. Place it in the refrigerator and let cool completely before serving, at least 6 hours. Cheesecake is delicate, so be gentle.

4. TO MAKE THE RED CURRANT GLAZE: While cake is cooling in the oven, in a small saucepan, combine the cornstarch, sugar, lemon juice, and water and cook over very low heat, stirring, until the mixture starts to thicken, about 4 minutes. Immediately stir in the currants and cook, stirring occasionally, until the mixture begins to bubble up slightly and thicken, 10 to 12 minutes more. Remove from the heat and let cool. The glaze can be prepared up to 3 days in advance of serving and stored in the refrigerator.

5. The cheesecake will keep in the refrigerator for up to 1 week. Serve it chilled, with a spoonful of currant glaze on top and a cup of coffee.

DARK CHOCOLATE AND ROASTED BEET ICE CREAM

JEFFREY It's easy to forget that ice cream was around in Europe even before it became an all-American dessert. The ingredients—milk, cream, eggs, and sugar—plus the blocks of ice stored during pre-refrigeration summers, made it a luxurious treat for the wealthy. As ice and sugar became cheaper in the nineteenth century, ice cream became much more common. In small towns in eastern Europe, ice cream was sold at local candy shops. A close family friend who grew up in Dubienka, Poland, before the Second World War remembers fondly how a shop owner would give out free ice cream to children who helped him churn it.

Something about the sweetness of beets and their deep crimson color feels so in line with the Ashkenazi dessert tradition, although I doubt that Jews from Dubienka were experimenting with vegetable-flavored ice creams. I like to leave the mint out and use it simply as a garnish, but Liz thinks the ice cream is best with the mint infused, as described in the recipe. We both agree, however, that the chocolate should come from a high-quality bar. Note that this is a longer, more involved recipe and requires an ice cream maker.

MAKES ABOUT
1 PINT ICE CREAM

---

9 ounces whole beets (about 3 medium), scrubbed

½ cup plus 2 tablespoons whole milk

½ cup heavy cream

¼ cup loosely packed fresh mint leaves (optional)

2 large egg yolks

¼ cup sugar

2 ounces dark chocolate

Kosher salt

Chocolate shavings, for garnish

Sprig of fresh mint, for garnish

---

1. Preheat the oven to 400°F. Wrap the beets individually in aluminum foil and place them on a baking sheet. Roast the beets until they are fork-tender, 40 minutes to 1 hour, depending on the size of the beets (larger beets take longer). Remove from the oven and set aside to cool. When cool enough to handle, peel the beets (the skin should peel off easily under cold running water). Quarter the beets and liquefy in a blender with 2 tablespoons of the milk. If your beets don't completely liquefy in the blender, pass the mixture through a fine-mesh strainer lined with four layers

(continued) ▶

▶ (Dark Chocolate and Roasted Beet Ice Cream, *continued*)

of wet cheesecloth to remove the solids. Set the beet liquid aside.

2. In a small saucepan, combine the cream, remaining ½ cup milk, and mint (if using) and heat over low heat. Using the bottom of a jar or glass, muddle the mint into the milk-cream mixture to release its flavors. Cook over low heat, stirring occasionally, for about 15 minutes. Meanwhile, in a small bowl, whisk together the egg yolks and sugar until light in color and set aside. If using mint, remove the leaves from the milk-cream mixture with a slotted spoon.

3. Increase the heat to medium-low and stream a couple of tablespoons of the hot milk-cream mixture into the sugar-egg mixture, whisking continuously. Pour the sugar-egg mixture into the pot with the hot milk-cream mixture to make a custard. Stir continuously until it thickens and turns a pale yellow, about 10 minutes. Do not let the custard

boil. The custard is ready when it coats the back of a spoon. Remove from the heat and pour into a large bowl to let cool slightly.

4. Meanwhile, melt the chocolate in the top of a double boiler. Stir the melted chocolate into the custard, then stir the beet liquid in.

5. Place the chocolate-beet ice cream base into an airtight container or your ice cream maker's canister, covered with a lid or plastic wrap, and refrigerate until chilled, at least a couple of hours or up to overnight.

6. In your ice cream maker, churn the ice cream base according to the manufacturer's instructions. Store finished ice cream in the freezer; transfer it to the fridge 15 to 20 minutes before serving to soften it a bit. Garnish with chocolate shavings and a sprig of mint.

GRANDMA FAY'S APPLESAUCE CAKE

 LIZ

I first came across a formula for applesauce cake while looking through my grandmother's old recipe box. I was immediately drawn to this quick bread because it featured warming spices like cinnamon and allspice and was a great way to use all the applesauce I'd been making. Applesauce cake was hardly a Fay Alpern original. Apples found their way into many Jewish desserts, and applesauce cakes like this one started making appearances in cookbooks in the 1940s. My theory is that with the increased nutrition awareness of the 1940s, housewives began using applesauce to cut down on the fat in their cakes while still baking something flavorful and rich—similar to the use of applesauce in vegan baking. Also, applesauce cakes were usually pareve, neither meat nor dairy, making this an easy cake to keep around for any occasion. This recipe is super simple, and you likely have these ingredients around the house.

**MAKES 1
9 X 5-INCH LOAF**

¼ cup vegetable oil, plus more for the pan

1½ cups raisins

¾ cup packed light brown sugar

1 large egg, beaten

¾ cup Apple-Pear Sauce (page 26) or store-bought applesauce

1½ cups pastry flour or all-purpose flour

¾ teaspoon baking soda

¾ cup chopped walnuts

⅛ teaspoon kosher salt

¾ teaspoon ground cinnamon

½ teaspoon ground allspice

1. Preheat the oven to 325°F. Grease a 9 x 5-inch loaf pan with the oil.

2. Place the raisins in a medium bowl and pour boiling water over them. Meanwhile, in a separate medium bowl, whisk together the ¼ cup of oil and the brown sugar with a fork or a whisk until the sugar is well integrated. Whisk in the egg, then stir in the Apple-Pear Sauce.

3. In a separate bowl, stir together the flour, baking soda, walnuts, salt, cinnamon, and allspice. Drain the raisins and stir them into the dry ingredients.

4. Pour the dry ingredients into the bowl with the apple-pear sauce mixture and stir to combine. Pour the batter into the prepared loaf pan. Bake for about 1 hour, until a toothpick inserted into the center comes out clean. Serve warm, with coffee or tea, for dessert or for breakfast.

RUTH'S APPLE STRUDEL

JEFFREY

This recipe is almost identical to the one I wrote down while trailing my grandmother in the kitchen as a young boy. The dessert is best at room temperature, surprisingly, when the apple mixture has cooled and set a bit. It can be served after meals, or, preferably, late at night with herbal tea in a glass mug and with great company. Unlike a classic Austrian strudel, Grandma Ruth's dough doesn't require pulling and stretching—or butter. Take your time and be sure to roll it thinly and evenly, and it will come together.

SERVES 10 TO 12

FOR THE DOUGH:

½ cup vegetable oil, plus more for greasing the pan

3 cups all-purpose flour, plus more as needed

½ cup sugar

2 teaspoons baking powder

2 large eggs, beaten

¼ cup warm water

FOR THE FILLING:

3 pounds McIntosh apples (if not available, use Braeburn, Cortland, or Granny Smith), peeled, cored, and thinly sliced

1 tablespoon sugar

2 teaspoons ground cinnamon

⅔ cup strawberry jam, store-bought or homemade (page 30)

2 tablespoons fresh lemon juice

2 teaspoons matzo meal or cornstarch

1. Preheat the oven to 375°F. Grease a 9 x 13-inch baking pan with oil.

2. TO MAKE THE DOUGH: In a large bowl, gently stir together the flour, sugar, and baking powder. Stir in the ½ cup oil, eggs, and warm water to form a dough. Set aside.

3. TO MAKE THE FILLING: In a large bowl, coat the apple slices with the sugar, cinnamon, jam, lemon juice, and matzo meal.

4. Divide the dough into two equal parts. On a floured surface, roll each ball of dough until it is approximately ¼ inch thick. Press one sheet of dough against the bottom and up the sides of the prepared baking pan and fill with the apple mixture. Place the second layer of dough on top of the apples, tucking the dough into the pan. Poke holes in the top of the dough with a fork to vent steam while baking.

5. Bake for 50 minutes to 1 hour, or until fully browned on top. Serve warm or preferably at room temperature. The strudel can be stored in an airtight container at room temperature for a few days or in the fridge for up to a week.

ANNA'S PASSOVER SPONGE CAKE

Adapted from Anna Gershenson

Everyone loves to complain about Passover desserts, including me. But this sponge cake is moist, with a delicate lemon flavor, making it a delicious dessert even after the holiday is over. The key is to aerate the potato starch and matzo cake meal, and to avoid overbeating the egg whites, as outlined in the recipe.

Anna Gershenson, who shared this recipe with us, famously always baked two for her Passover seder, one for the guests and another for her mother. This is not unlike Jeffrey's Grandma Ruth, who always brought three apple strudels to High Holiday celebrations: one for the guests, one for Jeffrey, and a third for one of his sisters. I suppose that some cakes are just too good to be shared, even on Passover. This recipe should be made in a straight-sided metal tube pan, ideally one with a removable bottom.

MAKES 1 CAKE;
SERVES 10 TO 12

¼ cup sifted
potato starch

¾ cup sifted matzo
cake meal

10 large eggs, at
room temperature

1¼ cups sugar

⅓ cup fresh
lemon juice

1 tablespoon packed
grated lemon zest

Pinch of salt

Butter or oil for
greasing the pan

Fresh fruit,
for serving

---

1. Preheat the oven to 350°F.

2. Sift together the potato starch and matzo cake meal into a bowl three times to aerate. If you don't have a sifter, you can use a fine-mesh strainer. Set aside.

3. Separate the eggs and place the whites and yolks in separate large bowls. Using a hand mixer, beat the egg yolks on medium-high speed. Gradually add the sugar, 1 tablespoon at a time, occasionally scraping down the sides of the bowl to incorporate all the sugar. Beat for 5 minutes until the yolks look

bleached and thick. Gradually add the lemon juice and beat for 5 minutes more. Add the zest during the last minute of beating.

4. Using a hand mixer with very clean beaters, beat the egg whites on medium speed until foamy, about 1 minute, then add the salt. Continue beating until the egg whites are thick and firm and hold soft peaks, about 3 minutes more.

5. Using a rubber spatula, fold the starch mixture into the egg yolks, one-third at a time, folding it in quickly but gently, until

the dry ingredients are fully incorporated. Then gently fold in the egg whites, a bit at a time, until completely incorporated. Stir gently, being careful not to deflate the egg whites.

6. Pour the batter into a greased straight-sided metal tube pan, preferably one with a removeable bottom.

7. Bake for 50 to 55 minutes until the cake top is brown and springs back when touched. It should not be loose or wobbly. Remove from the oven. Let cool completely, then invert the pan. Alternatively, to prevent the cake from deflating too much, you can cool the cake using our friend's family's teacup method. Once the cake has cooled for about 5 minutes, flip a teacup upside down and invert the tube pan so its protruding center rests on the upside-down cup. The cake will still deflate, but it will do so facing downward and so will retain its height. When cool, using a sharp, thin knife, separate the edges of the cake from the edges of the pan. Slice and serve with fresh fruit.

ORANGE-SPICED RYE HONEY CAKE

JEFFREY

Honey cake emerges from its hibernation around the High Holidays in the fall, when honey and other sweet foods are eaten to usher in a sweet new year. But as much as this is an early fall cake for the holidays, its warming spices make it a perfect winter cake that works both for dessert and in the morning with a cup of coffee.

The rye adds a rustic feel, a feature of older Jewish and rural French honey cake recipes. Try cutting out the sugar altogether if you prefer a more subtle sweetness. We often bake our honey cake in a loaf pan, but for special occasions, a Bundt pan looks beautiful. If using a standard 10- or 12-cup Bundt pan, you'll need to double this recipe, and let it cool for an hour before removing it from the pan.

MAKES 1
9 X 5-INCH LOAF;
SERVES 10 TO 12

1½ cups vegetable oil, plus more for greasing the pan

3 large eggs

1 cup sugar

1 cup pure honey

¾ cup lukewarm coffee (brewed and cooled slightly)

1 teaspoon packed grated orange zest

1½ cups all-purpose flour

1 cup rye flour

2 teaspoons baking powder

½ teaspoon baking soda

½ teaspoon kosher salt

2 teaspoons ground cinnamon

¼ teaspoon ground ginger

¼ teaspoon ground cloves

---

1. Preheat the oven to 350°F. Generously grease a 9 x 5-inch loaf pan with oil.

2. In a large bowl, whisk together the 1½ cups of oil, the eggs, sugar, honey, coffee, and orange zest. In a separate large bowl, whisk together the flours, baking powder, baking soda, salt, cinnamon, ginger, and cloves.

3. Make a well in the center of the flour mixture and pour in the egg mixture, then stir with a fork or a whisk until the batter is smooth and free of lumps.

4. Pour the batter into the prepared pan and bake for 50 to 55 minutes, until set in the middle—the cake should hold firm when lightly pressed on top. Be careful not to leave it in the oven for too long or it will dry out.

5. Let the cake cool in the pan for at least 30 minutes (1 hour for a Bundt cake) before very carefully inverting it and removing the pan. Slice and serve with fresh fruit and tea.

∼NINE∼

BEVERAGES

JEFFREY I was one of those unfortunate children whose parents didn't allow him to drink soda. To be sure, I overdosed on sugary soft drinks whenever my mother wasn't looking—at friends' houses or at summer camp—but at home with my family I was stuck with plain seltzer if I wanted a bubbly fix. There was one exception, however: my parents allowed me to drink Dr. Brown's sodas whenever we ate at the Jewish deli. I ordered cream soda or root beer and the occasional black cherry—really any flavor but Cel-Ray. This was Dr. Brown's notorious celery-flavored soft drink. I never actually tasted it, but based on that pale green can, how could I? Celery-flavored soda had to be gross.

One Passover, when I was about eleven, my father brought home 2-liter bottles of the stuff for the weeklong holiday (Passover was the other soda loophole). I couldn't believe it. "Cel-Ray?" I remember yelling, in near-tantrum mode. "You bought celery soda instead of cream soda?!?" It seemed ludicrous. In protest, I waived my soda privileges that holiday.

Years later, as an adult, I met my friend and deli aficionado David Sax at the 2nd Ave Deli. He ordered a Cel-Ray. I asked, somewhat incredulously, "Did you really just order that?" He replied flatly, "There's nothing better with pastrami." David forced me to take a sip. Holy crap, it was amazing. Like a more refreshing version of ginger ale. Paired with the hot pastrami and spicy deli mustard, it was heavenly. I was shocked. I felt an urge to drink Cel-Ray all the time just to make up for all those celery soda–less years. In the heat of the summer, I also appreciated celery soda's cooling properties.

The day after my lunch with David, I called my father. It had been fifteen years since our soda fight, but it's never too late for a mea culpa, right? I reminded him of my intransigence and shortsightedness as a preteen, then I apologized. "I just wasn't ready for Cel-Ray then," I confessed. Ever since, I haven't ordered anything else to drink with a deli sandwich. Liz and I have even been taking it a step further, making our own Celery Syrup (page 299) so we can re-create the experience at home. We've been playing around with other less conventional syrups, too, like Caraway Syrup (page 300), Cucumber-Dill Syrup (page 297), and Rhubarb Syrup (page 300).

Yet as much as I appreciate a refreshing soda when at a deli, perhaps my mother's strict rules paid off, because I tend to prefer less-sugary drinks. Since I began making lacto-fermented pickles (see chapter two), I've been deeply excited by fermented beverages and tonics. "Before there were tanks of compressed CO_2 to carbonate sweet syrups into sodas, there was the natural carbonation produced by fermentation," writes Sandor Katz in *The Art of Fermentation*. The less-sugary beverages we include in this chapter fall into a loosely defined category called kvass, a kind of catchall Slavic term for fermented sour drinks, which, in most cases, are quite healthy and invigorating. Some of the kvass recipes in this chapter call for the same fermentation process as many of the lacto-fermented pickles from chapter two. In Russia, where kvass is ubiquitous, the term generally refers to a fermented drink made from stale rye. This rye kvass served an important function in Russia and beyond for centuries. In Europe as a whole, water from wells and rivers was contaminated, so drinks had to be prepared specially. Kvass was, at times, a safer alternative to water. It was said, "Even if it turns your nose aside, at least it's kvass, not water."

When Liz and I first began cooking together, we were making lots of borscht. We took a traditional approach and incorporated the sour liquid from fermented beets, called *rossel* in Yiddish, to provide that sour kick. But the *rossel* was too good to only use for soup. We began producing the *rossel* for beet kvass by fermenting beets with ginger and straining the liquid, which turns an otherworldly magenta that Liz and I continually marvel at. The fermentation process essentially pulls all the color and vitamins from the beets.

As was the case with borscht, once we began serving the beet tonic at outdoor markets around New York, sometimes spliced with fresh-squeezed lemonade, Ukrainian immigrants would find us, order a drink, and tell us about drinking kvass as children back home. Poles sipped our beet kvass and reminisced about *barscz*, yet another version of the drink. But mostly, the same folks who were most excited about the health benefits of kombucha and turmeric found our booth.

I like to think of myself, and the beverage recipes in this book, as a bridge between the old-timers and the contemporary health nuts. It excites me to imagine what would happen if folks from different generations all tried these beverages in their homes. They could be neighbors in New York City, and generations apart, but the power of kvass might just bring them together without their even knowing it.

〰️

LIZ ➙

Like many of my American Jewish friends, I didn't grow up with much alcohol around me. My mother's maiden name is Sober, and there's a joke in my family that that entire branch of her family lives up to the reputation. To be honest, I hadn't seen more than a single glass of syrupy Manischewitz—the American standard for overly sweet sacramental wine—at my family's holiday table, and even then it was just for ritual purposes.

Back in Europe, however, wine and spirits played an important role. Vodka, brandy, schnapps, slivovitz, mead, wine, and fruit aperitifs were all available and enjoyed, mostly by men, on special occasions like holidays, weddings, and other *simchas*. Even families with limited means would provide drinks for their neighbors when a celebration was held at their home. For one of my favorite Jewish holidays, Purim, it became customary to drink so much that you'd mix up the main characters in the story, confusing the villain, Haman, for the hero, Mordechai.

The relationship between Ashkenazi Jews and alcohol goes beyond the holidays, however, and ties in to commerce. Since Jews in Europe were unable to own land for centuries, many worked as tavernkeepers and brewers servicing a non-Jewish clientele. Jews were also active as merchants in the Polish and Ukrainian liquor trades. This special relationship between Ashkenazi Jews and the European alcohol trade only lasted through the mid-nineteenth century, however, when changing political realities in Europe forced many Jews out of the alcohol profession.

My personal relationship to booze really blossomed when I moved to Quebec as a college student—where the drinking age is eighteen—and encountered the legacy of legendary Jewish bootlegging billionaire Edgar Bronfman. In Montreal, I discovered a Jewish community in which drinking felt like a healthy part of the culture. I began taking part in a weekly *tisch*—a Hasidic-style celebratory gathering at which guests sing songs and the drinks flow freely. Every Friday night, following Shabbat dinner, we'd sit around the table with our rabbi, toasting with whiskey late into the evening with cheers of "*L'chaim!*"—to life. Manischewitz wine was nowhere to be found. At a *tisch*, there's a spiritual and communal feeling that underlies the singing and toasting, taking the act of drinking one step beyond rote ritual blessings. When I share a *l'chaim* over a Pickle Brine Bloody Mary (page 305) or Sour Dill Martini (page 306), I continue to think of my nights at those *tisches*, when I felt fully present in the moment, clinking glasses and sharing drinks with my community.

BEVERAGES
⇒ RECIPES ⇐

BEET AND GINGER KVASS

LIZ

Beet kvass was a by-product of preserving leftover beets from the root cellar in brine. Our kvass is like a natural beet soda that aids in digestion thanks to its probiotic properties. Be sure to review our fermentation tips (page 44) before you begin the process. Using a splash of beet kvass from a previous batch kick-starts the fermentation process, but it's not necessary. This recipe calls for extended wait times.

MAKES 2 QUARTS KVASS

---

2 quarts filtered water

¾ teaspoon kosher salt

3½ pounds beets, peeled and halved

3 ounces fresh ginger, scrubbed and coarsely chopped

Splash of beet kvass from a previous batch (if available)

FOR SIMPLE SYRUP (OPTIONAL)

¼ cup boiling water

¼ cup sugar

1. Fill a gallon-size crock or glass jar with the filtered water. Add the salt and stir until it has dissolved. Place the beets and ginger in the crock and add a drop of kvass from a previous batch, if available.

2. Use a plate or wooden board to cover the beets and keep them beneath the brine. Cover the crock with a clean kitchen towel and let sit at room temperature for 7 to 10 days. On day 7, taste the kvass. The flavor should be full-bodied and earthy with a hint of sour, but it shouldn't taste like vinegar. If it isn't to your liking yet, let sit for another day or two. When ready, remove any large pieces of yeast by straining the liquid through a fine-mesh strainer and pouring into a glass vessel with a tight-fitting screw-on lid. Reserve the beets for making Clove and Spice Pickled Beets (page 72).

3. For a less-sour, slightly sweeter drink, make a simple syrup by pouring the boiling water into a small bowl and stirring in the sugar until it has completely dissolved. Let the simple syrup cool completely, then stir it into the kvass, 1 tablespoon at a time to taste.

4. Whether or not you are sweetening the kvass, note that the drink is particularly delicious when slightly carbonated. Leave the sealed bottle at room temperature for about 4 hours before storing in the refrigerator. Additional natural carbonation will build up after several days in the refrigerator, so open carefully. Serve chilled. The kvass will stay delicious in your refrigerator for up to 4 months.

LONG-FORGOTTEN LETTUCE KVASS

JEFFREY

Liz and I almost couldn't believe that lettuce kvass was a thing until fermentation guru Sandor Katz sent us an academic paper about the forgotten Jewish tradition of turning bitter lettuce into a refreshing drink. Lettuce kvass was apparently all the rage among Jews in Poland and the Ukraine between the First and Second World Wars.

The recipe calls upon the same lacto-fermentation technique as Beet and Ginger Kvass (page 290) so be sure to review our fermentation tips (page 44) before you begin. Lettuce kvass is best served chilled. And while it may seem like it will mix well with seltzer or booze, you'll find that lettuce kvass is best on its own, when it can be its own eccentric self. Note that this recipe calls for a quick prep time but an extended wait time.

MAKES 2 QUARTS KVASS

---

2 quarts
filtered water

1½ teaspoons
kosher salt

5 tablespoons honey

1 head romaine
lettuce, cleaned and
coarsely chopped

1. Pour the filtered water into a half-gallon jar or ceramic crock. Add the salt and 2 tablespoons of the honey and stir until dissolved. Place the lettuce in the water.

2. CREATE A SEAL: If fermenting in a crock, use a plate or wooden board to cover the lettuce and keep it beneath the brine—the weight of the plate is enough to keep the leaves submerged. If fermenting in a jar, use an empty smaller jar to do the same (see page 45 for detailed sealing instructions). Cover with a kitchen towel to keep out dust and bugs and let sit at room temperature for 4 days.

3. Strain the liquid completely, discarding the lettuce, and pour it into a glass vessel with a tight-fitting screw-on lid. Pour the remaining 3 tablespoons honey into the bottle, seal tightly, and shake to dissolve the honey. Let sit at room temperature for 4 days to create natural carbonation. If the weather is particularly warm, the carbonation may take less time. You can test it by opening the jar; if you hear the release of gas, you're in business. If not, close it up and let it sit out for a little longer. Store in the refrigerator for up to 4 months. Carbonation will continue to build up slightly, so open carefully.

FROM LEFT: **Russian Rye Kvass** (page 293),
Parsley Kombucha (Tea Kvass) (page 295),
Beet and Ginger Kvass (page 290), **Long-Forgotten Lettuce Kvass** (page 291)

RUSSIAN RYE KVASS

Rye kvass was traditionally brewed using stale rye bread, herbs, and fruit. Kvass is still sold in Russia today from street carts, not unlike how it was sold a century ago on the streets of Moscow and Kiev, and even the Lower East Side. Yet rye kvass today is mass-produced, just like any other soft drink, without a hint of rye.

Try this recipe when you have leftover rye bread on hand and brag to your Russian friends that you're brewing kvass at home. Don't be surprised if they invite themselves over to try it and then tell you it doesn't taste anything like kvass. They're used to the commercial stuff, but this kvass is way better. Liz and I have found that using rye starter adds an unexpected fruity essence to the drink, like a nectar, without adding any fruit. This recipe calls for champagne yeast, which is inexpensive and can be found in most beer supply shops or online (see Resources, page 327). Active dry yeast also works in a pinch. "Borukh's [kvass] . . . explodes from the bottle as though shot from a gun," writes Sholem Aleichem in his story *Motl, The Cantor's Son*. While ours is not as powerful as Borukh's kvass, use caution when opening the cap to your rye kvass bottle, since carbonation and pressure do build rather quickly. That's why your rye kvass should be bottled in plastic. Note that this recipe requires extended wait times, so plan ahead. Also, the yield on this recipe varies depending on what rye bread you use.

MAKES 1½ TO 2 QUARTS KVASS

---

1 pound rye bread (stale or fresh), sliced, store-bought or homemade (page 100)

1 gallon water

1 tablespoon rye starter (page 102; optional)

1½ teaspoons champagne yeast (½ teaspoon active dry yeast is a fine substitute)

⅓ cup honey

½ cup plus ½ teaspoon sugar

About 8 small sprigs of fresh mint

1 raisin

---

1. Preheat the oven to 400°F. Place the bread directly on the oven rack and bake for about 7 minutes, or until the bread is well toasted and completely firm when pressed in the middle of the slice. If using stale bread, this process may take less time. Remove and let cool.

2. Bring the water to a boil, then remove it from heat. Break the bread into small pieces and drop them into the boiled water. Let the bread and water steep until the liquid cools to room temperature, about 2 hours.

(continued) ▶

▶ (Russian Rye Kvass, *continued*)

3. Strain the liquid from the bread, retaining the liquid in a ceramic, glass, or food-grade plastic vessel. This is easiest to do using cheesecloth or a thin, clean kitchen towel, because you will want to squeeze as much of the liquid out of the bread as possible. This will be more difficult than you think, so put some muscle into it. You'll never get it all, but squeeze for a couple of minutes, then discard the soggy bread.

4. Stir the rye starter (if using), yeast, honey, the ½ cup of the sugar, and the mint into the rye liquid, mixing well. Cover with cheesecloth or a kitchen towel and let sit at room temperature for 10 to 12 hours or overnight. I like to start this process in the morning and then come home in the evening to an active and effervescent liquid. If it's colder than usual in your kitchen, consider waiting an additional 6 hours.

5. Strain the mixture well to remove the mint and any leftover sediment. Pour it into a plastic bottle with a tight-fitting screw-on lid. Be sure to leave one-quarter to one-third of the bottle empty. Add the raisin and remaining ½ teaspoon sugar to the bottle, then seal. Leave at room temperature to carbonate until the plastic bottle expands and/or the raisin floats to the surface, about 2 hours. Store the kvass in the refrigerator, where it will continue to carbonate slightly. It will keep for several weeks. If the bottle looks like it's expanding at all, just open the lid and release the pressure. White sediment will fall to the bottom of the bottle. That's normal. Serve cold, alongside dried sardines and *pelmeni*, while sitting at the Russian baths or relaxing at home.

PARSLEY KOMBUCHA (TEA KVASS)

Parsley kombucha is our light and refreshing take on the fermented tea that's become a health food staple. This kombucha reminds some people of sparkling kosher grape juice. That seems fitting.

If you have a friend who makes kombucha, they will definitely have a SCOBY (symbiotic colony of bacteria and yeast) to give you. A new SCOBY, also called a mother, forms each time you brew kombucha, so once you start the process, you'll have more mothers than you'll know what to do with. If you don't know anyone who makes kombucha, you can either (a) purchase a SCOBY online or from a fermentation store (see Resources, page 327), or (b) make your own mother by purchasing kombucha from the store and letting it sit out at room temperature for about two weeks. If choosing option b, you'll notice that a layer will form at the top of the kombucha. This layer, which resembles a jellyfish, is your SCOBY, and it will grow and expand to fit the container in which it is placed. SCOBYs are delicate and must be kept in kombucha, in the fridge, if they are not being used to brew. Note that this recipe calls for a quick prep time but an extended wait time.

MAKES ABOUT
1 GALLON KOMBUCHA

3½ quarts
filtered water

¾ cup sugar

2 bunches fresh
parsley

2 cups store-bought
live-cultured
kombucha or
kombucha from a
previous batch

1 kombucha SCOBY

1. Bring the filtered water to a boil. Stir in the sugar until it has dissolved. Remove from the heat and add the parsley. Let the parsley and hot water steep until the water cools to room temperature. Note that the resulting tea will remain clear.

2. Remove all the parsley, setting aside 2 sprigs and discarding the rest. Pour the parsley tea into a 1-gallon crock or jar (a glass vessel with a spout at the bottom is ideal), then pour in the kombucha, add the SCOBY and reserved sprigs of parsley, and stir. Cover with cheesecloth or a clean kitchen towel and secure with a rubber band or twine. Let sit at room temperature for 1 to 2 weeks. As with most fermented foods and beverages, the time it takes for the kombucha to brew varies with the room temperature and your

(continued) ▶

personal taste preferences. The taste will also vary depending on the starter kombucha you've used and the SCOBY. After day 7, taste the kombucha daily. The flavor should be sour, but it shouldn't taste like vinegar. Once you're happy with the taste, remove the parsley stems and the SCOBY and store the SCOBY in the fridge in a glass jar with 2 cups of your recent batch of kombucha (or enough to keep the mother completely submerged). Bottle the rest of the kombucha in a glass vessel with a tight-fitting screw-on lid.

3. To carbonate, let the kombucha sit in the bottle with lid screwed on tightly at room temperature for 2 to 3 days before refrigerating. This will allow time for carbonation to develop in the bottle. Once you're in the groove of making kombucha, start another batch right away.

Note The ideal way to brew kombucha is to set up a continuous brew system. Using a vessel made of glass with a spout on the bottom (imagine a lemonade dispenser) allows you to brew kombucha over and over again. When your batch is finished, bottle your kombucha through the spout (no need to strain it!), leaving your SCOBY in enough kombucha to keep it submerged in liquid. Prepare more parsley tea (with sugar), let it cool, and pour it right back into the dispenser to begin the process all over again. I find that this method encourages me to keep up my kombucha brewing, and also makes it easier to taste during the fermentation process.

SODA SYRUPS

JEFFREY → Before Coca-Cola or Pepsi, Dr. Brown's on the Lower East Side of New York began selling a seltzer flavored with celery seeds and sugar in 1869. Cel-Ray, as it was called, "provided a better counterpoint to the heavy, briny meats than sweeter, fruit-flavored sodas," wrote food historian Gil Marks, explaining how it became a fixture of the Jewish deli in the 1930s.

I find it ironic that sugary sodas, the scourge of nutritionists, began as healthful tonics. Seltzer was considered medicinal in nineteenth-century America, and in Philadelphia in 1807, a doctor sweetened the fizzy water to make it more pleasant to drink for his patients. I get it. I drink ginger ale when I have an upset stomach, and I prefer Alka-Seltzer to other pain relievers because the effervescence feels curative.

While I'm often content with plain seltzer, I find the infusion of familiar Ashkenazi flavors mixed into bubbly water to be extremely refreshing. These soda syrups and the drinks you can mix from them make a great party trick and are also a nice way to bring a bit of that Ashkenazi spirit into your everyday eating and drinking. For a cocktail party, they're nice virgin drinks, and as you'll see with the Celery Collins (page 301) and the Seeded Rye (page 305), they also make a great base for cocktails.

Cucumber-Dill Syrup

JEFFREY → I think of this as the perfect midsummer soda. Mix with seltzer for a truly refreshing drink.

⊁ MAKES 1½ CUPS SYRUP ⊰

1 English cucumber (about 1 foot long), peeled

½ cup water

1 cup sugar

1 small bunch fresh dill

1. If you have a juicer, run the peeled cucumber through the juicer and strain the juice through a fine-mesh strainer.

If you don't have a juicer, place the cucumber in a blender and blend until

(continued) ▶

▶ (Soda Syrups, *continued*)

liquefied, then run the juice through a strainer until you have ½ cup of cucumber juice. Set the juice aside and refrigerate.

2. In a small saucepan, bring the water to a boil. Stir in the sugar until it dissolves. Remove from the heat.

3. Add the fresh dill to the hot syrup and let steep for at least 2 hours. When cool, remove the dill, squeezing out any remaining syrup clinging to the herb. Stir the cucumber juice into the infused syrup. Pour into a jar and store in the fridge.

4. To serve, mix 3 tablespoons of the syrup with 6 to 8 ounces of seltzer water. Serve over ice. This syrup will stay fresh for 2 to 3 days in the refrigerator.

Celery Syrup

JEFFREY

Make your own version of Cel-Ray to drink while eating a pastrami sandwich (page 210) or a knish (page 195). Or use the syrup to make a Celery Collins (page 301) for when you're sitting on the porch with friends. Note that this syrup is a rich simple syrup, meaning it has more sugar than water. As such, a little goes a long way.

⇥ MAKES ABOUT ⇤
1 CUP SYRUP

½ cup water

1 cup sugar

1½ tablespoons celery seeds

1. In a small saucepan, bring the water to a boil. Stir in the sugar until it dissolves. Remove from the heat. Add the celery seeds, stir, cover, and let steep for 2 hours.

2. Strain the syrup through a fine-mesh strainer. Pour into a jar and store in the fridge. To serve, mix 1½ tablespoons of the syrup with 6 to 8 ounces of chilled seltzer, or to taste. Serve over ice.

Caraway Syrup

 Toasting caraway seeds will make your house smell like rye bread is baking. If anyone comes home and is disappointed, just make them a Seeded Rye cocktail (page 305) and they'll quickly get over it.

※ MAKES ABOUT ※
1½ CUPS SYRUP

⅓ cup caraway seeds

1¼ cups water

1 cup sugar

1. In a nonstick sauté pan, toast the caraway seeds over medium heat, stirring often, until brown and fragrant, about 10 minutes. Ideally, your seeds will turn dark but should not burn.

2. In a small saucepan, bring the water to a boil. Stir in the sugar until it dissolves. Remove from the heat and add the toasted caraway seeds. Stir and let steep for at least 2 hours.

3. Strain the syrup through a fine-mesh strainer. Pour into a jar and store in the fridge. To serve, mix 3 tablespoons of the syrup with 6 to 8 ounces of chilled seltzer, or to taste. Serve over ice.

Rhubarb Syrup

JEFFREY Perfect for when rhubarb is in season. Mix with seltzer for a refreshing pink soda with a sour rhubarb kick.

※ MAKES ABOUT ※
1½ CUPS SYRUP

1 pound fresh rhubarb stalks, coarsely chopped

2 cups water

1 cup sugar

Fresh lemon juice, for serving

1. Place the rhubarb and water in a small saucepan and bring to a boil over medium heat. Cook until the rhubarb is soft and falling apart, 10 to 15 minutes.

2. Strain the liquid through a fine-mesh strainer into a bowl. Return the liquid to the saucepan and add the sugar, stirring until it dissolves. Let cool, then pour into a jar and store in the fridge.

3. To serve, mix 3 tablespoons of the syrup with 6 to 8 ounces of chilled seltzer and a generous squeeze of fresh lemon juice, or to taste. Serve over ice.

COCKTAILS

LIZ →
Around the Jewish holidays each year, I see cocktail recipes passed around that incorporate Manischewitz into martinis and margaritas, but we can do better.

These cocktails provide a great way to fuse the flavors we use in Ashkenazi cooking, like pickle brine, celery seed, caraway, and dill, with the creativity of mixology. These flavors mesh with some of my favorite liquors. Note to the novice: These cocktails are simple and straightforward, so dive right in and integrate one or more into your next gathering.

Celery Collins

LIZ →
This cocktail is light and refreshing, and takes advantage of summer ingredients, making it the ultimate summer cocktail to serve at your Latvian picnic (page 313).

⇥ MAKES 1 COCKTAIL ⇤

4 to 6 cucumber slices

2 ounces gin

1 ounce Celery Syrup (page 299)

1½ ounces fresh lime juice

6 ounces seltzer

1. In a cocktail shaker, use a muddler or the bottom of a thin jar to muddle the cucumber slices, reserving one for garnish.

2. Fill the shaker with ice and pour in the gin, syrup, and lime juice. Shake vigorously until cold.

3. Pour into a tall collins glass filled with ice, top with seltzer, stir, and garnish with the reserved cucumber slice.

FROM LEFT: **Cucumber Dill Syrup** soda (page 297), **Celery Syrup** soda (page 299), **Caraway Syrup** soda (page 300), **Rhubarb Syrup** soda (page 300)

Seeded Rye

 This is a warming winter drink for rye whiskey lovers, evoking one of the tastiest Jewish breads.

⇥ MAKES 1 COCKTAIL ⇤

1 ounce rye whiskey

1 ounce Caraway Syrup (page 300)

1½ ounces soda water

1 teaspoon fresh lemon juice

Lemon twist, for garnish

Place all of the ingredients except the lemon twist in a rocks glass. Add 1 ice cube and stir. Garnish with the lemon twist.

Pickle Brine Bloody Mary

 This recipe offers an alternative use for three of my favorite recipes: the brine of our sour dills (page 50), which adds a sour, effervescent base; Carrot-Citrus Horseradish (page 176) for a spicy kick; and dilly beans (page 56) for a unique and colorful garnish. Scale it up and make a pitcher.

⇥ MAKES 1 COCKTAIL ⇤

8 ounces tomato juice

1 tablespoon fresh lime juice

1 tablespoon fresh lemon juice

2 tablespoons lacto-fermented pickle brine (store-bought or from Classic Sour Dills, page 50, or Crisp Garlic Dilly Beans, page 56)

1 to 2 tablespoons store-bought horseradish relish or Carrot-Citrus Horseradish Relish (page 176)

Splash of Worcestershire sauce

1 tablespoon hot sauce (optional)

Pinch of kosher salt

Pinch of freshly ground black pepper

1 ounce vodka

Dilly bean (page 56) or sour dill pickle spear (page 50), for garnish

Combine all the ingredients except the dilly bean, stir well, and taste for spice level. Adjust the levels of horseradish, salt, and pepper as needed. Garnish with the dilly bean and serve immediately in a tall glass over ice.

Sour Dill Martini

 LIZ This sour dill martini is a close relative to the "extra dirty" martini, which features olive juice added to the simple blend of gin or vodka and vermouth. The pungent pickle brine we add here lends a bit of sour and a splash of dill to the mix, flavors that easily complement the strong liquor.

⇥ MAKES 1 COCKTAIL ⇤

2½ ounces vodka or gin

2 tablespoons lacto-fermented sour pickle brine (store-bought or from Classic Sour Dills, page 50, or Crisp Garlic Dilly Beans, page 56)

½ ounce vermouth

Cornichon (or dilly beans, page 56), for garnish

Fill a cocktail shaker with ice and pour in all the ingredients except the cornichon. Shake vigorously until cold, then strain into a martini glass. Garnish with the cornichon.

ACKNOWLEDGMENTS

WHEN WE SET OUT TO WRITE THIS BOOK, we met with our agent, Nicole Tourtelot, at one of our favorite cafés in Brooklyn and connected with her instantly. She was our people, and since then, she's shepherded us through a sea of unknowns and helped make this book a reality.

We were fortunate enough to work with two incredible editors on this project, Kara Rota and Will Schwalbe of Flatiron Books. They believed in this book, and in us, right from the start, and they helped us to find and fine-tune our voice. In fact, the whole team at Flatiron matched our passion with their enthusiasm, and we're incredibly appreciative.

Lauren Volo and Marianna Velasquez, our talented photographer and stylist, respectively, brought our dishes and stories to life through their photos and compositions. Working with the two of them was among the most gratifying parts of this whole process.

We owe a great deal of thanks to Seena and Harrison Peck in the Berkshires and to Cynthia Lagdameo in Brooklyn. They graciously opened their homes for our photo shoots and smiled with joy as we filled their kitchens with smells of the Old Country. And to Adamah Farm, for encouraging us to pick berries and cucumbers and explore its fields for our photos.

Without Jackie Lilinshtein, our third partner in The Gefilteria, we would never have taken the leap of faith to be where we are today and write this book. Thank you. And to some of the other original Gefilteria family members: Molly Alpern, Steve Bennet, Erica Braudy, Alice Chai, Rachel Davidson, Danielle Durchlag, Adam Esrig, Zach Stern, The Way We See the World crew, and all our other friends who cooked with us, showed up at events, placed orders, spread the word, and carried us through the ups and downs of entrepreneurship.

We are so grateful to those who read our proposals and chapters and offered sage advice and input when we needed it most. Thank you, Orit Gat, Gabriella Gershenson, Marisa Robertson-Textor, Kim Taylor, Temima Fruchter, Emma Alpern, and Stephen Klein.

We owe many thanks to our fellow cookbook authors, food friends, teachers, scholars, and mentors: Noah Bernamoff, Frank Carollo, Andrew Coe, Jayne Cohen, Mitchell Davis, Devra Ferst, Shannon Sarna Goldberg, JJ Goode, Sandor Katz, Leah Koenig, Jonathan Milder, Gil Marks (*z"l*), Irene Pletka, Eddy Portnoy, Shlomo Raskin, David Sax, Naama Shefi, David Siegel, Adeena Sussman, Ari Weinzweig, Clark Wolf, and Jane Ziegelman.

We are deeply grateful to the testers who contributed to tweaking and tasting the dishes in this book. Julia Braun, Mira Evnine, Austin Reavis, Lauren Utvich, and Caroline Lange deserve particular recognition for their thoughtful and diligent attention to our recipes, but there are many others: David Aamar, Brahm Ahmadi, Leah Katz-Ahmadi, Anna Altman, Miriam Aronoff, Judith Belasco, Leah Byrne, Erika Davis, Samuel Frommer, Lisa Goldman, Anna Goren, Molly Goren, Shuli and Adam Herbert, Stephanie Hewson, Shoshana Kasle, Jesse Leiken, Fran Levine, Hanakyle Moranz, Amy Robinson Oost, Erik Oost, Deena Prichep, Kat Romanow, Richard Semegram, Zack Schulman, Zoya Treyster, David Wolkin, and Nitzan Ziv.

The recipes in this book were inspired by stories from so many people, including Jacqueline Crockett, Malgo Bakalarz-Duverger, Anna Gershenson, Oscar Green (*z"l*), Noah Goldstein, Dr. Alexandra (Sasha) Grigorieva, Aunt Yetta Kovitz, Stephanie Levine, Joan Nathan, Dorly Ninio, Celia Ores, Michelle Ores, Rachel Przetycka, Zak (the Baker) Stern, Laura Silver, Lilya Vinets (*z"l*), Edith Wolpin, and Bessie Weinstein (*z"l*).

To the institutions, organizations, and communities whose resources were invaluable during the process of writing this book: ROI, Genesis and BIMA at Brandeis University, YIVO, and Adamah Farm.

And a sincere thank-you to our wide community of friends, near and far, who care deeply about the foods and the philosophies found in this book. It is because of you that we have the strength to lead this passion-driven life. There are too many of you to name, but this book was written for you.

LIZ A HUGE THANK-YOU to Jeffrey, my co-conspirator in a book, a business, and a philosophy of life. Thank you to my loving family—Carol and Michael Alpern, Jesse and Erika Alpern, Grandma Beverly Sober and Grandma Fay Alpern (*z"l*)—all of whom are infinitely enthusiastic about this crazy gefilte life I've been living and without whom I could never be living it.

To my roommates and chosen family, who let me take over the kitchen for two years of testing, tasting, successes, and failures. Michelle Ben David, Jill Ariela Putterman, and Jennifer Martin are more a part of this book than they could ever imagine, and I plan to feed them forever with my gratitude for their generosity of spirit and space.

To Joan Nathan, who took a chance on me many years ago and without whom I never would have been able to jump headfirst into the world of food.

JEFFREY I COULDN'T HAVE ASKED FOR a better writing and business partner than Liz Alpern. I've also been blessed with an amazing family, including two of the most supportive parents, who raised me with a deep love and appreciation of my culture, and who made sure that our family and its stories were a huge part of my life. I'm grateful to my uncles, Michael and Mark; my sisters, Dahlia and Shuli; my brother-in-law, Adam; and my niece and nephews for sharing stories with me and for their continued support.

Thank you, Grandma Ruth, for your strength and courage throughout your life. You survived some of the worst atrocities the world has ever seen, and yet you spent your life sharing love, culture, and delicious food with your family. You inspired so much of my life. And I owe so much to Grandpa Joe (*z"l*), Grandpa Julius (*z"l*), Grandma Lily (*z"l*), and Great-Grandma Frieda (*z"l*).

And I'm forever grateful for the support of my partner, Rachel Davidson, who has been heavily invested in this project from the beginning and who not only put up with a refrigerator of schmaltz and pickles for a year but also willingly talked about Jewish food ad nauseam with me, tested recipes, offered feedback on the ideas in these pages and on the dishes themselves, and showed so much enthusiasm and encouragement through the whole process. Thank you for everything.

SAMPLE MENUS

⊱ PEASANT LUNCH ⊰

You'll find us eating this lunch more often than not.

Everything Bagel Butter

Peasant Potato Salad

Leek Soup with Beet Greens

Sauerkraut or Sauerruben

Spiced Herring in Oil

Beet and Ginger Kvass

Jewish Rye

⊱ THE LATVIAN PICNIC ⊰

In summertime, when watermelon and grapes are in abundance, pickle them up in quantity for all your picnicking needs. These foods are all eaten at room temperature and are easily transportable. This menu is perfect for sharing with friends while lounging on a blanket in the park.

Sweet Pickled Watermelon Rind

Sweet Vinegar–Brine Pickled Trout

Mustard Slaw

Cardamom Pickled Grapes

Smoked Whitefish Gefilte Terrine

Bessie Weinstein's Schnecken and Honey Sesame Chews

Bialys

Lewando's Leek Frittata

Long-Forgotten Lettuce Kvass

Spiced Blueberry Soup

⚹ SUNDAY BRUNCH ⚹

This brunch spread can be mostly prepped in advance. Make your butter, jams, and pickled trout the week before and prep your mustard slaw, blintzes, and celery syrup the night before. The day of, simply bake off your bread and cookies and fry the blintzes with your guests' help. Makes for a great party with a DIY feel.

Bialys, Bagels, or Seeded Honey Rye Pull-Apart Rolls

Everything Bagel Butter

Summer Harvest Jams

Sweet Vinegar–Brine Pickled Trout

Mustard Slaw

Sweet and Savory Blintzes

Black-and-White Cookie Sticks

Celery Collins Cocktails or Pickle Brine Bloody Marys

⚹ A NIGHT IN GREENPOINT, BROOKLYN ⚹

Greenpoint is the Polish hub of Brooklyn, and this menu will give you a taste of what you can find there.

Jewish Rye

Classic Sour Dills

Żurek (Sour Rye Soup)

Pierogi

Rye Kvass

⚹ WEEKNIGHT ASHKENAZI FIX ⚹

Whip this up in no time after work.

Mixed Greens with Pickle Brine Salad Dressing

Pan-Fried Trout with Herbed Mashed Potatoes or Crispy Chicken with Tsimmes

Bow-Tie Kichel

⚹ CLASSIC DELI NIGHT ⚹

Invite a crowd and plan ahead for this epic meal of deli classics.
Be sure to start curing your pastrami at least ten days before the big
night, and let your rye starter refresh overnight the night before.

Spicy Whole-Grain Mustard

Classic Sour Dills

Jewish Rye

*Roasted Garlic Potato
and Kasha Knishes*

Pierogi

Chopped Liver Pâté

Home-Cured Pastrami

*Bow-Tie Kichel and
Seasonal Fruit Compote*

*Celery Syrup soda or Long-
Forgotten Lettuce Kvass*

⚹ DELI NIGHT, QUICK AND DIRTY ⚹

If you're craving a night of delicious deli but you're a little short on
time, use this menu to take some shortcuts. Simply purchase a prebrined corned beef and boil and steam the day-of. Mustard and dilly
beans should be made a few days in advance but require very little
active cooking time.

Spicy Whole-Grain Mustard

Crisp Garlic Dilly Beans

Mustard Slaw

Pickle Brine Bread

*Crispy Kasha Varnishkes with
Brussels Sprouts*

Home-Cured Corned Beef

Seasonal Fruit Compote

Celery Syrup soda

Seeded Rye cocktails

⚜ COCKTAIL PARTY ⚞

Serve the borscht in tiny shooter cups that can be easily passed around to guests. Deviled eggs are perfect for serving on trays, and the corned beef and pastrami can be served at room temperature for guests to assemble into sandwiches on their own.

Lilya's Summer Beet Borscht
(served chilled)

Cholent Deviled Eggs

Chopped Liver Pâté

Jewish Rye or Rachel's
Buckwheat Bread

Home-Cured Corned Beef
or Pastrami

Bow-Tie Kichel

Sour Dill Martinis

Celery Collins cocktails

⚜ SPRING/SUMMER DINNER PARTY ⚞

As the temperatures warm up, share cooling dishes with friends and family. The cucumbers should be perfect for pickling and the leftover brine can be transformed into bread. The ice cream is the ideal way to end a fresh meal like this one.

Classic Sour Dills

Pickle Brine Bread or Rachel's
Buckwheat Bread

Leek Soup with Beet Greens

Pan-Fried Trout with Herbed
Mashed Potatoes or Braised
Sauerkraut and Potato Gratin

Dark Chocolate and Roasted
Beet Ice Cream

Parsley Kombucha or
Cucumber and
Dill Syrup sodas

Sour Dill Martinis

⚜ FALL/WINTER DINNER PARTY ⚞

Cozy up with friends around the table with the warming flavors and spices of this menu.

Clove and Spice Pickled Beets

Seeded Honey Rye
Pull-Apart Rolls

Spiced Blueberry Soup
(served hot)

Autumn Kale Salad

Braised Sauerkraut and
Potato Gratin

Cheesecake with Currant
Glaze and Caraway Crust

Russian Rye Kvass or
Caraway Syrup sodas

Seeded Rye cocktails

⁂ SHABBOS DINNER WITH FRIENDS ⁂

Whether you're serving lighter Ashkenazi fare in the springtime or hosting a cozy winter meal in the fall, this traditional menu (with a bit of a twist) has something for everyone and every season.

Classic Challah or Classic Challah with a Marble Rye Twist

Rustic Matzo Balls in Classic Chicken Soup or Mushroom and Barley Soup

Sunflower Salad or Autumn Kale Salad

Herbed Gefilte Terrine or Crispy Kasha Varnishkes with Brussels Sprouts

Kimchi-Stuffed Cabbage or Roast Chicken with Barley and Vegetables

Ruth's Apple Strudel

⁂ AUTUMN HIGH HOLIDAY MEAL ⁂

In the fall, we celebrate a series of Jewish holidays, starting with the New Year and up through the harvest holiday of Sukkot. This menu highlights the flavors and colors of the season. If you've been preserving all summer, the pickle spread should already be in your fridge, and most of the remaining produce needed can be found at the farmers' market.

Cardamom Pickled Grapes, Sweet Pickled Watermelon Rind, Crisp Garlic Dilly Beans

Classic Challah with a Marble Rye Twist

Old World Stuffed Gefilte Fish

Beef Kreplach in Classic Chicken Soup or Full-Bodied Vegetable Broth

Autumn Kale Salad

Cauliflower and Mushroom Kugel

Crispy Chicken with Tsimmes or Kimchi-Stuffed Cabbage

Orange-Spiced Rye Honey Cake

⚹ HANUKKAH FEAST ⚸

Fermented vegetables like kimchi and sauerruben help balance out
the heavy, fried foods of Hanukkah. The addition of a Hanukkah
goose here hearkens back to centuries of Ashkenazi Jewish
tradition. Plus, geese are most readily available during Hanukkah,
as they are also a traditional Christmas main dish.

*Sauerruben or
Ashkenazi Kimchi*

Mushroom and Barley Soup

*Seeded Honey Rye
Pull-Apart Rolls*

*Fried Sour Pickles with
Garlic Aioli*

Root Vegetable Latkes

Apple-Pear Sauce

*Alsatian Roasted Goose with
Apples and Onions or
Kimchi-Stuffed Cabbage*

*Honey Sesame Chews
(as giveaways) and
Wintry Compote*

⚹ PASSOVER SEDER ⚸

This menu combines some really exciting elements like homemade
matzo and a whole stuffed fish with classic Passover dishes like
matzo balls and braised brisket, as well as pickled vegetables to
help soothe your stomach after a heavy Passover meal.

Sauerkraut or Sauerruben

Make-at-Home Matzo

Old World Stuffed Gefilte Fish

*Rustic Matzo Balls or
Passover Lokshen "Noodles" in
Classic Chicken Soup or
Full-Bodied Vegetable Broth*

*Mixed Green Salad with
Pickle Brine Salad Dressing*

*Wine-Braised Brisket with
Butternut Squash or Braised
Sauerkraut and Potato Gratin*

*Anna's Passover Sponge Cake
and Seasonal Fruit Compote*

CHOOSE YOUR OWN LEFTOVER ADVENTURE

Because resourcefulness is the name of the game.

Note Not all of these ideas can be found in this cookbook. Think of some of them as just a jumping-off point.

➡ I made butter (page 18), and now I have buttermilk.

> Be a badass: follow the recipe for **farmer's cheese** (page 21), but act like the buttermilk is actually whole milk.
>
> Use it for muffins, cakes, and cookies.
>
> Drink it straight. Sometimes it'll have floating butter globules, and it's kind of sweet.
>
> Can't stress buttermilk pancakes enough.

➡ I have all this whey from making farmer's cheese (page 21) and feel bad getting rid of it.

> Do some weight training, then make a banana-berry smoothie and use the whey for extra protein instead of a powder.
>
> Use it to soak beans or grains instead of water to give added flavor.

➡ I skimmed the foam while making strawberry jam (page 30) and it looked strangely appetizing. Thoughts?

> Believe it or not, it makes a really good, flavorful syrup for pancakes.

➡ **I bought too many cucumbers for making pickles.**
There's no such thing as too many cucumbers.

> Make more **Classic Sour Dills** (page 50) in a smaller jar.
>
> Juice the cucumbers for **Cucumber-Dill Syrup** (page 297)

➡ **I made pickles and all I got (besides the yummy pickles) was a jar full of brine.**
If this book is good for anything, it's for what to do with your leftover pickle brine.

> **Pickle Brine Salad Dressings** (page 80)
>
> **Pickle Brine Bread** (page 96)
>
> **Sour Dill Martini** (page 306)
>
> **Pickle Brine Ice Cream** (just kidding)

➡ **The Garlic Aioli (see page 54) for Fried Sour Pickles calls for just an egg yolk. I quadrupled the recipe and have all these unused egg whites. What do I do?**

> Make meringues.

➡ **What do I do with the extra green cabbage from making Ashkenazi Kimchi (page 68)?**

> **Have you seen our sauerkraut recipe** (page 60)? Weigh the cabbage and adjust the salt ratio accordingly.
>
> Try **Mustard Slaw** (page 185).

➡ **After I eat all the sauerkraut, I'm left with extra sauerkraut brine.**

> Make Żurek (page 124) and instead of using rye starter to flavor the soup, use sauerkraut brine.
>
> Drink it as a shot.
>
> Swap it in for pickle brine in one of the salad dressings.

➡ I don't exactly have extra sauerruben—I'm just not sure what to do with it.

> Use the brine for **Pickle Brine Salad Dressings** (page 80).
>
> Eat the fermented vegetables paired with **Pickle Brine Bread** (page 96) and **Everything Bagel Butter** (page 18). That's Liz's favorite snack.

➡ I have all these extra sesame and poppy seeds from challah baking and bagel making.

> Turn them into **Honey Sesame Chews** (page 270).
>
> Save them and use them to season **croutons** (see page 38).

➡ And what about the leftover challah?
If you're planning on making extra challah, you should freeze some once it cools and warm it up in the oven before serving (on a low temp). If not . . .

> First choice is, of course, challah French toast. But you knew that.
>
> Make **Seasoned Croutons** (page 38).
>
> Challah kvass anyone? Use the **Russian Rye Kvass** recipe (page 243) and give it a shot.
>
> Try your hand at an old-fashioned challah kugel.

➡ There was extra bialy filling (see page 109) that I didn't use.

> Mix it with butter and spread on everything.

➡ I have extra raw beets on hand from making borscht (page 117).

> Make **Clove and Spice Pickled Beets** (page 72)
>
> Make **Sweet Beet Horseradish Relish** (page 174)
>
> Make **Dark Chocolate and Roasted Beet Ice Cream** (page 275)
>
> Make **Beet and Ginger Kvass** (page 290)

➡ And what about the beet greens?

Treat them like you would kale or spinach and sauté them as a side with onions and garlic.

Shred some up and use for **Leek Soup with Beet Greens** (page 122).

Shred some and throw them into **Crispy Kasha Varnishkes with Brussels Sprouts** (page 201) to add some color and flavor (and iron).

➡ What do I do with this extra chicken from making soup?

Make **Grandpa Joe's Famous Chicken Salad** (page 192).

Stuff some of the meat into your **Rustic Matzo Balls** (page 133).

➡ I have leftover raw carrots and celery from making chicken soup (page 130) and vegetable broth (page 123).

Make **Carrot-Citrus Horseradish Relish** (page 176) with the carrots.

Use the carrots for **Crisp Chicken with Tsimmes** (page 230).

Celery is great as a garnish for a **Pickle Brine Bloody Mary** (page 305).

Grandpa Joe's Famous Chicken Salad (page 192) calls for celery.

➡ What do I do with excess leeks from making leek frittata?

When life hands you extra leeks, make a small batch of **Leek Soup with Beet Greens** (page 122).

Or, hey, plan ahead and make the spinach and leek filling for **kreplach** (page 139) and freeze it until you're ready to make the dough.

Sauté like an onion, just be a bit more gentle, and make soup (like potato leek).

➡ I have all this extra Carrot-Citrus Horseradish Relish (page 176) that I made for gefilte fish. What can I do with it?

Make **Pickle Brine Bloody Marys** (page 305)

Spread it on a sandwich. It'll give it some extra bite.

Use it as an unconventional garnish on lots of things.

➡️ **I threw a deli night extravaganza but still have all this extra corned beef (page 207).**

> Throw a brunch with corned beef hash as a featured item.

➡️ **Ditto with the pastrami (page 210).**

> Make a pastrami hash. Hey, why not?
>
> Make a Montreal breakfast classic, mishmash, but instead of chopped-up hot dogs with scrambled eggs, add some chopped-up pastrami.
>
> Cut some up and mix it into the potato filling for the knish, and you'll have a pastrami knish.

➡️ **I made knishes (page 195) and wound up with some extra potato knish filling.**

> Make a few crepes, wrap it up, and you have yourself a potato blintz.
>
> If you have enough, for whatever reason, pass it off as the mashed potato side for **Pan-Fried Trout** (page 229). No one will know.

➡️ **Somehow I have extra potato filling from Savory Blintzes (page 224).**

> Why don't you wrap 'em up in the knish dough from the **Roasted Garlic Potato Knish** (page 197)?

➡️ **Can I use this extra filling from the Sweet Blintzes (page 224)?**

> Make some knish dough (page 195), add stewed cherries, and wrap it up to make Jeffrey's father's favorite treat: a cherry cheese knish.
>
> Use as a filling for **Pastry-Style Hamantaschen** (page 264).
>
> Make sweet **Pierogi** (page 140).

➡️ **Whenever I make the Crispy Chicken with Tsimmes (page 230) or Roast Chicken with Barley and Vegetables (page 232), I always have extra chicken.**

> You should obviously use the meat to make a **chicken salad** (page 192).

➡️ **What do I do with leftover meat from Alsatian Roasted Goose or Duck with Apples and Onions (page 234)?**
There shouldn't be any leftovers, but if there are . . .

> Use the meat to make a **chicken** (well, goose) **salad** (page 192).
>
> Make a rich soup using the carcass. Check out the **Classic Chicken Soup** recipe (page 130).

➡️ **What do I do with the leftover semicooked cabbage from Kimchi-Stuffed Cabbage (page 245)?**

> Slice it up and sauté with sliced onions, cooked slowly so they caramelize, and serve as a side with **Pierogi** (page 140) or **Beef Kreplach** (page 135).
>
> Make a hearty winter borscht with cabbage and tomatoes. Lilya would approve.

➡️ **There are all these extra dried fruits that I didn't use for the chicken and tsimmes recipe (page 230).**

> Make **Wintry Compote** (page 101)!
>
> Use it in homemade granola or trail mix.

➡️ **I have rhubarb left over from making Strawberry-Rhubarb Compote (page 259).**

> It's time to make **Rhubarb Syrup** (page 300) for sodas.

➡️ **I bought a whole bunch of parsley when all I needed was a sprig or two for garnish.**

> **Parsley Kombucha** (page 293) has your name written all over it.

WATER BATH CANNING 101

Canning using glass jars and screw-top lids is an effective way to keep your high-acid foods in the pantry for a long time. A proto-canning method using paraffin wax and jars with lids was a common feature of older Jewish pantries.

If canning, do *not* adjust the vinegar amounts or sugar amounts of the recipes.

If using spice bundles with cheesecloth for any of the pickled recipes, remove the spice bundle before canning.

Note that brand-new unused canning jars usually come presterilized, but even so—or if reusing jars—sterilize them first by washing them thoroughly and placing them in a stockpot with water. Bring the water to a boil and then reduce heat to low and simmer until you are ready to begin the canning process. To sterilize lids and rings, place them in a small saucepan, cover with water, and bring to a simmer just before use. Retrieve them with tongs or a magnetic lid lifter right before sealing your jars. Presterilized jars should be warmed before canning, but do not need to be boiled.

MATERIALS:

Deep stockpot

Round metal rack that fits in the stockpot

Mason or Weck jars for canning

Brand-new canning lids with screw-top rings

Jar lifter (useful, but optional)

Magnetic lid lifter (optional)

Canning funnel

Clean kitchen towel

1. Fill a stockpot three-quarters of the way with water and bring the water to a boil. Place a round metal rack at the bottom.

2. When your jam, applesauce, or pickles are ready to be canned, carefully retrieve empty sterilized jars from the simmering water and place them on a clean kitchen towel. For applesauce and jam, pour the finished products into the jars using a canning funnel, leaving ¼ to ½ inch of headspace. For

pickled shallots, beets, and watermelon rinds, use a slotted spoon or a wooden spoon to fill the jar with the pickled items, leaving 1 inch of headspace, then pour the brine over, leaving ½ inch of headspace. Run a wooden skewer, chopstick, or thin rubber spatula around the inside of the jar to remove any air bubbles.

3. Wipe the jar rims with a damp clean kitchen towel, place the lids on the jars, and secure with rings, twisting to tighten, then carefully set the jars on the rack in the pot of boiling water so they're covered by 1 to 2 inches of water. Process (boil) for the amount of time the recipe requires (see list below).

4. Turn off the heat, remove the jars with a lid lifter or tongs, and set on a kitchen towel on the counter to cool for 12 to 24 hours, or until they've reached room temperature. Pretty soon after they've come out of the water bath, the jar lids should ping, the sign that the seal has taken hold. The center of the lid will turn inward so it's concave. Once the jars are at room temperature, test the seal by removing the ring, grabbing the lid with your fingers and lifting a few inches. If the lid stays on, it's a healthy seal. If not, or if you're unsure if a jar has sealed properly, don't take the chance on storing it at room temperature—leave it in the fridge and keep it for the time recommended in the original recipe.

SUGGESTED WATER BATH CANNING TIMES

Applesauce	15 minutes for pint-size jars and 20 minutes for quart-size jars
Jam	5 minutes for pint-size or half-pint jars
Pickled shallots	10 minutes for quart-size jars
Pickled beets	30 minutes for pint- or quart-size jars
Pickled watermelon rinds	10 minutes for pint- or quart-size jars

If you live above 1,000-feet elevation, check the National Center for Home Food Preservation site (nchfp.uga.edu) for accurate boiling times.

RESOURCES

SOURCING SPECIFIC INGREDIENTS AND MATERIALS:

- CHEESE CULTURES AND RENNET: *Cheese and Yogurt Making,*
  https://cheeseandyogurtmaking.com

- KOMBUCHA SCOBY: *Kombucha Brooklyn,* www.kombuchabrooklyn.com

- FERMENTATION INGREDIENTS, SUPPLIES, AND EQUIPMENT: *Midwest Supplies,*
  www.midwestsupplies.com and Lehman's Hardware and Appliances, www.lehmans.com

- BARLEY MALT SYRUP: *Check at your local natural grocery store or large chain natural
  grocery store. Generally on a shelf near the honey.*

- WHOLE UNROASTED BUCKWHEAT GROATS: *Bob's Red Mill Brand, found in many natural food
  stores or online at www.bobsredmill.com/organic-raw-buckwheat-groats.html*

- PINK (CURING) SALT: *This is also known as Prague Powder #1 or Pink Curing Salt #1
  (6.25 percent sodium nitrite). While in large quantities it can be dangerous (even lethal),
  our Corned Beef and Pastrami recipes call for small quantities that render It harmless. Keep
  it out of the reach of children und do not confuse pink curing salts (which are dyed so as not
  to confuse it with regular salt) with Himalayan pink salt, which is a simple pure salt whose
  mineral composition colors it pink. To purchase, inquire at your local butcher shop or search
  online where many third party retailers sell it.*

- PASTURE-RAISED KOSHER MEAT: *Grow and Behold ships nationwide,*
  http://growandbehold.com

- GOOSE: *Check your local butcher shops around Hanukkah and Christmas.*

- PASTURE-RAISED KOSHER GOOSE IN NEW YORK: *Yiddish Farm,* https://yiddishfarm.org

- ARTISAN CERAMIC CROCKS: *Ogusky Ceramics,* www.claycrocks.com

- FOOD-GRADE PLASTIC VESSELS: *For the fermented vegetables and beverages in this book,
  we encourage you to use wood, ceramic, glass, or food-grade plastic vessels. When it comes
  to plastic, your options generally include 5-gallon buckets or larger plastic barrels, which
  can be helpful as you scale up and ferment in larger quantities. The term "food-grade
  plastic" refers to containers or receptacles made from high-density polyethylene (HDPE).
  Each plastic container will contain a number on the bottom of it, so look for #2 HDPE.
  Unlike standard Tupperware (no matter how dense it seems!), food-grade plastic is safe for
  fermentation, so be sure look for this symbol below:*

NOTES

INTRODUCTION

5 "Jewish cooking today has a reputation for blandness, not entirely unearned. A hundred years ago, however, the label would have never stuck." Jane Ziegelman, *97 Orchard: An Edible History of Five Immigrant Families in One New York Tenement* (New York: HarperCollins Publishers, 2010).

1. PANTRY STAPLES

16 "People wanted to guard the valuable rendered fat." Andras Koerner, *A Taste of the Past: The Daily Life and Cooking of a Nineteenth-Century Hungarian-Jewish Homemaker* (Oberlin, OH: UPNE, 2006).

24 "And her face always looked strained and worried, as if her shipload of sour cream had just sunk." I. L. Peretz, *In the Mail Coach* (1893) trans. Golda Werman, in *The I. L. Peretz Reader*, ed. Ruth R. Wisse (New York: Schocken Books, 1990), p.114.

35 "Schmaltz became to Ashkenazi cooking what olive oil was to Mediterranean food." Gil Marks, *Encyclopedia of Jewish Food* (Hoboken: John Wiley & Sons, Inc., 2010).

37 Jews have been rearing geese and ducks for centuries. Claudia Roden, *Book of Jewish Food: An Odyssey from Samerkand to New York* (New York: Penguin: 1999), p. 111.

37 "The smell of smoking goose fat became the traditional scent of Hanukkah." Michael Wex, *Rhapsody in Schmaltz: Yiddish Food and Why We Can't Stop Eating It* (New York: St. Martin's Press, 2016), p. 78.

2. PICKLES

42 "In other societies people digested their heavy starch diet with the assistance of sauces, chili peppers, olive oil, or sugar-based products." John Cooper, *Eat and Be Satisfied: A Social History of Jewish Food* (Northvale, NJ: Jason Aronson, Inc., 1993).

44 Old-fashioned recipes call for about 10 percent of the pickle brine to be salt. Andrea Chesman, *The Pickled Pantry: From Apples to Zucchini, 150 Recipes for Pickles, Relishes, Chutneys & More* (North Adams, MA: Storey, 2012), p. 37.

47 Soaking cucumbers in ice water before pickling helps firm them. Penn Extension: extension.psu.edu/food/preservation /safe-methods/quick-process-pickles.

3. BREADS

84 "It is impossible to think of any good meal, no matter how plain or elegant, without soup or bread in it." M. F. K. Fischer, foreword to Julia Older and Steven Sherman, *Soup and Bread* (New York: Penguin, 1981).

85 "Then on the seventh, the Sabbath, they enjoyed light and golden challah." Andrew Coe, Serious Eats: newyork.seriouseats.com/2014/03 /jewish-corn-rye-comeback.html.

85 could stay fresh for up to a week or longer. Stanley Ginsberg and Norman Berg, *Inside the Jewish Bakery: Recipes and Memories from the Golden Age of Jewish Baking* (Philadelphia: Camino Books, Inc., 2011), p. 59.

85 Rye bread was a nutritional foundation of the Ashkenazi diet. Hirsz Abramowicz, *Profiles of a Lost World: Memoirs of East European Jewish Life before World War II* (Detroit: Wayne State University Press, 1999), pp. 102, 104–106.

85 "It is no wonder that the aroma of fresh baked rye bread smelled like perfume. People could do even the most strenuous work having eaten only plain rye bread with sour soup or with barley soup laced with a little milk." Hirsz Abramowicz, *Profiles of a Lost World*, pp. 102, 104–106.

85 "eating black bread on holidays." Mary Antin, *The Promised Land* (Boston:Houghton-Mifflin, 1912), p. 127.

100 "The old style Jewish rye starter is made by taking the previous day's fully baked rye bread . . . and cutting it up and using that to feed your starter culture." Ari Weinzweig, *Rye Bread, Bridges and a Vote for Really Big Loaves, Zingerman News*. November 2008, p. 17.

4. SOUPS AND DUMPLINGS

114 "The truth of the proverb was borne out on a daily basis in the immigrant soup pot." Jane Ziegelman, *97 Orchard*, p. 45.

117 "contains everything . . . and it can be refrigerated and reheated in perpetuity, always better the next day . . . The crucial ingredient . . . is a large, hungry family, surviving together." Aleksandar Hemon, "Borscht," *The New Yorker*, November 22, 2010, p. 95.

122 the classic spring soup *schav*. Hirsz Abramowicz, *Profiles of a Lost World*, p. 100.

122 Adding acidity is common with Ashkenazi soups. John Cooper, *Eat and Be Satisfied*, p. 156.

127 Among the types of mushrooms eaten by Jews in Europe. Gil Marks, *Encyclopedia of Jewish Food*.

127 "Mushrooms were one of the few things they [Jews] bothered to bring in from the Old Country. There was even a little mushroom wholesale district on Houston Street." Jane Ziegelman, in conversation on October 1, 2015.

130 "How could one greet so important a guest as the Holy Sabbath with only *borscht* or barley soup? That would be a profanation." Hirsz Abramowicz, *Profiles of a Lost World*, p. 107.

5. APPETIZING AND LIGHTER SIDES

148 "After the harsh winter's groats, and bread and garlic *borscht*, it was a delight to eat *schav* [sorrel] *borscht* with new potatoes, crumbled farmer's cheese with green onions, and the early summer vegetables and fruit." Abraham Rosenberg, 1961, jewishgen.org/yizkor/brzeziny /brz098.html.

149 The methods of preservation. Gil Marks, *Encyclopedia of Jewish Food*.

149 "It could be claimed that each Jew eats a herring a day. It is the food of the poor, but it is also the delicacy of the rich." Edouard de Pomiane, *The Jews of Poland: Recollections and Recipes* (Paris: Pholiota Press, Inc, 1929), p. 90.

159 "Beat 3 eggs with some salt, pour over the leeks and cook like a frittata." Fania Lewando, *The Vilna Vegetarian Cookbook: Garden-Fresh Recipes Rediscoverd and Adapted for Today's Kitchen* (New York: Schocken Books, 2015).

173 "Gefilte fish without *chrain* is punishment enough." Yiddish proverb.

174 Horseradish grew wild outside of the cities in eastern Europe. Mayer Kirshenblatt and Barbara Kirshenblatt-Gimblett, *They Called Me Mayer July: Painted Memories of a Jewish Childhood in Poland before the Holocaust* (Berkeley: University of California Press, 2007).

6. DELI SIDES AND SPECIALTIES

180 Most Jewish immigrants from central and eastern Europe. David Sax, *Saveur Magazine* 134: saveur.com/article/Travels/Meats-of-the-Deli.

181 It's been said that the deli. Jane Ziegelman, *Deli Man*, Dir. Erik Anjou. Cohen Media Group, 2014, Film.

181 Jewish deli owners were cooking from memories of a world. David Sax, *Save the Deli: In Search of Perfect Pastrami, Crusty Rye, and the Heart of Jewish Delicatessen* (Boston: Houghton Mifflin Harcourt, 2009).

186 Generally, it's easiest to peel the eggs. J. Kenji López-Alt, Serious Eats, seriouseats.com/2014/05/the-secrets-to-peeling-hard-boiled-eggs.html.

204 The latke . . . took quite a culinary journey. Gil Marks, *Encyclopedia of Jewish Food*.

210 "When Romanian Jews settled on New York's Lower East Side, beef was more plentiful and replaced goose as the protein of choice, and pastrami started to be served hot, as a sandwich." David Sax, *Saveur Magazine* 134: saveur.com/article/Travels/Meats-of-the-Deli.

7. MAINS

218 "taste, temperature and texture [rather] than the appearance of the food, for eating is a gustatory rather than visual pleasure . . . there is little effort to appeal to the eye with garnishes, color contrast or arrangement." Elizabeth Herzog, Margaret Mead, and Mark Zborowski, *Life Is with People: The Culture of the Shtetl* (New York: Schocken Books, 1995), p. 371.

219 "heighten their enjoyment of their subsequent feasting." John Cooper, *Eat and Be Satisfied*. p. 173.

219 So indispensible was the Sabbath meal. Hirsz Abramowicz, *Profiles of a Lost World*, p. 107.

220 Jewish immigrants on the Lower East Side. Jane Ziegelman, *97 Orchard*, p. 113.

8. DESSERTS

254 Walnuts. Gil Marks, *Encyclopedia of Jewish Food*.

254 For many immigrants. Stanley Ginsberg and Norman Berg, *Inside the Jewish Bakery*.

254 "The thought of cake or anything baked, except perhaps the lightest fruit tart, seems excessive after a full meal." Mimi Sheraton, *From My Mother's Kitchen: Recipes & Reminiscences* (New York: HarperCollins Publishers, 1979).

257 "The compote that traditionally closes the seder meal." Michael Wex, *Rhapsody in Schmaltz*, p. 17.

264 The predominant type of hamantaschen these days. Gil Marks, *Encyclopedia of Jewish Food*.

266 Black-and-whites originated in upstate New York and were adopted by New York's Jewish bakeries as they increased their cookie inventories. Stanley Ginsberg and Norman Berg, *Inside the Jewish Bakery*.

266 "The thing about eating the black-and-white cookie," Jerry says to Elaine in a classic episode of *Seinfeld* (Larry David, George Shapiro and Howard West). (1993.) *Seinfeld* [Television series]. Epidose 13, Season 5, "The Dinner Party." Studio City, CA: Castle Rock.

271 a baker in Chicago. Gil Marks, *Encyclopedia of Jewish Food*.

9. BEVERAGES

286 "Before there were tanks of compressed CO₂ to carbonate sweet syrups into sodas, there was the natural carbonation produced by fermentation." Sandor Ellix Katz, *The Art of Fermentation* (White River Junction, VT: Chelsea Green Publishing, 2012), p. 148.

287 "Even if it turns your nose aside, at least it's kvass, not water." David Christian and R. E. F. Smith, *Bread and Salt: A Social and Economic History of Food and Drink in Russia* (Cambridge, U.K.: Cambridge University Press, 2008), p. 288.

287 Even families with limited means. Elizabeth Herzog, Margaret Mead, and Mark Zborowski, *Life Is with People*, p. 297.

288 tavernkeepers and brewers. Jacob Goldberg, "Tavernkeeping," in *The YIVO Encyclopedia of Jews in Eastern Europe*: yivoencyclopedia.org /article.aspx/Tavernkeeping.

293 "Borukh's [kvass] . . . explodes from a bottle as though shot from a gun." "Motl, the Cantor's Son," Sholem Aleichem, as translated by Hillel Halkin in *The Letters of Menakhem-Mendl and Sheyne-Sheyndl and Motl, the Cantor's Son* (Yale University Press, 2002), p. 146.

297 "provided a better counterpoint to the heavy, briny meats than sweeter, fruit-flavored sodas." Gil Marks, *Encyclopedia of Jewish Food*, pp. 96, 541.

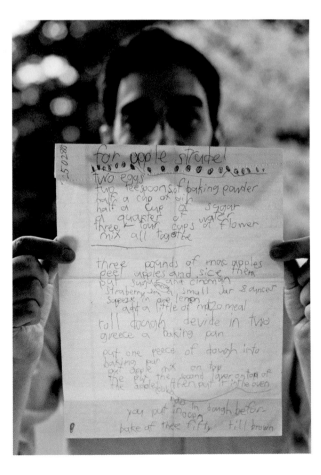

SELECT BIBLIOGRAPHY

Adler, Tamar. *An Everlasting Meal: Cooking with Economy and Grace*. Scribner, 2011.

Aleichem, Sholem. *The Letters of Menakhem-Mendl and Sheyne-Sheyndl and Motl, the Cantor's Son*. Translated by Hillel Halkin. Yale University Press, 2002.

Avnon, Naf, and Uri Sella. *So Eat, My Darling: A Guide to the Yiddish Kitchen*. Massada Ltd., 1982.

Bernamoff, Noah and Rae. *The Mile End Cookbook: Redefining Jewish Comfort Food from Hash to Hamentaschen*. Clarkson Potter, 2012.

Child, Julia, Louisette Bertholle, and Simone Beck. *Mastering the Art of French Cooking*. Knopf, 1961.

Cohen, Jayne. *The Gefilte Variations: 200 Inspired Re-Creations of Classics from the Jewish Kitchen, with Menus, Stories, and Traditions for the Holidays and Year-Round*. Scribner, 2000.

Edlin, Rosabelle, and Shushannah Spector. *Adventures in Jewish Cooking*. Galahad Books, 1964.

Gethers, Judith, and Elizabeth Lefft. *The World-Famous Ratner's Meatless Cookbook*. Ballantine Books, 1983.

Katz, Sandor Ellix. *Wild Fermentation: The Flavor, Nutrition, and Craft of Live-Culture Foods*. Chelsea Green Publishing, 2003.

Kirshenblatt-Gimblett, Barbara. "Food and Drink," *The YIVO Encyclopedia of Jews in Eastern Europe*. http://www.yivoencyclopedia.org/article.aspx/Food_and_Drink.

Koenig, Leah. *Modern Jewish Cooking: Recipes & Customs for Today's Kitchen*. Chronicle, 2015.

Levinson, Leonard Louis. *The Complete Book of Pickles & Relishes*. Hawthorn Books, Inc., 1965.

Levy, Faye. *International Jewish Cookbook*. Warner Books, Inc., 1991.

Luard, Elizabeth. *Old World Kitchen: The Rich Tradition of European Peasant Cooking*. Melville House, 1987.

Miller, Daphne. *The Jungle Effect*. William Morrow, 2008.

Nash, Helen. *Kosher Cuisine*. Random House, 1984.

Nathan, Joan. *Jewish Cooking in America*. Knopf, 2001.

Nathan, Joan. *Joan Nathan's Jewish Holiday Cookbook*. Schocken, 2004.

Pierson, Stephanie. *The Brisket Book: A Love Story with Recipes*. Andrews McMeel Publishing, 2011.

The Settlement Cookbook. Simon & Schuster, 1969.

Sheasby, Anne. *The Ultimate Soup Bible: Over 400 Recipes for Delicious Soups from Around the World with Step-by-step Instructions for Every Recipe*. Barnes & Noble, 2005.

Sheraton, Mimi. *The Bialy Eaters: The Story of a Bread and a Lost World*. Broadway Books, 2000.

The Spice and Spirit of Kosher-Jewish Cooking. Lubavitch Women's Organization, Junior Division, 1977.

Strauss, Edith Dosen. *Cooking is an Art*. The Edith Rosen Strauss Org. Inc., 1961.

Wex, Michael. *Rhapsody in Schmaltz: Yiddish Food and Why We Can't Stop Eating It*. St. Martin's Press, 2016.

INDEX